Sooner Doughboys Write Home

Sooner Doughboys Write Home

THE UNIVERSITY OF OKLAHOMA
AND WORLD WAR I

Edited by David W. Levy

Foreword by Joseph Harroz Jr.

University of Oklahoma Press : Norman

This book is published with the assistance of the McCasland Foundation, Duncan, Oklahoma.

Library of Congress Cataloging-in-Publication Data

Names: Levy, David W., 1937- editor. | Harroz, Joseph, Jr., writer of foreword.
Title: Sooner doughboys write home / edited by David W. Levy ; foreword by Joseph Harroz Jr.
Description: Norman : University of Oklahoma Press, [2025] | Includes bibliographical references and index. | Summary: "In November 1918, a week before the armistice ending World War I, the president of the University of Oklahoma wrote to every student, former student, and member of the faculty who had served in the military during the war. He asked each of them to write him a letter describing his experiences and impressions. This book contains a selection of more than fifty of those letters. Together with volume editor David W. Levy's introduction and annotations, the letters offer insights into what this group of young men, most of them from farms and small Oklahoma towns, saw and felt as they were thrust into a strange and often dangerous new world"—Provided by publisher.
Identifiers: LCCN 2024023906 | ISBN 9780806195278 (hardcover)
Subjects: LCSH: World War, 1914–1918—Oklahoma. | United States—Armed Forces—Oklahoma—History—20th century. | World War, 1914–1918—Personal narratives, American. | World War, 1914–1918—Europe—Personal narratives, American. | University of Oklahoma—Alumni and alumnae—History—20th century. | Brooks, Stratton D. (Stratton Duluth), 1869–1949—Correspondence.
Classification: LCC D570.85.O5 S66 2025 | DDC 940.3/766—dc23/eng/20241002
LC record available at https://lccn.loc.gov/2024023906

The paper in this book meets the guidelines for permanence and durability of the Committee on Production Guidelines for Book Longevity of the Council on Library Resources, Inc. ∞

For Joshua Richard Levy-Sprigge

CONTENTS

FOREWORD
By Joseph Harroz Jr.

Since its inception, the University of Oklahoma's enduring value has been its people. From our university's first president, David Ross Boyd, to the students, faculty, and staff of today, to the thousands of OU alumni across the world, it's our people who define our legacy.

This is one of the reasons this book, compiled and edited by OU historian Dr. David Levy, is so powerful. Levy has brilliantly brought to light the very personal experiences of the "Sooner doughboys"— "doughboy" being a popular nickname given to American soldiers during World War I.

The admiration I have for those who have served our country runs deep. My father, who came to OU as a first-generation student in 1947, was in the ROTC and spent much of these formative years in the Armory—a landmark that's been a cornerstone of service, leadership development, and civic duty at OU for over a hundred years. Following his medical residency, he served as a captain in the U.S. Air Force before returning to Oklahoma City for a long medical career.

The profound respect I have for our servicemembers and veterans is one of the reasons it is a privilege to write this foreword.

In the fifty-three letters presented here, we read the firsthand accounts of OU students and faculty as they experienced life in the trenches, inside a submarine, in mobile medical units, and in training sites at home and abroad. These letters provide a glimpse into the lives of these everyday soldiers to whom we can trace our OU lineage, revealing their humanity as they fought to preserve democracy and instill lasting peace.

It was the foresight of one of my predecessors—OU's third President, Stratton Duluth Brooks—that led to the creation of this book, a project over a century in the making. It was Brooks who, in the waning days of the war, wrote to every OU student, alumni, and faculty member who served in the armed forces with a request: to write a letter describing their wartime experiences. Some seventy men ultimately responded, and the letters were filed and archived. Decades later, Professor Levy stumbled across them while researching for the second volume of his history of the university.

As Levy notes, the OU community at the time of the First World War was a largely patriotic lot. Case in point: around the time of the Great War, over three-quarters of the university's students, alumni, and faculty who served in the armed forces volunteered as opposed to being drafted.

Those associated with OU will recognize many of the letter writers' names, including Walter Stanley Campbell (1887–1957). Campbell, who had served on OU's English faculty since 1915, served six months in France, becoming a captain in the Field Artillery. Under the name Stanley Vestal, he wrote two dozen books on the American West and Indigenous Americans. At OU, he founded the Professional Writing Program, which has produced dozens of writers whose work has been published over the years.

Another well-known OU alumnus and faculty member featured in these pages is Joshua Bryan Lee (1892–1967), who graduated in 1917 with a reputation for eloquence. Lee served with the 135th Infantry in France, where he was tasked with providing entertainment and raising morale among the troops. After serving fourteen months in the war, he returned to the university to chair the Public Speech Department, a position he held until his successful bid for the U.S. House of Representatives in 1934. He was elected to the U.S. Senate in 1937 and was sometimes mentioned as a possible vice presidential candidate in 1940. He ended his career practicing law in Norman.

Sooner Doughboys Write Home is an invaluable contribution to the vast compendium of scholarly literature on World War I. Through these letters, readers will move beyond the historical facts and get a glimpse into the hearts and souls of men who dedicated months, years, and sometimes their lives, to their country.

Not only that, but readers will also see how the service continued after these veterans returned home. Many completed their degrees at OU or continued to serve with distinction on the OU faculty. Others went on to become prominent lawyers or physicians or to otherwise lead and serve their communities, in Oklahoma or across the nation.

These letters remind us that those who call OU home have always been about the business of changing lives. And the Sooner doughboys' stories continue to inspire us today as we uphold our university's fundamental purpose: We Change Lives.

In his letter to these OU servicemen, President Brooks expressed his hope that their letters would be bound and kept in the university annals. Thanks to David Levy, we can finally fulfill that wish. I encourage you to read these letters not only to learn about the lives and legacies of those who have gone before us but also to be inspired to forge your own.

ABBREVIATIONS

AEF	American Expeditionary Forces
APO	Army Post Office
BH	Base Hospital
BN; Btn; Bat	Battalion
CAC	Coast Artillery Corps
ChO	*Chronicles of Oklahoma*
CO	Commanding officer
Cpl.	Corporal
DO	*Daily Oklahoman*
FA	Field Artillery
FSBn	Field Signal Battalion
GHQ	General Headquarters
Hq	Headquarters
HS	Hospital Ship
KP	Kitchen Police / Kitchen Porter
MG	Machine gun
OD	*Oklahoma Daily*
OU	University of Oklahoma
Pvt	Private
QH	Quartermaster Headquarters
QM	Quartermaster
QMC	Quartermaster Corps
RD	Rapid Deployment

S.O.S.	Services of Supply
TC	Transportation Corps
Trn	Transferred
USAT	United States Army Transport
USN	United States Navy
USSC	United States Submarine Chaser
USSO	United States Submarine, Class O

Introduction

B<small>Y</small> the beginning of November 1918, the Great War appeared, at long last, to be dragging itself to a conclusion. Recognizing the historic significance of the moment, Stratton Duluth Brooks, president of the University of Oklahoma, sat down at his desk and composed a letter. On November 6, five days before the armistice that actually ended the fighting, Brooks sent copies of that letter to every University of Oklahoma student, every former student, and every member of the faculty who was serving in the armed forces during the war and for whom the University had a mailing address.[1] His letter contained a request:

> The one thing that I want to ask of you is that from time to time you write a letter giving your experiences in detail, and particularly your impressions during your service in the war. My purpose is to have these letters bound in volumes and kept in the archives of the University. . . . I very much hope that you will find time, and have the inclination, to write us often.
>
> With best wishes, and appreciating the noble service you are rendering, I am,
>
> Sincerely yours,
Stratton D. Brooks
President of the University

1. For the full text of Brooks's November 6, 1918, letter, see the Stratton D. Brooks Collection (not his Presidential MSS), University Archives, Western History Collections (WHC), University of Oklahoma Libraries, Norman, Oklahoma.

1

Back in April 1917, when President Woodrow Wilson asked Congress to declare war against Germany, Oklahomans were far from unanimous in their support of America's entry into the bloody European conflict. In fact, a considerable number of the state's citizens were dubious about the whole enterprise. By 1917, for example, there were probably around 10,000 Oklahoma residents who had been born in Germany and perhaps another 30,000 American-born Oklahomans who had at least one German-born parent.[2] Many of these Oklahomans with German connections no doubt resented (and had reason to fear) the exuberant and contemptuous denunciations of German militarism, German motives, German *Kultur*. It is not surprising that many of them wanted no part of this war. Similarly, by 1917, there were more than 1,800 Ireland-born residents in the state and more than 10,000 Oklahomans with at least one Irish parent.[3] Many of these Oklahoma citizens with Irish loyalties harbored deep reservations about the United States rushing in to save the evil and oppressive British Empire.

Oklahoma was also home to a great many members of the Socialist Party. Only six months prior to America's entry into the war, more than 45,000 Oklahomans had voted for the Socialist candidate for the U.S. presidency; that number was around 15 percent of Oklahoma's total vote, by far the highest percentage of any other state.[4] Presumably, a fair

2. For German population growth in Oklahoma, see Richard C. Rohrs, *The Germans in Oklahoma* (Norman: University of Oklahoma Press, 1980), 19–22; or Rohrs, "Germans," in *The Oklahoma Encyclopedia of History and Culture* (Oklahoma City: Oklahoma Historical Society, 2009), 1: 579–80.

3. Patrick J. Blessing, *The British and Irish in Oklahoma* (Norman: University of Oklahoma Press, 1980), tables 3 and 4; and Larry O'Dell, "Irish," in *Oklahoma Encyclopedia*, 1: 743–44.

4. Garin Burbank, *When Farmers Voted Red: The Gospel of Socialism in the Oklahoma Countryside, 1910–1924* (Westport, Conn.: Greenwood Press, 1976); Jim Bissett, *Agrarian Socialism in America: Marx, Jefferson, and Jesus in the Oklahoma Countryside, 1904–1920* (Norman: University of Oklahoma Press, 2002); James R.

number of them subscribed to their party's official position of opposition to the war. Religious and philosophical pacifists were another group who resisted entry into the conflict; they saw every war as barbaric and immoral, and could detect no redeeming moral attributes in this one.[5] And beyond all these ethnic, political, and ideological opponents of the war were large numbers of everyday Oklahoma farmers, many of them tenants, who were simply unconvinced of the necessity to disrupt the current prosperous economic climate. Many of them saw no reason to send their sons overseas to die in a faraway war for purposes that seemed pointless and remote. In the summer of 1917, there was even a short-lived rural uprising against the war and the draft, called the Green Corn Rebellion. Around the same time, a small and obscure group of antiwar radicals, calling themselves "the Jones Family," sprang up in parts of Cleveland County, the very same county in which the University of Oklahoma carried on its work.[6]

Opposition to the war was so widespread that federal, state, and local authorities, as well as unofficial vigilante groups, felt justified in resorting to some unusual (and questionable) measures to counter the "disloyal," the "pro-German" the "lukewarm," and to challenge directly these unwilling "traitors" and "slackers" to do their part.[7] Supporters of

Scales and Danney Goble, *Oklahoma Politics: A History* (Norman: University of Oklahoma Press, 1982), 62–79; and Oliver Benson et al., *Oklahoma Votes, 1907–1962* (Norman: University of Oklahoma Bureau of Government Research, 1964).

5. See, for example, Marvin E. Kroeker, "'In Death You Shall Not Wear It Either': The Persecution of Mennonite Pacifists in Oklahoma," in Davis D. Joyce, ed., *"An Oklahoma I Had Never Seen Before": Alternative Views of Oklahoma History* (Norman: University of Oklahoma Press, 1994), 80–100.

6. Nigel Anthony Sellars, *Oil, Wheat, & Wobblies: The Industrial Workers of the World in Oklahoma, 1905–1930* (Norman: University of Oklahoma Press, 1998). For a review of the literature on the Green Corn Rebellion, see Daniel Hanne, "The Green Corn Rebellion, Oklahoma, August, 1917: A Descriptive Bibliography of Secondary Sources," *ChO* 79 (Fall 2001): 343–57.

7. James H. Fowler, II, "Tar and Feather Patriotism: The Suppression of Dissent in Oklahoma During World War One," *ChO* 56 (Winter 1978–79): 409–30; and

the war in Norman, for example, erected a "slacker pen" on Main Street, a wooden cage where those who declined to contribute sufficiently to the War Stamp Drive or the Liberty Loans or the Red Cross, were confined in the public view of their neighbors until they agreed to mend their ways.[8] Towns and individuals with German sounding names were strongly urged to change them. Studying the German language was widely considered inappropriate, as was worshiping or even conversing in German or reading German language newspapers. There were not infrequent acts of violence against critics of the war or against their property.

Despite these harsh measures, resistance toward the war persisted among local citizens. In light of that sentiment, the enthusiasm for the war on the campus of the University of Oklahoma seems especially remarkable.[9]

On April 4, 1917, the day the Senate acceded to Wilson's request for a declaration, and two days before the House of Representatives did the same, the new student editor of the *Oklahoma Daily*, Fayette Copeland (soon to be in the army himself and, after the war, a professor and the mainstay of academic journalism at the University for four decades) published an editorial entitled "Prepare." With the war almost upon them,

---

Fowler, "Creating an Atmosphere of Suppression, 1914–1917," *ChO* 59 (Summer 1981): 202–23. For the nationwide treatment of dissenters, see Horace C. Peterson and Gilbert C. Fite, *Opponents of War, 1917–1918* (Seattle: University of Washington Press, 1968).

8. "Slacker Pen Used to Urge Slothful," *DO*, September 22, 1918, D11. See also Michael C. Morton, "Cooperation and Conflict: A Case Study in Harmony and Discord in Cleveland County, Oklahoma, 1889–1959" (master's thesis: University of Oklahoma, 1980), ch. 2.

9. For an overview of the wartime activity on the Norman campus, see David W. Levy, "'Practically a Military School': The University of Oklahoma and World War One," *ChO* 84 (Summer 2006): 132–61.

Copeland wrote "it is time that Sooners were thinking of the part which they may have to play." He thought that "it is probable that 50 per cent of the student body would answer the call. Some would do so immediately while others would wait until after school is out [in June]." He offered a suggestion: "Why not organize a volunteer training corps among the students by which the rudiments of military science might be learned?" If they drilled every day "even with sticks or baseball bats for guns," they might be just as patriotic as if they enlisted.[10]

The principal question in those early April days was, as Copeland had predicted, whether the young men on campus should leave school now or wait until June. The day after Copeland's editorial, the University's faculty gathered as "a war cabinet" and announced that any young man who enlisted before the end of the semester would receive full credit for his course work provided he had passing grades when he withdrew.[11]

A mass meeting of male students occurred on the oval on Wednesday afternoon, April 11. At the time, there were 907 men enrolled at the University; 850 of them appeared at the gathering.[12] The air resounded with patriotic speeches. Josh Lee, the silver-tongued graduating senior who had won a prestigious national oratorical competition and who had ahead of him an illustrious career first as chair of the University's Speech Department and then as a U.S. congressman and senator, opened the proceedings. He made a stirring speech, calling for "sane patriotism" and declaring that "the Sooner war cry, 'Oklahoma Fights' that has often been heard upon the gridiron was the slogan to which all loyal Sooners must rally and show that they do mean what they say. . . . The time has

10. Fayette Copeland, Jr., "Prepare," *OD*, April 4, 1917, 2.
11. *OD*, April 5, 1917, 1. Within a week, however, it was discovered that some students were leaving school "intending" to enlist, but not actually doing so, "hoping by this method to get credit . . . without attending the remainder of the year or taking the final examinations." The abuse was countered by a requirement that "a written statement of his enlistment from his company commander" would be needed before credit could be granted. *OD*, April 12, 1917, 3.
12. *OD*, April 12, 1917, 1.

passed for talk and we must act."[13] Lee was followed to the platform by Stratton Brooks. The president proposed that the men would remain at school but would form a volunteer regiment. They would drill on Monday, Wednesday, and Friday afternoons, from 4:30 to 6:00, and attend military lectures on Tuesdays and Thursdays. Attendance was to be compulsory. When Brooks had finished, the much-esteemed history teacher and dean of Arts and Sciences, James ("Uncle Buck") Buchanan, suggested that a vote be taken on the president's proposal. It passed without a single dissent. The men then sang "The Star-Spangled Banner," "America," "Dixie," and (of course) "Boomer Sooner." The next morning's headline in the *Oklahoma Daily* said it all: "SPIRIT OF WAR INVADES SOONERLAND."

A whirlwind of activity ensued. Brooks sent urgent telegrams to Washington asking that an army officer be dispatched to Norman to train the students; he also asked for any army rifles the government could supply.[14] The *Daily* printed relevant passages from the "Infantry Drill Regulations."[15] A fifteen-page "Military Rules of the University of Oklahoma" was distributed.[16] A selection committee named the regimental officers, chosen from among eighty-five eager volunteers. Two battalions were organized, each with three companies. One company was set aside for faculty members.[17] The director of the University's band asked all

13. Ibid. Lee enlisted after his graduation and served in France. See his letter to President Brooks, below.

14. Edwin K. Wood, "The University of Oklahoma in World War" (master's thesis, University of Oklahoma, 1923), 11.

15. *OD,* April 14, 1917, 4.

16. For a copy, see Stratton D. Brooks, Presidential MSS, University Archives, WHC, Box 12, Folder 11.

17. There is some discrepancy in numbers between Edwin Wood's 1923 thesis (n. 14, above) and the 1918 *Sooner Yearbook.* Wood reported (13) that 3 battalions, consisting of 12 companies, were formed; the *Yearbook* (279–96) pictures and lists membership of 2 battalions and 6 companies. I have taken the view that Wood's figures represented the theoretical structure of the regiment, while the *Yearbook* comes closer to depicting the reality. In any case, the University's regiment was

musicians to report to him for the purpose of forming a thirty-piece regimental band.[18] Fraternities and sororities began canceling their spring dances. Unfortunately, it was too late to stop the Junior Prom. But its organizers pledged that "the Stars and Stripes will reign supreme . . . and red, white, and blue will predominate all declarations." All proceeds would be sent to the Red Cross.[19] Astonishingly, revered football coach Bennie Owen announced that spring football practice would be canceled so the players could drill alongside the other men. "A bomb has completely shattered every branch of Sooner athletics for the remainder of the season," declared the *Daily*.[20] On April 4, fifty students at the Medical School in Oklahoma City declared that they would be organizing a volunteer hospital company just in case it was needed. Two weeks later the U.S. Surgeon General advised the young doctors to apply for commissions in the reserve and urged the medical faculty to teach during the summer to help train medical men for the war effort.[21]

On April 10, a day before the men had their mass meeting, female students, led by Marian Brooks, the president's daughter, held their own meeting and organized a Red Cross chapter. By the end of the month, 160 women students were enrolled in First Aid and other home nursing classes.[22] (It is regrettable that President Brooks did not send his November 6 letter to women students and alumni about *their* experiences and impressions during the war. Many of them rendered notable service as nurses or through the YMCA/YWCA, the Red Cross, or other formal

---

disbanded a month later, on May 11, in favor of the conscription policy adopted by Congress.

18. *OD*, April 12, 1917, 1.

19. Ibid.

20. Ibid.

21. *OD*, April 5, 1917, 1; Mark R. Everett, *Medical Education in Oklahoma: The University of Oklahoma School of Medicine and Medical Center, 1900–1931* (Norman: University of Oklahoma Press, 1972), 136.

22. *OD*, April 11, 1917, 1; Wood, "University of Oklahoma in World War," 9–10. Wood errs in placing the women's meeting on April 9.

or informal organizations. A record of their service would have been as valuable and interesting as that of their male counterparts.)

⁂

The intense and pervasive pro-war atmosphere that so inflamed the student body (and served to silence any potential dissent) was, at least in part, inspired and encouraged by the examples set by the faculty. The most popular, influential, and respected members of the faculty rushed into prominent roles in support of the war.

The Oklahoma Council of Defense was the statewide institution most responsible for promoting patriotic feelings and countering any outright objection or lukewarm support of the war.[23] The official secretary of the council was none other than Stratton Brooks, and the council's director of wartime publicity was Chester Westfall, a professor of Journalism. If his work as secretary of the council was not demanding enough, President Brooks also took on the job of chair of the council's "Science and Research Committee." On top of that, from July 1917 until April 1918, Brooks was the Federal Food Administrator for the state of Oklahoma. To assist with these heavy duties, he turned over parts of the Administration Building (Evans Hall) to an army of twenty women secretaries and typists.[24] (It was thanks to these helpers that he was able to send out the letter he wrote right before the end of the war to so many recipients in so many different locations.) Brooks placed the University into the service of the war effort in other ways as well: turning the extension service into a virtual propaganda agency on behalf of the war; approving a score of new war-related courses in seven different departments; and authorizing

23. O. A. Hilton, "The Oklahoma Council of Defense and the First World War," *ChO* 20 (March 1942): 18–42. For the council's own version of its wartime activities, see *Sooners in the War: Official Report of the Oklahoma State Council of Defense, from May 1917 to January 1, 1919: Containing the War Activities of the State of Oklahoma* (Oklahoma City: Oklahoma State Council of Defense, 1919).

24. "President Stratton D. Brooks and His Work," *Sooner Yearbook, 1918,* 26.

the regular publication and distribution of *Sooners in the War Service,* a newsletter sent to men in the military.[25]

The Oklahoma Council of Defense created county branches, where, predictably, the most questionable enforcement measures were invented and implemented. The head of the Cleveland County Council was Roy Gittinger, a professor of History and the dean of undergraduates. The goal of the County Council, Gittinger would later write, "was to get results that would redound to the winning of the war, to see that every American citizen did his whole duty in every crisis, and to put a quietus upon disloyalty wherever and whenever it attempted to rear its hydra head." Under Professor Gittinger, the local council put a "loyal man on guard in every school district" and "dealt firmly with slackers of every description, putting the fear of God into their hearts and, at least, an outward semblance of loyalty to their country."[26] Assisting Gittinger was a popular and pugnacious professor of Chemistry named Guy Y. Williams. He had been a circus acrobat in his youth, and for many years he entertained and astounded his students by placing one hand on the corner of his desk and slowly lifting his body until it was parallel to the floor; into his sixties he would occasionally spring into a handstand or enter the classroom through the transom. Williams was active in those parts of Cleveland County where the war was regarded with less enthusiasm than it was on campus. He was described as "a very efficient member of the unofficial 'strong-arm squad' maintained by the council."[27]

Other professors were well known among the students for their ardent support of the war. Six highly regarded teachers (the historian E. E. Dale; Arts and Sciences dean "Uncle Buck" Buchanan; director of the School of Education, Warren Phelan; and three professors at the law school) gave patriotic lectures on why America was in the war to young soldiers

25. Wood, "University of Oklahoma in World War," 28–30.

26. Gittinger's comments were part of the State Council's official report, *Sooners in the War,* 33.

27. Wood, "University of Oklahoma in World War," 24.

at nearby military bases.[28] Coach Owen agreed to serve as the lieutenant colonel of the new student regiment. Professor of German, Roy Temple House, became chief translator in Europe and was decorated for his services by the government of Belgium; he made numerous speeches promoting the war when he returned to the United States. Arthur Adams, director of the Business School, left Norman for wartime service at the Federal Trade Commission. Other professors served at the Bureau of Standards or the War Department or with the YMCA.[29]

Thus, every day the young men and women on campus saw their teachers and mentors passionately endorsing the war effort and just as passionately disparaging those who harbored reservations about the conflict and about performing their patriotic responsibilities. These teachers were powerful models of what constituted proper attitudes and appropriate behavior.

Within days of America's entry into the war, some of these students ignored the pleas to remain in school for the remaining two months of the semester and began to disappear from the campus. On April 11, the day before the mass meeting on the oval, the *Daily* listed on its front page the names of no fewer than thirty students who had enlisted during that first week. Subsequent issues of the paper kept adding new names. "Each passing day in Soonerdom sees a few more vacant chairs in the classrooms as Oklahoma sons answer the call to the colors," said the *Daily*.[30] The following day, a professor of speech announced that her plans for presenting two plays had to be dropped because members of her class

28. Ibid., 50.
29. On Coach Owen, see *OD*, April 12, 1917, 1; on Professor House, see Wood, "University of Oklahoma in World War," 6; on Adams, see Daniel Wren, *Collegiate Education for Business Administration at the University of Oklahoma: A History* (Norman: Michael F. Price College of Business, 2002), 25.
30. *OD*, April 11, 1917, 2.

had enlisted. A "pageant of Oklahoma history," scheduled for May 12, had to be canceled "on account of the enlistment of many needed in the cast."[31] It was only natural that the examples of those who had left school so readily raised uncomfortable questions in the minds of those who stayed behind: were they less patriotic? Less courageous? Should they also sign up without delay?

Under the circumstances, the University's enrollment figures were troubling. The College of Arts and Sciences had claimed 1,730 students during the 1916–17 academic year but only 1,662 in 1917–18. Fine Arts dropped from 466 to 381, Medicine from 85 to 75, and Law from 175 to 87. Perhaps predictably, both Nursing and Engineering experienced small increases in enrollment.[32]

It did not get better. On May 22, 1918, thirteen months after America entered the war, the *Oklahoma Daily* suspended publication because of "sudden and heavy enlistments from the business staff of the paper.... The war has been directly responsible for the end. Both the business manager and the circulation manager were called into service upon extremely short notice." The paper's final issue before the suspension carried a sobering front-page assessment: "A large number of those who would have been here this year, under ordinary conditions, are now across the sea; many of the students who enrolled in the fall have left to enter . . . military service; some of those who will complete the year's work will answer their country's call during the summer months, and will not return in the fall."[33] The newspaper did not resume publication until January 31, 1919, a gap of more than eight months.

The situation at the University was a reflection of the general crisis in American higher education caused by the war. The U.S. Bureau of Education estimated that male enrollment might have declined by as much

31. Ibid., April 23, 1917, 1.
32. Compare the enrollment statistics in the *University Catalogue* for 1916–17 (p. 435) with those in the *Catalogue* for 1917–18 (p. 454).
33. *OD*, May 22, 1918, 1, 2.

as 40 percent by the fall of 1917 (offset slightly by a small increase in female enrollments).[34] Many schools suffered losses even more severe than the University of Oklahoma, and some were threatened with closing. Members of the national administration (including that former university president, Woodrow Wilson) were alarmed by the emergency. It was, after all, the universally accepted belief that "college men" made the best military officers. Could the depleted colleges continue to supply officers if college men left their campuses to enlist or were drafted as privates? Some expressed concern for the possible shortage of college-educated men once the war had ended.

The eventual federal answer to the problem of keeping men in college was the Student Army Training Corps (SATC). The program, authorized by Congress in August 1918, deferred college men from the draft if their college agreed to operate like an army training camp. All able-bodied males had to enroll in the SATC and, along with their regular schoolwork, wear uniforms, operate under military discipline, and drill under the supervision of regular army officers. Fraternity and sorority houses became barracks. Calisthenics, guard duty, bayonet practice, marching to meals—all would become routine. For all practical purposes, the government took over colleges and universities, supplying equipment and buildings. Participating schools received $900 for each student-soldier, thereby alleviating the financial catastrophe caused by declining enrollments. The University of Oklahoma was one of 525 American colleges that joined the SATC on October 1, 1918, and the campus became more like a military installation than an institution of higher education. Looking back a quarter century later, Roy Gittinger

34. David O. Levine, *The American College and the Culture of Aspiration, 1915–1940* (Ithaca: Cornell University Press, 1986), 27. See also Carol S. Gruber, *Mars and Minerva: World War I and the Uses of the Higher Learning in America* (Baton Rouge: Louisiana State University Press, 1975); and Samuel P. Cappen, "The Effects of the World War, 1914–18, on American Colleges and Universities," *Educational Record* 21 (January 1940): 40–48.

wrote that "from October 1 to December 21, 1918, when the SATC was disbanded, the university was practically a military school."[35]

⌖⌖⌖

Tallying up the numbers of Sooners who served in the military during the Great War proved to be a tricky undertaking. As a result, the figures vary. For example, Gittinger, in his history of the University, states that 38 members of the faculty joined the military, but in an appendix to that book he lists 41 names.[36] The numbers that follow here are taken from the accounting in a 1923 master's thesis by Edwin K. Wood, entitled "The University of Oklahoma in World War."[37] According to Wood, more than 2,300 students, former students, and members of the faculty contributed to the war effort in some way or other. Of these, 1,139 were part of the armed forces: 972 in the army; 147 in the navy; and 20 in the marine corps.[38]

Of this total, by Wood's count, 885 (77.6 percent) volunteered and 254 (22.4 percent) were drafted under the Selective Service Act of May 18, 1917. It should be noted that across the nation this breakdown was much different. According to the National Archives Foundation, about 2 million American men volunteered for military service in World War 1 and 2.8 million were drafted—a breakdown of 41 versus 59 percent.[39] Of those University of Oklahoma men in the army or the marine corps, 444 (45 percent) saw duty overseas. At least 487 of the 1,139 University of

35. Roy Gittinger, *The University of Oklahoma: A History of Fifty Years, 1892–1942* (Norman: University of Oklahoma Press, 1942), 111.

36. Ibid., 106–7, 214–16.

37. Other attempts at estimating numbers of those in service were made in both the 1918 and the 1919 University yearbooks. The 1919 yearbook was entitled *Victory Sooner.*

38. Wood, "University of Oklahoma in World War," 21.

39. "Mobilizing for War: The Selective Service Act in World War 1," National Archives Foundation, www.archivesfoundation.org/documents/mobilizing-war -selective-service-act-world-war/.

Oklahoma–connected men (43 percent) were commissioned officers. Among the 468 army officers, 396 were first or second lieutenants. There were 16 naval officers and 3 officers in the marine corps. Four University men reached the rank of lieutenant colonel, and eleven others ended their service as majors.[40]

It was inevitable that some of them never made it back home. Three members of the faculty died: one in combat and the other two in the horrific influenza pandemic of 1918.[41] Among the University's students and former students twenty-one died during the war, twelve in combat, six from influenza, and three from other diseases.[42] One of those dying from the flu was Eloise Eagleton, a young nurse who had graduated in 1914 and came back to school to earn her MA in 1918. She was struck down by the disease while working in a military hospital in Waco, Texas. Eagleton was the only University-connected woman to die in the war. Among men who came home wounded, seven were exposed to poison gas, eleven were hit by enemy fire, and one (Sergeant Gerald S. Tebbe from the class of 1916) suffered both gassing and wounds on August 8, 1918.[43]

Within a few weeks, the letters requested by President Brooks on November 6, 1918, began to arrive. A small handful of them were typed, but the great majority were scrawled out by hand, and some of them, smudged and hastily composed, were almost indecipherable. Some letters did

40. Wood, "University of Oklahoma in World War," 21.

41. On the flu pandemic, see John M. Barry, *The Great Influenza: The Epic Story of the Deadliest Plague in History* (New York: Viking, 2004); and Alfred Crosby, *America's Forgotten Pandemic: The Influenza of 1918* (Cambridge: Cambridge University Press, 2003).

42. *Victory Sooner*, 9–18, published each deceased person's picture, with details of the cause of death. The 1919 *University Catalogue, 1919*, also lists names and details, 77–78. See also Gittinger, *University of Oklahoma*, 107–9. Wood, "University of Oklahoma in World War," gives a slightly different accounting.

43. *Victory Sooner*, 21–24.

not get sent until well into 1919—delayed because other duties took precedence, or by the common tendency to postpone things one is not required to do, or because the military's proclivity to move personnel about from place to place resulted in Brooks's request sometimes not catching up with the intended recipient for months.

In the end, around seventy men wrote to Brooks. No doubt this was fewer than he had hoped, and the letters were never "bound in volumes" as he had originally suggested. As each letter arrived, it was dutifully placed into a box, filed away in alphabetical order, and deposited in the *personal* papers of Stratton Brooks (not in his *presidential* papers). There, in that box, the letters have rested for more than a century. I stumbled across them quite by accident while searching for something else. It was unclear whether any person had looked at them since they were first deposited. Recently, the staff of the Western History Collections at the University has placed the letters into protective plastic envelopes in order to preserve them for the future. In the pages that follow, readers will find fifty-three of the most interesting and revealing of these old letters.

As John Keegan noted in his celebrated book *The Face of Battle* (1976), the vast preponderance of writing about warfare has been written from the perspective of the general headquarters: biographies of important generals and diplomats, discussions of grand strategies, details of weaponry, trials of supplying troops in the field, histories of particular branches of the military, the strain of a conflict on the national economy or the civilian population. Great battles are usually described as if they were looked down upon from a great height ("The 4th Division moved up to the front in good order and, after a rest, twice attempted to break through the enemy's lines," or "There was some confusion on the left flank as the machine guns were late in taking up their positions," and so forth). Stories of warfare, in short, have not often been told from the point of view of the ordinary men who fought in the battles. For one thing, as Keegan points out, it is only since the nineteenth century that many ordinary soldiers could read or write.[44] Perhaps it is not entirely accurate to call the writers of the letters published here "ordinary," because in 1917, ordinary young American men did not go to college. But the viewpoints of these letter writers were not the same as the viewpoints of the generals; these letter writers did not look down on the Great War from above but described and tried, as best they could, to make sense of the aspects of it that they themselves experienced as participants.

Taken as a whole, therefore, these letters constitute a remarkable repository of reminiscence and feeling. These young men, or "doughboys" (as they were nicknamed), shared, to a striking degree, a set of beliefs and attitudes.[45] They were unashamedly patriotic and quite certain that their own country was better than any other. They were determined to carry out their duties conscientiously. They were contemptuous of the German enemy and modest about their own (sometimes prodigious) efforts and achievements. They expressed a desire to return home as soon as possible and to resume their education or take up again the jobs they had left. Almost nothing is said in these letters of a religious nature, and there are few references to immediate family—wives, girlfriends, parents. There are none of the complaints about their officers and few complaints about the food that are commonly associated with military life. The letters betray a poignant and appealing innocence of the wider world into which these young men had been abruptly thrust.

44. For Keegan's critique of traditional military history scholarship and his argument for seeing the story from the point of view of the ordinary soldier, see his *The Face of Battle* (New York: Viking Press, 1976), ch. 1.

45. The term "doughboys" was inherited from the Mexican War of the 1840s and the Civil War of the 1860s. It was first used to denote infantry and then other military personnel during World War I. There are several theories about how the term originated and became attached to common soldiers. See Elizabeth Nix, "Why Were American Soldiers in WWI called Doughboys?" History (website), last modified September 18, 2018, www.history.com/news/why-were-americans -who-served-in-world-war-i-called-doughboys.

For many of them, it was a world of dreary inactivity and boredom, punctuated by moments of breathtaking violence and danger.

Most of these youngsters had come from farms or small rural Oklahoma towns. For many of them, Norman (population of around 5,000 at that time) was the largest place in which they had ever lived, and Oklahoma City (population of around 78,000) perhaps the biggest city they had ever even seen. Suddenly they were herded onto crowded trains and deposited in crowded training camps where they were drilled and hardened into the military life. From there many of them were delivered to embarkation posts on the East Coast; they got acquainted with Hoboken, New Jersey; with Baltimore, Maryland; with Manhattan and Brooklyn. They were put into huge transport vessels that carried them across an ocean filled with prowling enemy submarines that were trying to send them down to watery graves. They landed in France where they found people who had strange customs and who did not usually speak English. Many of them got to see Paris and many were sent into Germany as part of the army of occupation. All the while, they kept a sharp eye out for old classmates from Norman, eager to share a quick drink or a hurried chat about the whereabouts of mutual friends. They took part in constant drills and long hikes. They learned a great deal about artillery bombardments and poison gas and trenches and going "over the top," about taking orders and giving orders, about machine guns and tanks, about life on troop transports, about submarines carrying torpedoes and airplanes carrying bombs. Some of them saw their friends killed or terribly wounded.

And each, in his own way, tried to write about some of these things to the president of his old school.

※※※※

In the course of editing these letters, I have tried to let the writers speak in their own voices. This has meant restricting editorial intrusions except when necessary to clarify the writer's intent. Bearing in mind that many of these men were responding to President Brooks hastily and while dealing with other duties and other personal concerns, I have ignored minor spelling and grammatical errors if those mistakes did not seem to obscure the writer's meaning. With regard to format, I have presented certain standard elements, such as salutations and signatures, in a consistent style. For example, I have used a colon after each letter's salutation. Finally, in rare instances where a word was illegible or indecipherable, I have indicated so in brackets [ ].

Letters from Sooner Doughboys

Lawrence Edgar Beattie

AMERICAN RED CROSS
ON ACTIVE SERVICE
WITH THE
AMERICAN EXPEDITIONARY FORCE

L. E. Beattie–Cpl.
B.H. 84 Med. Det. U.S.A.
A.P.O. 794 Am. E. F.

Perigueux, France,[1] Dec. 19th, 1918

Dear Old "U" and Friends:

As the rain descends this evening upon a once more peaceful soil, the inhabitants of which are this moment singing with unabounded [*sic*] joy the praise that justly falls upon the newly proclaimed "Citizen of Paris", our own beloved President, announced on his arrival as the Liberator of the World,[2] such it seems to me forms a most beautiful and appropriate setting for the near dawn of Christmas Day, the Birthday

---

Lawrence Edgar Beattie (1892–1965) was born in Kansas, but moved to Alva, Oklahoma. He was a senior and active in student politics in 1917. After enlisting, he served in France with the Medical Corps, Base Hospital 84. After the war, Beattie attended the University's law school and was president of the Oratorical Association and vice president of his law class. He received his degree on June 8, 1920, and practiced law in Ardmore, Oklahoma, until his death.

1. Périgueux, a city of around 33,000 at the time, is located about 300 miles southwest of Paris.

2. On December 13, 1918, a week before Beattie's letter was written, President Woodrow Wilson arrived in France to participate in the preliminary peace negotiations at the end of the war. He was the first U.S. president to cross the Atlantic while in office. Everywhere he went in Europe, Wilson was greeted by enormous crowds and hailed as the leader of the country that had saved Europe from German victory and as the prophet of a new world order, heralding a new era of peace and prosperity.

of the only "Prince of Peace"; and as that day approaches nearer and nearer happy memories of home once again are recalled, and with home must be coupled the dear old recollections we hold in our memory of the plain little campus, separated from us by the waves of a wild ocean, for upon that spot is situated our own beloved Alma Mater. But thoughts here are numerous and diversified. The routine of the army life, our daily work, stories of the front, French people and their customs, expectations and anticipations of the future, and a longing for home are all found in that conglomerate mass from which is formulated the thought of the A.E.F. boy.

Located in the outskirts of the City of Perigueux on the left bank of the beautiful Lisle, within the Province of Dordogne, is our hospital. Hills covered with vegetation, forests, ancient structures, and the serpentine windings of the magnificent French roads form the environment of our camp. Mediaeval history is continually recalled in one's mind as your eyes gaze upon the crumbling, rock built chateaus, the remnants of city walls, and lookout towers found within our neighboring city. Monuments of Rome's ambitions are still famous landmarks in this region,[3] and within Perigueux an ancient arena casts upon that ever moving screen "Imagination" a picture of an amphitheater filled with people eagerly awaiting the lions and their prey, or perchance some gallant knight who has challenged some sturdy rival.

But your mind must soon return to realities, for the hospital is no place for a dreamer when the wounded are thick around you, needing the immediate attention of a surgeon, perhaps to save the life of some mother's son. As we labored day by day and frequently nights in the operating pavilion, warfare in many of its features was brought home to us in a way never before realized. Wounds of all types and sizes were before our eyes to demonstrate the inhuman instruments of warfare that must have

3. Périgueux had been an important Roman center from Julius Caesar's victory over the Gauls around 50 BC until the barbarian invasions around 410.

been used by Imperial Wilhelm's[4] Workers in an endeavor to send Democracy to its grave. Victims of the Kaiser's poisonous gases[5] left marks upon our memory that are not pleasant to review. Surgical and medical genius by its constant watchfulness and research discovered many ways and means of aiding the distressed, thus preserving many a seemingly hopeless case. But there were those who fighting the battle for life failed to conquer this or that disease or infection, and it was for those that Prof. Lewis Salter[6] assisted the band in playing the droleful [*sic*] march to the little cemetery across the road. No more are new wounds being made in living flesh, no longer are all hospitals endeavoring to secure a larger capacity, for now the task is preparation for evacuation, and such is a difficult one.

Spare time in this vicinity has been at a premium. We have seen the beauties of France only from one viewpoint, except for the slight glimpses of the moving panorama caught from the door of a French box car as we came crawling southward from Le Havre[7] to our present place of

4. During the war, the chief villain for Americans was Kaiser Wilhelm II (1859–1941), Germany's last emperor. Wilhelm II reigned from 1888 until his forced abdication on November 9, 1918, two days prior to the armistice.

5. The large-scale use of poison gas by the Germans began in April 1915 at Ypres, Belgium. When inhaled, the terrifying new weapon caused convulsions, blindness, vomiting, and asphyxiation. Gas masks were not developed and distributed until later in the war. Soon chemical weapons were being developed by nations on both sides. Perhaps as many as 100,000 deaths and 1.3 casualties overall may be attributed to the use of poison gas. Public revulsion over the use of gas resulted in its being banned in 1925 by the Geneva Protocol. See Charles E. Heller, *Chemical Warfare in World War I: The American Experience, 1917–1918* (Fort Leavenworth, Kans.: U.S. Army Command and General Staff College, 1984).

6. For Lewis Salter, see his letters of January 15 and April 2, 1919, below.

7. As will be seen from these letters, many American military transports entered France through the major port of Le Havre, and many Oklahoma men first encountered French culture there. (Almost two million British soldiers also came through Le Havre during the war.) On the country's northern coast in the Normandy region and on the English Channel, Le Havre had a population of around 140,000 in 1918.

abode. Orleans, perhaps, with its historical maid,[8] is the most noted point we passed. We had reached Le Havre after a voyage across the channel from Anglo-land, which in turn had been preceded by a night's journey from Liverpool. The latter's harbor lights on the night of September 12th had presented to our eyes the most welcome sight since our vision of the Statue of Liberty, for we had practiced deck walking thirteen days, and on the 13th we again stepped on Allied soil.

Although our voyage had been full of anticipations of what might occur,[9] it was never interrupted, and we now patiently await the time to set sail upon that broad expanse of water, this time free of hidden enemies lurking beneath the rolling waves, and to journey peacefully westward toward the one great Emblem of Liberty, knowing that such statue holds high in her hand a guiding torch and represents the hearts within our nation as it welcomes the homeward bound A.E.F.

Best wishes to all in Soonerland.

Still a Sooner,

Lawrence E. Beattie

8. Orléans, a historic city on the Loire River, is around 200 miles south of Le Havre. Its population during World War I was around 70,000. The "maid of Orléans" was the martyred Joan of Arc (1412–1431).

9. The fear of German submarines, called U-boats, preying upon trans-Atlantic shipping, both merchant and military, was pervasive. Every ship that ventured across the Atlantic Ocean, whether a solitary vessel or part of a convoy, was in danger of being torpedoed and sunk by these fearsome underwater weapons. During the course of the war, German "subs" sank almost a dozen battleships, around 15 cruisers, and thousands of civilian merchant and fishing vessels. Germany's insistence upon "unrestricted submarine warfare" was a major catalyst for America's entry into the war in April 1917. See Richard Compton-Hall, *Submarines and the War at Sea: 1914–1918* (London: Macmillan, 1991).

Joseph Samuel Belt

Pvt. J. S. Belt
H.Q. Co. 144 Inf.
A.E.F. A.P.O. 796

Rugny, Yonne,[1]
France. Jan. 16, 1919

Dr. Stratton D. Brooks.

Dear Sir:

With pride in the services which I have rendered unto my Country, and appreciating the opportunity to thus aid in any way the institution of my respect and pride, and to be represented in its Volumes as a graduate and alumnus member of those who have served in the American Expeditionary Forces, I feel the inclination and due respect to write in answer to your appreciable letter.

I have kept no diary as all identification and information about our person was necessarily dispensed with before we swung into action, and since the signing of the Armistice for lack of experiences of interest.

To all soldiers in the infantry marching becomes second nature and none is considered efficient unless he can "hike" ten kilometers[2] on sheer determination and "grit" after his physical ability is exhausted.

Joseph Samuel Belt (1894–1974) was born in southwestern Oklahoma. He graduated from the University's law school in June 1918, and enlisted on May 29, 1918, a few days before receiving his diploma. Belt was with the 14th Infantry in France. He was discharged on May 15, 1919. Upon his return, he practiced law in Norman until moving to Amarillo, Texas, and then to Houston.

1. Rugny, a small village in the Yonne department, is around 130 miles southeast of Paris.
2. 6.2 miles.

We left Hoboken,[3] enroute to Brest, France,[4] where we disembarked and proceeded to Bar Sur Aube.[5] Being stationed among the villages thereabout we underwent a period of training and schooling. From there we went by way of Epernay[6] where we again left our train of box cars at night. There we could hear the roar of guns and see the Heavens lighted by their continuous flashes.

Beside the depot were trenches partly demolished used for protection against almost nightly air raids.

This town "smelt above the earth"[7] with the savagery of the Huns. There also is the largest Champaigne [sic] factory in the World. Dispensing with the modernism of the United States it might be said to rival the Busch Brewery[8] in magnitude.

We left immediately and were stationed not a great way from Rheims, my organization being at Juvigny.[9] Here we experienced our first

3. Hoboken, New Jersey, is directly across the Hudson River from New York City and part of the giant metropolitan complex. Hoboken became the chief embarkation point for troops heading to France. By the end of the war, around three million men passed through the city on their way to the war. In 1919, Hoboken had a population of nearly 70,000.

4. Like Le Havre, Brest was a major landing point for Americans coming to fight in France. Its location at the westernmost tip of France, along with its excellent harbor, made it the logical disembarking place for American troop transport ships. The U.S. Navy opened a base there in February 1918. Brest's population was around 75,000 during the war.

5. About 150 miles east of Paris, Bar Sur Aube is in the midst of the champagne industry of northeastern France. Because of its proximity to some of the major battlefields of the war, it was an important staging area for American troops.

6. Epernay, on the Marne River in northeastern France, was at the center of some of the fiercest fighting of the war. Its population at the time was around 21,000.

7. William Shakespeare, *Julius Caesar,* act 3, scene 1.

8. The Anheuser-Busch brewery, in St. Louis, Missouri, was opened in 1852. It eventually expanded to 140 acres and hundreds of structures.

9. Rheims and Juvigny are both in the Marne department. The former is a major city, the site for the coronation of the kings of France and home of a famous

air raid at night. The Hun plane circling over the town with the well known hum of the Boche[10] engine.

Strong lights searched the air, and bursting shells of shrapnel, some aimed, some fired at random made a Fourth of July at a high altitude. At an opportune moment the bird man made a sudden descent, threw out a flare of blinding light at the same time dropping two bombs.

Leaving there after further training we proceeded toward the Champaign [sic] Front. It is quite romantic in our memories that as we waited for nightfall on the approaches of the great Hindenburg system[11] preparatory to swinging in that our long looked for mail was distributed. Here among desolation and destruction inconceivable to the human mind without being actually witnessed, among the sights of lingering horrors and the meditations of our fate, we read our letters from home, self-possessed though haunted with curiosity and eagerness.

As night approached the Bat[t]alions in column formation with the combat wagons distributed majestically proceeded, an approaching storm of American pride, of German dread.

---

cathedral, which was damaged by a German bombardment in 1914. The prewar population was more than 115,000, but mass flight from the city reduced the number to 76,600 by 1921. Juvigny, where Belt was stationed, is a tiny village about 25 miles from Rheims.

10. Both "Boche" and "Hun" were derogatory terms applied to Germans, especially to German soldiers.

11. Called the Siegfriedstellung by the Germans, the Hindenburg Line (named by the British after German field marshal Paul von Hindenburg) was a series of defensive fortifications, built in late 1916 and early 1917, that stretched from Arras in far northern France, southward for 94 miles to near Soissons. Consisting of trenches, concrete pill boxes, machine gun emplacements, and barbed wire, and several miles deep, the line was intended to shorten the German line and conserve German infantry resources after the Battle of the Somme. The Germans fell back to the line in mid-March 1917. After a momentous artillery barrage, the Allies breached the defenses on September 29, 1918.

The seventy first brigade preceded the seventy second. On the night of October 10, 1918 we swung into action opposing the Prussian Guards.[12]

We were twenty three days under fire, advancing to a depth of thirty kilometers[13] supported by French troops on each wing.

The victory and I hope the undying fame of the 36th Division was here won.

May those who gave their lives for this victory receive their rewards in the next world forever, while mourned by their kinsmen and their noble services imprinted on our memories, and honored by their Country, their names will illuminate pages of new American history and descend to our posterity for generations to come, among and leading the traditions that has placed the United States of America above the World.

As for other impressions many may be had at a glance.

As Rome fell in 444 A.D. so did Germany in 1919 "Deep in ruin as in guilt."[14]

Primitive Europe still lingers in the path of modernism.

Vast Russia in all her weakness portrays a nation of social ignorance.

France in her heroic defense as a nation is now luminous, our debt of 1776 is paid. Future destiny is faintly conjectural.

Commerce and industry, World economics are now problematic, while the diplomacy and statesmanship must under[go] a supreme test.

---

12. Begun in 1740 by Frederick the Great, the Prussian Guard began as the personal bodyguard of the king of Prussia and then the Kaiser. It was still in existence during World War I. By then, the restructured Guard consisted of 26 infantry divisions and 10 machine gun companies. The Guard participated in the initial invasion of Belgium and France in August 1914. Later, it played an important role in the defense against the French offensive in 1917. The Prussian Guard was disbanded upon German demobilization at the war's end.

13. 18.6 miles.

14. From William Cowper's "Boadicea: An Ode" (1780), writing of ancient Rome:
Rome shall perish—write that word
In the blood that she has spilt;
Perish, hopeless and abhorr'd,
Deep in ruin as in guilt.

Hoping to return home soon and pursue the legal profession the mastery of which was a pleasant though difficult task in the University of Oklahoma.

Yours sincerely,
Joseph S. Belt

Odd Charles Blakely

Correspondence Room, Brooklyn Branch of the
Navy Young Men's Christian Association
167 Sands Street, Borough of Brooklyn
New York City

Brooklyn N.Y.
Dec 20 1918

Dear Sir:

In reply to your letter, regarding the activities in which the service placed me, having kept a log, I hope that these notes will have served a good purpose and take pleasure in sending them to the university.

I enlisted in the Navy May 30, 1917 and was sent to the St Helena training station, Norfolk Va. On Aug. 4, I was transferred to the USS Nevada.[1] I served in the fleet as a signalman until Feb 6, 1918, when I was transferred to the "Armed Guard"[2] and was stationed at the "City Park Barracks," Brooklyn N.Y. But for fleet maneuvers the six months I served on the "Nevada" was uneventful.

On Feb 13–18 I was detailed as convoy signalman to the English ship, "SS Vennachar" and landed at London Mar 1. The convoy though

Odd Charles Blakely (1895–1973) was born in Norman. After the war, he returned to school, earning his law degree at the University in 1920. He practiced law in Shawnee, worked for a while at Tinker Air Force, and moved to Oklahoma City, where he lived from 1960 until shortly before his death. He died in Memphis, Tennessee, in October 1973.

1. The USS *Nevada* was a new battleship, launched in 1914. It was the first battleship to be powered by oil rather than coal. The *Nevada* remained in American waters during Blakely's assignment. The ship arrived in Britain in August 1918 and served as a convoy escort for the rest of the war.
2. The Armed Guard was formed in 1917 to protect both merchant ships and troop transports from U-boats.

attacked by a submarine landed safely. I sailed from Liverpool Mar 14 aboard the USMS St Louis,[3] and landed at New York Mar 23, 1918.

I have made six convoy trips, two to England, three to France and one to Gibraltar. I have been detailed to English, Japanese, Italian and American cargo transport ships. Each of my trips across the sea was equally interesting. I returned to New York Dec 18, [19]18.

Sincerely yours,
Odd C. Blakely
QMs U.S.N.

3. The SS *Vennachar* was a British oil tanker. In April 1916 it had been attacked by a U-boat off Scotland and was damaged. The *St. Louis* had been a passenger ship before the war, sailing between New York and Liverpool. In March 1917 it was given an armed guard of 26 men and provided with guns. A month after Blakely's trip home, the *St. Louis* was taken over by the U.S. Navy and used as a troop transport. In January 1920, while docked at Hoboken, New Jersey, the *St. Louis* was destroyed by a fire.

Abraham Lincoln Blesh

Base Hosp. Camp Sheridan Ala.

Nov. 25–18

My Dear Pres Brooks:

This letter of yours, very much appreciated, found the staff of this Big Base in reaction from the fearful strain incident to the epidemic of "Flu" which seems to have swept pretty much over the entire world.[1] Following that all my trained help was ordered on to some other Post leaving me to rebuild my shattered "doll house" as best I could. This Uncle Sam of ours, no matter what he does to one's machine, still has a habit of exacting 100% at the muzzle of the gun. There are no excuses accepted. Who enters the Med. Corps leaves excuses behind. Especially is that true of Chiefs of Service, for upon their devoted heads is visited all the sins of everyone under him. I have built several such nice little "doll houses", had 'em all finished up nice, very pretty and serviceable things they were, when a barrage of Uncle Sam's telegrams wiped them out and I had to rebuild. I'm just digging out from such a barrage at this moment. But

---

Abraham Lincoln Blesh (1866–1934) was already a prominent physician by the time the war started. A graduate of Northwestern University, he studied in Vienna before entering practice in various places in Kansas and Wisconsin. He moved to Guthrie, Oklahoma, in 1894 and then to Oklahoma City in 1908. In 1912 he was appointed professor of surgery at the University's School of Medicine. He served terms as president of the Oklahoma Medical Association and the Medical Association of the Southwest.

1. The worldwide 1918 flu pandemic was one of the worst such outbreaks in human history. More than a third of the world's population was infected and many millions died of the disease. There were somewhere around 650,000 to 675,000 deaths from the flu in the United States, far more than the number of combat deaths suffered by the nation in the Great War. See Alfred W. Crosby, *America's Forgotten Pandemic: The Influenza of 1918*, 2nd ed. (New York: Cambridge University Press, 2003); or J. M. Barry, *The Great Influenza: The Epic Story of the Greatest Plague in History* (New York: Viking Penguin, 2004).

now that the war is over I am hoping soon to get back among my friends once again. My only regret being that entering the service to get into the war, I did not get in but was compelled to do my fighting, bleeding, and dying in Tex[as] and Ala[bama]. This has been a bitter disappointment to me, therefore I'll say nothing of my "experience" in ["]the great war." I have done nothing but do the thankless work of training surgeons and corps-men for service overseas since first I came in. I have been nothing more than the teacher-surgeon I was at home but in a wider field. Personally I have operated upon 3500 soldiers in the 1 1/2 years of my service, besides organizing two enormous Surg[ical]. Depts, so large that in my wildest dreams, I would not have conceived that I could have done it. Even now I do not know how I did it. Then I've sat on innumerable Boards, which is a common garden variety of army affliction. Besides I've kept an avalanche of papers slipping along to Wash[ington], to moulder in the archives—another common disease of the army. But by now you would not recognize in the hardened sinner I am the quiet, mild-mannered, soft-spoken surgeon whom you used to know. My regards,

A. L. Blesh

Andrew Nimrod Boatman

WAR DEPARTMENT
Headquarters Port of Embarkation
Office of the Quartermaster and General Superintendent Army
Transport Service Newport News, Va.

November 26, 1918

Mr. Stratton D. Brooks,
President, University of Oklahoma

Dear Dr. Brooks:

I have just received your office letter of November 6th in which you request an account of my experience while in the Army. Unfortunately for myself I was assigned to duty in the Quartermaster Corps at the end of the First Training Camp and a greater part of the time have been on duty at this Port.[1] Consequently I have but little of interest to relate, however, I did slip away from here long enough to make two voyages to France in charge of an Army Transport and will relate some of my impressions and experiences on those two voyages.

After coming to this Port last winter I had tried on various occasions to get a Transport, but due to the fact that my Captain would not agree to relieve me I did not succeed until April of this year. On April 4th I received an order from the Commanding General of the Port, relieving me from duty here and directing that I proceed to Baltimore and take

Andrew Nimrod Boatman (1887–1966), from Okmulgee, Oklahoma, earned his bachelor's degree in 1914 and his law degree two years later. He enlisted on May 10, 1917, went to Officers Training Camp, and was commissioned a first lieutenant. As he indicates, he was transferred to the Quartermaster Corps and made two trips to France. He was discharged on December 15, 1918. After the war, Boatman practiced law in his hometown and was county attorney for Okmulgee County.

1. Newport News, Virginia.

charge of the U. S. A. C. T. "Minnesotan",[2] then being loaded at that Port. I had never been to sea and knew nothing about a ship—Then imagine my predicament when I was shown this big freighter and told that it was up to me to direct all affairs aboard with the exception of the actual navigation which was to be done by the civilian Captain.

The "Minnesotan" is one of the ships owned by the American-Hawaiian Line and was being operated by the Army on a Bare-Boat basis.[3] She was manned by a civilian crew and had twenty-four enlisted men of the Navy aboard as Gun Crew, Signal men, and Radio operators. In employing men for the civilian crew I had a rather interesting experience. We had one man sent to the ship of whom both the Captain and myself were suspicious from the beginning. Just before the ship sailed we had the office send a Secret Service man down to take charge of this man, and I am told that he was later interned for the period of the War. What he was up to I do not know but he was there for some purpose other than to work as a mess-man on the ship.

We sailed from Baltimore just at 12:00 O'clock on April 16th going via New York harbor. The Captain had proceeded to New York by rail in order to attend the conference of Masters held before the Convoy sailed. We reached New York harbor and the Captain came aboard at 11:45 on the night of April 17th. His instructions were to proceed to sea if we reached the harbor before midnight. The last ship of the Convoy

2. The USS *Cargo Transport Minnesotan* was built in 1912 by the American-Hawaiian Steamship Company, and was one of the company's many ships carrying sugar from Hawaii to the United States. During the war, the ship was first chartered by the U.S. Navy and, in August 1918, was transferred to the navy. It was used to carry cargo to France. When the war ended, the *Minnesotan* became a troop ship and took more than 8,000 American soldiers back home from France.

3. Taking a boat on a "bareboat basis" means chartering or hiring it, but without a crew and provisions. In this case, the government chartered the *Minnesotan*, armed it as described by Boatman, and hired a civilian crew.

had left at noon that day, but we went in pursuit, due to the fact that we had one of the fastest freighters in the Service.

On the following morning I had my first and only touch of seasickness, which did not last long. We went at full speed ahead until we picked up the Convoy about day light on the morning of the 19th. We had been going at a speed of about fourteen to fifteen knots but then we had to take up our position in the Convoy and proceed at a speed of about eight to nine knots, as the slowest ship in the Convoy must of necessity determine its speed.

There were about forty cargo ships in the Convoy, lead [sic] by an old crippled cruiser. We sailed along in Convoy formation and after we neared the danger zone began running a zig-zag course, the signals being given out by the Convoy commander something like the Quarterback gives out signals to a Foot-ball team, only that it was done by signal flags instead of by word of mouth. On the morning of May 1st we picked up the English Destroyers just at day-break. Their coming was to me a most thrilling sight. They were scheduled to appear about that time and I was up looking for them. Just as it was getting light in the East the look-out, high up in the "crow's nest" announced that he saw a group of five Destroyers appearing on the horizon and within a very few minutes they could be seen from the deck with the naked eye. There they were, five abreast, coming on at full speed, and before one could think twice they had taken up their positions about the Convoy and were on the look-out for "Fritz". These five were joined by the sixth English Destroyer about noon and about 2:00 P. M. the American Destroyers began to appear on the horizon, and soon we could see six of them all coming from different directions. They were here, yonder and everywhere, darting in and out like a Bird-dog on a warm trail.

We moved on in the same formation until about sunset when the Convoy began to split; the English Destroyers taking the English ships and some American Oil Tankers on in the General Eastwardly direction into the English Channel, while the American ships were turned to the Southward, being guarded by the Six American Destroyers. On all ships the closest look-out was now kept as we had been warned that the "subs" were very active and we were now in their territory; or rather, what was their territory before the American Destroyers came. Even at that early date it was being seriously doubted whether the U-Boat had any territory.

On the morning of May 2nd I got up and dressed just before day, as that is the most dangerous hour and the time when everyone is most likely to be needed. Since I saw nothing unusual I had lain down on my lounge and began to doze when I was awakened by the sound of an explosion and at the same time felt my ship give. I was sure "Fritz" had us but was relieved of my anxiety when I learned that it was only the discharge of the 5-inch gun on the bow of our ship. It seems that the Gun Captain on the forward gun mistook a fog-buoy for a periscope and fired without waiting to ask questions. When the ships were in Convoy, running without lights they put out a fog buoy on a long line back of the ship as a protection against collisions. On this particular occasion the English ship in question had not pulled in the line with the coming of day as was the usual custom and the wake left by the fog-buoy looked very much like the wake of a periscope. Without waiting to investigate, the Gun Captain fired, and all that was left of the buoy was a few splinters. This little incident furnished the only excitement we had on the voyage. We entered Brest harbor about 4:00 P. M. May 2nd, where we dropped anchor until the following morning.

Brest harbor is a very beautiful place and was a scene of great activity at that time. Near where we were anchored lay the "Leviathan", formerly the "Vaterland", on one side of which lighters were lined up taking off troops and baggage while on the other side coal and provisions were being put aboard for the return voyage.[4] As we left New York harbor we

4. The German ship *Vaterland* was seized by American authorities at the outbreak of the war. It was rechristened the *Leviathan* in September 1917. A huge

had seen her coming in on a return trip from France and then when we got to Brest we found her there. She had taken on her human cargo, crossed the Atlantic, and almost had the cargo discharged while we were making the voyage.

At 4:30 on the morning of May 3rd we sailed on South down the coast of France, where we saw at different places the ships' masts sticking out of the water, telling a story of the days gone by when the Hun was Lord of those waters. We were still guarded by five Destroyers of the French Navy while two American Hydroplanes were on duty overhead. Thus we sailed along until the after-noon of May 4th when we went inside the nets at Verdun Roads[5] to await orders to proceed up the Garonne River some sixty miles to the city of Bordeaux.[6]

When we arrived at the French Docks on the Garonne River near Bordeaux, I had assumed that I was a stranger in a foreign land, but was agreeably surprised to find a number of Oklahoma friends there, and more especially three graduates of Oklahoma University, namely, R. E. Jackson, '15, now 1st Lieutenant Q. M. C.; Chas. B. Memminger, '14, now 2nd Lieutenant Q. M. C., and Geo. A. Bucklin, '03, now American Consul at Bordeaux, France.[7] I had many pleasant chats with Mr. Bucklin

---

vessel of 54,000 tons, it transported military personnel from America to Brest, carrying more than 10,000 men at a time. By the end of the war, it had carried almost 120,000 across the Atlantic.

5. Boatman probably means Le Verdon-sur-Mer, where the Garonne River meets the Atlantic.

6. Bordeaux, a large center for the production of wine, is located on the Garonne River in southwestern France. At the outbreak of the war, it had a population of around 280,000.

7. Robert Ernest Jackson, from Checotah, Oklahoma, was stationed at Quartermaster Headquarters, Base Sector 2, France. He had been in the class of 1915. Charles Burrows Memminger (1892–1970), a 1914 graduate of the University, enlisted on May 7, 1917, and was commissioned a first lieutenant with the Quartermaster Corps in May 1918. He spent 11 months in France before becoming part of the Army of Occupation in Germany. After the war, Memminger practiced law in Atoka, Oklahoma, and served as a senator in the state legislature. George Augustus

and he seemed to be most eager to have me tell him of the University and of the many friends there. He is still a most loyal "Sooner" in spite of the fact that he has been away from Oklahoma a long time.

Bordeaux is the principal city in Southern France. It is about the fourth largest city in France, and in many respects is considered the second city of that country. Coming from the "New West" I was peculiarly impressed with the old and worn appearance of the town. The streets run in all directions, winding about as though they had lost their course, and are exceedingly narrow in most places. To see an American truck come tearing down one of these streets, noting the alertness of the driver and the general expression of life, as contrasted with the surroundings made me want to caution my fellow countryman to not move about so briskly lest he disturb the atmosphere of peace and quietness which prevailed.

On May 19th we left Bordeaux coming back to the mouth of the river to await a Convoy. Just after dark on the evening of May 21st we put to sea, coming out in Convoy with four troop ships, and reaching Cape Henry[8] on the morning of June 1st. Just before reaching land we were informed that a "Sub" had been sighted near where we were but we did not see it, however, we were not disappointed. This was the first appearance of German U-Boats off the Atlantic Coast and caused a great deal of excitement among certain classes, more particularly my civilian crew, most of whom left the ship as soon as they were paid, saying they were

---

Bucklin (1875–1954) was an important figure in the early history of the University of Oklahoma. He came to Norman as an undergraduate in 1897 and was immediately appointed as the secretary to President David Ross Boyd and soon thereafter named as the University's registrar. After earning a master's degree from Yale, he returned to the University to head the Sociology and Economics Department. In 1906, however, he left academic life to join the diplomatic service. He served in important positions all over the world, and during the war he was the American consul at Bourdeaux. See David W. Levy, *The University of Oklahoma: A History, Volume 1, 1890–1917* (Norman: University of Oklahoma Press, 2005), 66–68.

8. Cape Henry, Virginia, near Virginia Beach, is the southern entrance to the Chesapeake Bay.

afraid of the Submarines. Be it understood they were not Americans who were scared that way, but a lot of Aliens who had been attracted by the high wages being paid by our Government, and who had no patriotic feeling toward our nation. The American boys we had aboard stayed there and said "To Hell with the U-Boats".

On our second voyage we went the same route, leaving New York harbor with a convoy of about fifty cargo ships, at noon on June 18th. That was the largest Convoy that had then left for Europe and it was to me a most interesting sight. On June 23rd we encountered a most severe storm which lasted all day and well into the night. It swept all the buildings from the main deck that had been built there for temporary use by the Government, including the butcher shop, troop mess room, and other buildings. During the storm three of the ships fell behind and the next morning were from ten to fifteen miles back of us, having been ordered to put into Halifax and await a slower convoy.[9] About 9:00 O'clock in the morning one of them began to call for help saying she was being shelled by a submarine. The Cruiser with us went to her rescue but before she reached her the sub had disappeared. Later in the day a second one of the group began to call for help. It seems that the sub just lay off out of reach of their small guns and let them have the shells, but did no great damage. It only served to furnish a little excitement for all of us.

The morning of July 4th about 10:00 O'clock found us again dropping anchor in Brest harbor where we lay until the 6th. This time we went to La Pallice[10] and there I again found Lieut. Memminger and other friends; as a result I decided that this is a small world after all. At La Pallice the cargo was removed from the ship by German prisoners. One day while going over the ship I came upon a German Sergeant sitting on a bale of hay and intently studying some papers. I decided to take a look at his

9. Halifax is a port city on the coast of Nova Scotia.
10. La Pallice is a major French port, located between Brest and Bordeaux. It is the port for La Rochelle, a city of around 38,000 at the time of the war.

papers and picked up one of them. When I did this he jumped up and saluted. I did not return the salute, but just ignored him and when I was convinced that the papers pertained to his men, walked away. Those were the days when the tide was beginning to turn against the Germans and, as a result, the prisoners were very humble and polite.

When we returned to this Port, the latter part of August I was taken off the ship and put back in the office where I am likely to remain until allowed to resign my commission, which I am trying to do at the earliest date possible, now that the War is over and my services no longer needed. It goes without saying that I am coming back to Oklahoma to live just as soon as released from the Service.

A. N. Boatman
1st Lieut qmc

Charles Arthur Brake

Allentown Pa Nov 12, 18

Mr. Stratton D. Brooks

  Norman, Okla

Dear Sir and Friend at O.U:

I don[']t know whether I should begin this by "I take my pen in hand["] or jump on the subject like the people here seem to think all westerners do.

Perhaps it would be better if I tell first of my impression on entering camp.

I was first impressed with the idea of cleanliness and neatness. Of course I [am] speaking of my first station, Fort Riley Kansas.[1] I next noticed that every one was doing something and there was a certain air and feeling around you that made you feel like rolling up your sleeves and getting in it yourself.

My first blunder was committed when I entered the Adjutants office. Not knowing just where the forbidden ground lay, I soon was inside the boundaries where I was quickly told I did not belong.

Along with seventy one others I formed the student company 35.

Charles Arthur Brake (1894–1947), from Geary, Oklahoma, arrived at the University in 1914. He earned his MD in 1917 and was president of the Senior Medical Society. He became a first lieutenant and served with the Medical Reserve Corps, Camp Crane, Pennsylvania. He returned to Norman after the war and lived there for the rest of his life, serving as a physician at the Central State Hospital from 1924 until his death.

1. First opened in the 1850s, Fort Riley, located in north-central Kansas, was greatly expanded during the war under the command of the famous general Leonard Wood. Eventually it was capable of providing training to 30,000 to 50,000 men for overseas duties.

The first morning the bugle blew all to[o] early. We were rolled out at 5:00a.m. by our C.O. and told to take the Sitting up exercises or as the medical men say Upsitting. Which in truth they are to the average medical man. I began to wonder if they would never cease but we were dismissed and somebody said Chow! In the mad rush for the mess hall I was one of the last to get in. Judging by my appetite I didn't think there was enough food in sight to satisfy me alone. But it is wonderful how fast it can appear on the tables. And disappear too, only I believe more rapidly.

The first day of drilling and hiking in the morning followed by our lecture work in the afternoon was one of torture for instructors and students. We soon got so we could do our upsitting exercises alone and forms right etc.

There is just one mystery to be cleared. I don[']t see how any one brain can remember the different forms and reports the poor medical officer is compelled to make out. Yet they say it is easy.

As I reported to camp on Friday the next day we had equitations,[2] or as one expressed it, practice in flying. Many of the men had never been on a horse before. We were a great sight trying to mount. Finally every one succeeded in getting on. The next question was could he stay. That day[']s ride will ever be fresh in my memory. Up hill and down and some of them I would hesitate to walk down on foot. Over hurdles and ditches. To look back over the line and see the men was better than a circus. Some were hanging to the horse[']s mane. Others had their arms around his neck. Most of us however held on both to the front and back of the saddle. We all managed in some way to get back. When the signal to dismount was given most of us fell off just any way to get off whether right or wrong.

The results you can all [well?] imagine. I won[']t mention the part of our anatomy affected but will say we all preferred to stand rather than sit down.

2. The handling and riding of horses.

Perhaps no one fully realizes just what it means to a doctor to enter the army. He is compelled to obey orders where before he gave orders. And the exercise and mode of living is so much different. I will say one word of praise. I have never seen one of the "Docs" as we are called who wasn[']t "game" no matter how hard his task and to many the drills and hikes were tortures. The "Doc" always came in smiling.

During our first few weeks we were all willing for the lights to go out at 9:30p.m.

Perhaps this will prove of some interest and at some other time I will attempt to tell you some of the really ridiculous things done by the "Doc" when he reports to camp. But never the less he is a good fellow and generally makes himself popular. But I won[']t say any more being one myself.

I could write on for several more pages but I am saving that for a future letter.

Yours respectfully
Chas. A. Brake
1st Lieut M.C. USA

James A. Brill

AMERICAN YMCA
ON ACTIVE SERVICE
WITH THE
AMERICAN EXPEDITIONARY FORCE

Dec. 18 1918
Dijon[1]

Dear Dr. Brooks:

This missive probably will arrive too late for enclosure with the war letters from Sooners over here, but this is the first chance I've had of getting "Y[MCA]" paper since receiving your very kind letter.

When this arrived we had just pulled back into an old camp in the Argonne,[2] following the signing of the armistice, and there we waited and waited for orders either to go back to the S.O.S., or to "join the crowd" in the "Wacht am Rhine."[3]

James A. Brill, from Norman, was in the class of 1917. He enlisted in June (infantry) and during his eighteen months abroad, he fought at St. Mihiel and Champaigne, in France, and was part of the Army of Occupation that crossed into Germany after the war ended. In 1919, he returned to the College of Fine Arts as a voice major. He also briefly taught in the art faculty of the University (1919–20), and then settled in Oklahoma City, where he taught music.

1. Dijon is a major city, located about 190 miles southeast of Paris. A cultural center, famous for its architecture, wine, and cuisine, Dijon had a population of almost 80,000 during the war.

2. The Argonne is a large forest in northeastern France, very near the Belgian border. It was the scene of intense fighting in 1914 and 1915, and again in 1918.

3. When it became apparent that the French would be unable to supply the material needs of the American Expeditionary Forces, the Services of Supply (S.O.S.) was given the job of providing combat troops with logistical support, including food. The 640,000 noncombat servicemen attached to the S.O.S. did everything from unloading cargo ships, feeding troops, distributing clothing and equipment, manning hospitals, repairing railroad lines, delivering mail, and burying the dead. The S.O.S.

Just at the moment when I was sure I couldn't longer stand the monotony of it, I received an order to join the envied 3rd Army—that was the 11th of December, and I'm now on my way. Seems rather a funny way—to jog way down here to get to Coblenz.[4]

I'm enjoying the S.O.S. for the first time in my 15 months here. Have been in every mix up from Soissons[5] to Switzerland this year. But since I got "shanghaied" into office work I have not been in so much danger from "direct hits" and things.

And of course I have sketches from different points in the Vosges, the Wown, Argonne, Champagne, Toul and Marne Sectors. Also I had picked up a good many souvenirs, (with the university's museum in mind certainly[)], but gave most of them away perforce when this unexpected order reached me to proceed to Germany.

Among several good friends I've made over here, the most recent and one of the most valued is an artist I met at [*illegible word*] a few days ago. By accident I was quartered next to his home. Naturally I went out sketching one morning and the artist's wife, seeing me with drawing material, made me come in the house, introduced the husband and herself, and I had a delightful stay there as a result. (Altho I had to give them a valued sketch for "souvenir.") Le Monssieur is a native of Rheims, and, with a colleague, has been placed in charge of reconstruction work there.

---

was inaugurated in July 1917 and disbanded on August 31, 1919. Almost a third of the men in the S.O.S. were African Americans. The "Wacht am Rhine" was a patriotic German song dating back to the 1840s. Here Brill uses the title sarcastically to indicate the possibility of being sent with the Army of Occupation into Germany after the German surrender.

4. The Third Army was created by General Pershing to occupy Germany after the Armistice. Consisting of around 250,000 men, the army located its headquarters in Coblenz (after 1926, Koblenz), a major Rhineland city located where the Rhine and the Moselle Rivers meet. Its population in 1919 was 56,700.

5. The cathedral town of Soissons, in northeastern France, had a population of around 14,000; during the war it suffered from intense bombardment and was the scene of major western front battles in 1914, 1917, and 1918.

On my way down here, I rode with a compartment of returning prisoners (French) from Germany. They had many interesting tales and I had "Lucky Strikes."[6] Alors—

Am tired, but am faced by a big table of magazines, and will read myself to sleep tonight hoping for a pleasant tour of Dijon tomorrow morning.

Oh yes! I had the pleasure of saluting and talking to Lieut. Prent Lively yesterday at [*illegible word*]. He was returning casual from a hospital where he landed with quite a shrapnel peppering in October. He is distinctly the same as ever.[7]

Best wishes for the university and best regards to you and all others helping to maintain and boost its standard.

Sgt. James A. Brill
en route to Hq. 3rd American Army
Office of Chief Surgeon
Amer. E. F

6. Brill apparently traded cigarettes for the stories of the French prisoners.
7. William Prentice Lively (1894–1973), from Blackwell, Oklahoma, was a graduate of the University. He was a celebrated athlete on campus during his undergraduate days, and was to return to the University as a graduate student in 1919. In October 1918, while a first lieutenant in the 142nd Infantry, he was wounded in action. A "casual" officer or soldier is one who is detached from his unit for a special purpose or reason and who is awaiting an assignment.

Walter Stanley Campbell

Censored
W. S. Campbell
Capt F.A.U.S.A.
Amer. E. F.

Near Chateauroux[1]
October 4, 1918

Dear Dr. Brooks:

As the men say - this is a Hell of a War, but it[']s all we've got. Our outfit has been sent down here to help build a place about the size of Chicago for the Q.Ms. Take the star out of the service flag. I am wearing crossed pick and shovel on my collar now.[2] This place is more like a new oil town than anything else—all warehouses, new roads, freight trains, and mud. German prisoners wear their cooties[3] and work under guard of big niggers. One of these opined that "These can[']t fight. I killed six of 'em myself." That is a good gauge of the spirit and good humoured, confident pep of

Walter Stanley Campbell (1887–1957) had been a member of the University of Oklahoma English faculty since 1915. He graduated from Oklahoma's Southwestern Normal School and, in 1908, became the state's first Rhodes Scholar. He earned a bachelor's and a master's degree from Merton College, Oxford. When the war broke out, he enlisted and served six months in France, becoming a captain in the Field Artillery. Under the name Stanley Vestal, Campbell wrote two dozen books on the American West and American Indians. At the University he founded the Professional Writing program, which has produced dozens of publishing writers over the years. Campbell was inducted into the Oklahoma Hall of Fame in 1942. See Donald J. Berthrong, "Walter Stanley Campbell: Plainsman," *Arizona and the West 7* (Summer 1965): 91–104.

1. Châteauroux is a city in central France about 170 miles south of Paris. Its population during the war was around 26,000.
2. "Pick and shovel" is a synonym for laborious physical work.
3. "Cooties" are head lice, a persistent pest for both sides in the war. The term seems to have originated during World War I.

the new armies. The whole atmosphere is like that at a big Sooner pep meeting. And there are enough Sooners about to account for that.

Except for the fact that we are not doing the work which we expected to do and that we have never had any mail since leaving the States more than a month ago, everything is lovely—even the mud could not be beat.

It is reported, however, that the French are suffering from a dire short-age of vinegar, as they have sold it all at 3 francs the bottle to Yanks for white wine.

There is a destiny that makes my ways rough. I thought when I got into the army I was rid of grading themes. But now I have to censor the mail of some two hundred men, and believe me, Sir, they are prolific writers. I can[']t understand how the American public ever finds time to read the soldiers' mail and still subscribe to the newspapers. Some of it is so similar as to be practically identical. It would be a shock to the girls if they knew how shamelessly certain soldiers sent the identical let-ter to each of a dozen. All they need is an up to date process of redupli-cation. Uncle Sam has not issued any as yet.

I saw Frank McCain a few days ago. Vergil Hines and Don Walker are not far away and "Fat" Johnson[4] is reported to be somewhere around, though I have not seen him. The Sooners are very much in evidence.

4. George Franklin McCain (1893–1972), from Pontotoc County, Oklahoma, was a former star football player at the University. He was to return to the Univer-sity to finish his bachelor's degree in the College of Arts and Sciences in 1919. In 1924, he moved to Orlando, Florida, to teach high school football. Campbell prob-ably means Virgil Hine (1895–1939) of Muskogee, Oklahoma, who left school a few months before graduating to enlist; he became a pilot and then an instructor. Hine later moved to Coronado, California. Don Edward Walker (1895–1986) had been president of his junior class (1914), vice president of the Student Council, and sec-retary of the YMCA. His sister would marry Don Emery, a University Regent, and Walker worked for Emery at the West Franklin Petroleum Corporation in Ard-more. There are several "Johnsons" from the University in the military, and it is unknown to which one Campbell refers here.

People over here are very glad we came. In England they showed more enthusiasm than here, but their greeting took the form of a "goodbye, boys." Ten thousand of those in one day's march rather gets a man's goat. The French are at once more cheerful and more practical. It is always "Bon Jour" from an adult and "Un pennie" or "Biscuit" from a child.

The war is opening the eyes of all Americans to the vast superiority of American products, ways, and—in all humility—people. Europe viewed from the business end is a very different place from the Europe of the tourists.

All of us are animated with but one desire—to <u>finish</u> the war and get home. We are not [now?] fighting on because the war is not over.[5] We came over to settle it, so that we could return to our soft drinks and decent towns and jazz bands and Henry Fords and turkey dinners. There is going to be a riot when the fighting is over to get on board something that will float. Most of us never appreciated America properly, to judge by the sentiments expressed and felt on all sides. If you have any influence, pray use it to recover your English instructor[6] in case he is still serviceable.

Please give my very best wishes and affectionate regards to all your family and my friends in O.U. The University looks more like home to me than any place I've seen since I left it. I remain

Respectfully yours
Walter S. Campbell
Capt 335 F.A.
87 Div.
Amer. E. F. Via New York

5. It is worth noting that Campbell wrote this letter to President Brooks five weeks before the armistice.
6. Campbell, of course, is referring to himself.

Glenn Andrews Caskey

Dax, France
Jan. 3, 1919

Pres. Stratton D. Brooks
Uni of Oklahoma
Norman, Oklahoma.

Dear Sir:

I am in Southern France, at Dax, a city at the foot of the Phyrenees [*sic*] Mountains, and about twenty miles from the Atlantic coast[1]. It is a health resort and before the war was always crowded with tourists. Tropical climate and now in January, the flowers are in bloom, the bushes green, and the rubber & palm trees growing.

Dax is a beautiful city. It was principally used by the rich people of France as a winter resort. There are hot boiling water artesian wells here[,] and in front of the hotel where we are staying now there are fountains spouting hot boiling water all the time. This hotel was leased by the U.S. Govt. to be used for a hospital but now it is to be abandoned so we think we are going home.

I left Camp Grant Ill[inois],[2] in August 1918, and arrived at Brest France Sept the seventh. Our company came on the same ship Sec. Baker

---

Glenn Andrews Caskey (1894–1992) was born in Iowa, but moved with his family to Billings, Oklahoma, when he was a child. Caskey had just started his college career at the University of Oklahoma when he enlisted in May 1918. He was part of the Medical Department's Evacuation Hospital, serving eight months in France. He eventually returned to the University and received his bachelor's degree on June 3, 1923. He was an accountant, a chorus director, and a school superintendent in Oklahoma and Kansas. He moved to New Mexico in 1940.

1. The Pyrenees Mountain range forms a natural boundary between Spain and France.
2. Located near Rockford, Illinois, the training camp for infantry was opened in 1917 and became one of the largest camps in the country.

was on.[3] Our fleet was well convoyed. We saw many interesting sights and every day fish swimming by the side of our ship jumping from the water & trying to keep up.

We rested at Brest, then made a quick trip across France, stopping seventy-two hours at Le Mans, then on to the Verdun Front. We arrived there late in Sept. but in time for the Verdun & Argonne Forest Drive, the drive that ended the war.[4]

Our last night on the train brought us to Souilly.[5] In the morning we unloaded and marched to the side of a hill and waited all day. All day aeroplanes flew around & we saw 50 in one bunch and we tho[ugh]t that was wonderful but since then I've seen 150 mostly bombing planes all going to the [front] lines.

They told us every night behind the lines was like the fourth of July. We had our first one. Big flack lights, rockets flares, the flashes from the guns and the roar. Our company was divided and about 10 P.M. ambulances came and with lights out took us to three different hospitals. I went to American Red Cross Hospital 114. We had frequent air raids and

3. Newton Diehl Baker (1871–1937) had been a reform mayor of Cleveland before Wilson named him secretary of war (1916–21). Baker supervised the draft and chose John J. Pershing to lead the American Expeditionary Forces. After the war, he was frequently mentioned as a possible Democratic candidate for the presidency. See Daniel R. Beaver, *Newton D. Baker and the American War Effort* (Lincoln: University of Nebraska Press, 1966).

4. The trip from Le Mans to Verdun is around 285 miles. Before American entry into the war, Verdun, along the Meuse River in northeastern France, had been the scene of one of the most horrific battles of World War I. Between February and December of 1916, the French withstood the German advance, but with tremendous casualties (including 300,000 deaths) on both sides. When Corporal Caskey arrived there, in August 1918, Verdun, less than 20 miles from the Argonne Forest, became a staging area prior to the final battle leading to the armistice (September 26 to November 11). The offensive involved more than a million American troops and cost 26,700 American lives. It was the war's largest operation for American soldiers.

5. General Pershing set up headquarters in Souilly, about 20 miles from the Argonne Forest.

three boys from the hospital were killed in one raid. I worked in the operating room so saw and experienced many horrible sights.

We were back of the First Army in its advance west of the Meuse. The fighting was hard. The advance had to be made over hills & through thickets, which gave a big advantage to the enemy. There was no let up between the later part of Sept. and the end of the war. The road past our hospital was always crowded with trucks following close going and returning, with fresh troops going to relieve others, with long lines of German Prisoners, and ambulances bringing the wounded.

Since I've been over-here, I've received the Sooner War Pamphlet, and I appreciate it very much. I was also glad to [have] received your letter addressed to me.

I must close. We have orders to move and every-body is busy cleaning and packing up.

Sincerely yours

Cpl. Glenn Caskey

Evac. Hosp #20

American E. F.

Ross Anson Clare

Bad Salzig on the Rhine[1]

Dec. 21, 1918

My Dear Dr. Brooks:

Your nice letter of Nov. 6 just received. We were in camp at Fort Clark for about eight months, leaving there March 4, 1918. There is nothing there but Mexicans, negroes, sand, and cactus. Went to Camp Merritt, New Jersey by way of Chicago.[2] Left Camp Merritt March 18 and boarded the Niagara of the French line.[3] Had an uneventful trip across and good weather. One day out from port we sighted and exploded a contact mine. The force of the explosion broke windows in the cabins. Landed at Bordeaux on the morning of March 30. We made the trip across alone and without a convoy. Our captain used his wireless and went around the submarines. Was in camp at Bordeaux resting for a few

---

Ross Anson Clare (1891–1968) was born in Massachusetts, but moved to Oklahoma to attend the medical school in Oklahoma City. He graduated from the University in 1915. He enlisted in July 1917, and became part of the Medical Corps. Dr. Clare worked in the Toul and the Chateau Thierry sectors, in Field Hospital No. 27, and later joined the Army of Occupation. After returning to the United States, he moved to Ohio and then Indiana.

1. Bad Salzig, on the west bank of the Rhine River in western Germany, was a small town near Coblenz. It was one of the places where the American Army of Occupation was stationed.

2. Fort Clark had been in operation since the middle of the nineteenth century; it was located near Bracketville, Texas, a small town with a population of around 1,700 during this period. Camp Merritt (formerly Camp Tenafly) was located near Bergen, New Jersey, about ten miles from New York City. It was reactivated during World War I as a convenient place to keep men prior to their embarkation from Hoboken.

3. The Compagnie Générale Transatlantique, commonly known as "the French line," had been in existence since the mid-nineteenth century. It operated dozens of liners all over the world, but mainly on trans-Atlantic routes. During the war, 37 of its ships were requisitioned for wartime purposes such as troop transport.

days and then went to Arc en Barrois where we had some training. We first operated a hospital at Verdelot[4] in conjunction with the French. When I landed did not know a word of French, but soon picked up enough to get along alright. The French people treated us fine. From Verdelot we went to Chierry, just across the Marne from Chateau Thierry.[5] Here we had our first experience under a bombing raid. Was in Chateau Thierry several times and have been all over the city. In my next letter will tell of my experiences after leaving Chateau Thierry. With best regards I remain

A loyal Sooner

Pvt. 1/c Ross A. Clare
Field Hospital No. 27
A.P.O. #740
American E.F.

4. Arc en Barrois is a small village in northeastern France, about 160 miles southeast of Paris. Verdelot, another tiny village, is about 50 miles east of Paris and 15 miles south of Chateau Thierry.

5. Chateau Thierry was the scene of another battle that involved American troops, both army and marines. In June 1918, Pershing committed relatively new and barely trained units to stop a German offensive (headed for Paris, only 50 miles to the west). On June 3, the Americans and French forced the Germans back across the Marne. The encounter was part of the Battle of Belleau Wood (June 1–26).

William Edward Corkill

Coblenz, Germany
December 22, 1918

President Stratton D. Brooks,
Oklahoma University,
Dear Sir:

In accordance with the request in your letter of recent date asking for a statement from each alumnus of his adventures during the war[,] I will give a short summary of mine.

I am in Bat. "F" of the 10th F.A. 3rd Brigade, 3rd Division, Regular Army. I joined the 10th F.A. on Aug. 28 as a 2nd Lieut. at Douglas Arizona. On the 24th of March we entrained for Camp Merritt N.J. where we stayed for nearly a month, and "saw" N.Y. City during our stay there.

On the 22 April we embarked on the U.S.S. Tenedores [*sic*][1] for France where we landed after an eventful voyage on 7 May. We were in quarantine at Bordeaux for ten days. From there we went to Coetquidan, a F.A. training school, and trained intensively for over a month on the French "75" guns.[2] Then on the first of July we entrained for the Chateau

---

William Edward Corkill (1892–1972) was born in Texas, but moved to Henryetta, Oklahoma, where he was principal of the high school. Corkill graduated from the University in 1916. He enlisted on May 15, 1917, and was commissioned a second lieutenant with the Field Artillery three months later. Corkill remained in the army and served through World War II, and was discharged in 1947 as a colonel. He was living in Bexar, Texas, when he died.

1. Constructed in 1913 for the United Fruit Company, the *Tenadores* was turned over to the army in May 1917 for transport duties. In April 1918, the vessel was taken over by the navy. The *Tenadores* was grounded in heavy fog on December 28, and was unsalvageable.

2. Coetquidan was a French military training camp located in Britany, about 30 miles southwest of the city of Rennes. In June 1917, the French transferred the facility to the Americans for Field Artillery training. The French "75" was a

Thierry front but detrained about 20K[ilometers][3] short of that city. The first night off the train we reached a woods called the Great Forest and went into bivouac for the night. We had just finished caring for the horses & gotten between our blankets when a "whizz bang" an Austrian "88" opened up on a crossroads leading into our forest.[4] That one gun caused me more down right anguish than anything else during the rest of the war. This "88" fired for an hour and then let up without causing us any casualties, unless you call "shell shock" a casualty. The next day we moved our batteries up into position, about a mile & a half from the Marne river, which at that time was our front line. We had it pretty quiet then for two or three days & in fact I had begun to think that this war was more or less over talked & was not half as bad as I had expected. Then the 14 July came and about midnight that date the 5th German spring offensive began. The 15 July was the longest and saddest and altogether the worst day of my life. Many of my friends were killed by my side, and what was worse the Germans had begun to break through & cross the river. However the Americans held them and you know the rest; of how we straightened out that salient. Our Infantry was shot to pieces so badly there that after the second week they had to be relieved & then the 32 div infantry was brought up & we were attached to them and we stayed in until the boche was driven back to the Vesle [River].

We were then given a few days rest at Chateau Thierry, as that city was out of range by that time, and then were shipped to the Toul sector.

---

fast-firing and mobile artillery piece (20 to 30 rounds per minute), sometimes regarded as the first modern artillery weapon. Besides firing 75mm shells, the piece could also deliver poisoned gas shells. By the end of the war, the French had produced 12,000 of these weapons, 2,000 of which were in use by the American Expeditionary Forces.

3. 12.4 miles.

4. "Whiz-bangs" are high velocity shells that explode so quickly after their incoming sound is heard that soldiers have almost no time to duck for cover.

Our Infantry had not recovered in time for the St. Mihiel drive,[5]so we were attached to the 42 division (Rainbow)[6] during that push, if you choose to call it that, but to us it seemed like a picnic after what we had had on the Marne. Our casualties were much less during this drive than at Chateau Thierry. Next we were sent to the N.W. of Verdun where we were attached to the 4th division for the opening drive on the Argonne Forest.

When we reached Mont Fancon our own 3rd Division Infantry was put in and it was with them that we took Cierges, Nantillois, & Carmel.[7] This fighting was like the old style football game. It was plug, plug along a yard at a time, with heavy casualties every day and the enemy showing no signs of retreat. Our infantry was again shot to pieces after as plucky fighting as is known in history and had to be taken out, so we were attached to the 5th division. I might say right here that the 90th Division was on our left during this fighting and made a name for itself that will never die; and who would expect less from a division made up, as it was, of men from Okla. & Texas.

We were attached to the 5th Division then until the end of the war at 11 o clock 11/11/18. We took Brieulles, crossed the Meuse there & at Dun,

5. Saint-Mihiel was the site of a major battle, fought by American and French troops during the second week of September 1918. General Pershing hoped to break through the lines of the retreating German army. The effort met with considerable success until American troops were withdrawn to participate in the Meuse-Argonne offensive, beginning on September 26.

6. The famous 42nd (or "Rainbow") Division was organized in August 1917, in an effort to quickly send troops to France. It was made up of men from 26 state National Guard units from across the country. The exploits of this all-American unit were followed closely through the major battles of the war. The division endured over 14,000 casualties during the war. See James J. Cooke, *The Rainbow Division in the Great War, 1917–1919* (Westport, Conn.: Praeger, 1994).

7. Mont Fancon was in the heart of the monumental campaigns of the Meuse-Argonne and Verdun struggles from late September until the end of the war. Cierges is around 15 miles from Chateau Thierry; Nantillois is about 90 miles to the east; and Carmel de Verdun is 22 miles southeast of Nantillois.

took Liny, Fontaines and finally Brandeville and Louppay[8] where we were when the Armistice was signed.

On the thirteenth we received word that the 3rd Div. was one of the units in the army of Occupation, and to proceed at once toward Coblenz. We had been fighting and marching for over four months, half our horses killed, half the regiment made up of replacements & no rest, yet the news of a several hundred K. hike into Germany was received with enthusiasm. The hike proved to be more or less uneventful, the populous [*sic*] if not over joyed at our arrival were at least unconcerned, and in fact Lorraine[9] & Luxemburg were cordial in their greetings. We came onto the Rhine at Ober Wesel, and passed through St Goar, Holzfeld, Salzig, Boppard, Spay, Kapellen and finally Coblenz.[10] I think without a doubt that the Rhine Valley along this route is as pretty as anywhere else in Europe. We are now billeted at Kruft a few K out of Coblenz.

Yours Truly,
William E. Corkill
1st Lieut. 10th F. A.

8. All these are small towns along, or in the neighborhood of the Meuse River, north of Verdun and near the Luxembourg and German borders.

9. Lorraine was the much-disputed region in northeast France, near the Belgium, Luxembourg, and German borders. Along with Alsace, it had been taken by Germany as a result of the French defeat of 1871. Both regions would be restored to France after World War I.

10. These are towns along the Rhine. The distance between Oberwessel and Coblenz is around 30 miles.

Joe Clyde Creager

OFFICE OF THE ZONE MAJOR
20th ZONE
A.S., S.O.S.

February 1st 1919

Dr. Stratton D. Brooks,
  President—University of Oklahoma,
  Norman Oklahoma

My dear Sir:

Yours of many days past asking for a letter from the Sooners in the service telling of the adventures that we have had received today and also a copy of the "Sooners and the War" reminding us that we had not complied with your request. I have kept no diary and all my experiences have been recorded in my head but they will be hard to erase. I will relate them to you in order as they happened from the time that I left the camp in Texas to proceed East for France.

On July 6th 1918 my Division received the glad news that we should leave soon for the port of Embarkation. That didn't exactly suit me for I had the day before taken a "better half" and tho I was as anxious to go overseas as the rest I hated to have the joys of a honeymoon delayed.[1]

My section of the regiment left at 8 o'clock the morning of July 11th. We took the Southern Route thru all the big cities in the South but as I had the delightful job of train quartermaster I had no time for sightseeing for while the men were looking over the sights I was getting ice, water,

---

Joe Clyde Creager (1896–1967) completed two years at the College of Engineering before enlisting. He served with the 14th Infantry in France as a first lieutenant. When he returned from the war, he lived in several Oklahoma towns and worked for the Continental Oil Company, then headquartered in Ponca City.

1. On July 5, 1918, Creager married Georgia Goodwin in Fort Worth, Texas.

and provisions for the train and getting ready to move on the next lap. It took six days for us to reach New York. Went thru most of the big cities of the East via tunnels and therefore saw very little of them. On arrival in New York we were shot straight to Long Island and arrived there at 1 am. Stayed in the big camp till the 30th but was so closely watched and had so much work to do that it was impossible to see any of the glare of Broadway.

On July 30th we went aboard the SS Mauii [sic],[2] and sailed the next day. Made lots of friends among the crew for several of them were former "Sons of Pat" from Soonerland.[3] The trip was with out many incidents. I failed to have the usual malady of seasickness. The last two days a few of the Kaisers pets[4] attempted to annoy us but they seemed to forget we were Americans and that they were no match for our destroyers and gunners and as a consequence two or three sub crews are in watery graves today.

Landed the 12th of August at Brest and there sojourned in the former habitat of Napoleon-Pontenezan Barracks.[5] Didn't exactly like the first weeks that I spent in France for there was to[o] much water. I wasn't used to it for I had been raised in Western Oklahoma where that was a rare article. Leaving Brest in trains of many cars marked "8 chevaux-40 hommes,"[6] we travelled to Bar-sur-Aube. On the way we passed thru

2. The *Maui* was built in 1916 as a commercial passenger ship for travel from San Francisco to Hawaii. The navy acquired the vessel in March 1918, and it was employed as a troop transport until the end of the war.

3. Members of the Engineers' Club at the University styled themselves the "Sons of Saint Patrick" and were renowned for their exuberant celebrations of St. Patrick's Day.

4. U-boats.

5. Built by Napoleon, the Pontenezan Barracks, in Brest, were used during the war to house American troops arriving in France. These old quarters were uncomfortable and damp, but thousands of troops pouring into Brest spent time there while waiting to move eastward.

6. As several of these letters reveal, numerous American soldiers were amused by the railroad cars that were designed to carry "8 horses or 40 men."

the outskirts of Paris and thru several of the historic towns of the country.

After spending several days in training with the regiment I received orders to proceed to the 1st Corps School for instruction in Small Arms. There I spent a month doing various things in learning the art of war and I specialized in automatic arms. Ran into John Ward (Law School) and Chris Schalwachter [sic] (Engineers).[7] About the 1st of October I returned to the outfit and on reaching Divisional Hdq I was assigned to 144th Inf with prospects of a promotion. The next day we moved again. I went with my company to Brienne-le-Chateau[8] to act as a loading detail. There we worked night and day in 8 hour shifts in loading out for the unknown. During my hours off duty I looked the town over and visited the military school from which Napoleon received his commission. After riding two days we dismounted and returned to the familiar mode of traveling know[n] as hiking.

When the day was over we were in a small town near Chalons-sur-Marne.[9] There at night we could see the reddened sky and hear the big guns as they sent parcels over to Fritz. In the day time we could see the big balloons[10] and they appeared to be very close. Fritz paid us an occasional call with his night owls but failed to cause us any damage.

In one week we packed up again and started out—where we didn[']t know. Hiked all day and spent the night among the rats in a small

7. John P. Ward was an infantry lieutenant. He served 10 months overseas and suffered from poison gas during the battle of Argonne Forest. Christian H. Salwaechter, of the class of 1918, was a private in the 7th Corps of Engineers.

8. Brienne-le-Chateau, a small town of around 1,750 people, is located in north-central France, about 140 miles east of Paris.

9. Châlons-sur-Marne (renamed Châlons-en-Champagne in 1998) is the capital city of the Marne department, with a population during the war of around 31,000.

10. Both sides in the war employed balloons that hovered thousands of feet above the battle. They were useful both offensively and defensively in conveying, by telephone or signal flags, intelligence about enemy positions and movements. They also directed artillery fire on enemy positions.

village. Early the next day the journey was resumed. The next night found us in the old Hindenberg line above Suippes, in the Champagne sector between Rheims and Verdun.[11] There I found a very enticing dugout that had at some time been occupied by some German officers. After spending two nights there we started in. Felt rather queer when the first shell fell near me as we entered the reserve.

Our other brigade relieved the Marines that night and we lay on Blanc Mont[12] that night and the next day looking on from our "fox holes" in the white mud. Next night we started to leap frog our way to the assault line. Twelve hours found me changed from a platoon commander to a company commander for reasons easily imagined. Got a little of the German poison that night. First hard resistance was there and then we had a race most of the way for several days, occasionally finding a small party of the enemy. The fight was mostly against the artillery and we could hardly reach them with our rifles. All we could do was to pursue them vigorously and dodge the barns, oil tanks, iron mines, etc. that he was sending over. It was remarkable the many narrow escapes that we all went thru. They would look to[o] fishy on paper—such as having duds fall in the same shell hole, clothing and equipment being shot away and never touching you—having your side pardner killed beside you and many other things too numerous to mention. Was pretty well bruised up by being knocked off my feet by concussion and I was getting so that I could hardly talk from the whiffs of gas that I had gotten from time to time. My throat felt a great deal worse than it did the time that a retort exploded with me when I was generating chlorine.

11. Because of its central location in the Marne department of northeastern France, the village of Blanc Mont served as a staging area by both British and American forces. In 1918, the Americans stationed a brigade there. The town had been pillaged and badly damaged by the Germans during the first Battle of the Marne, 1915.

12. The Battle of Blanc Mont Ridge (northeast of Rheims) lasted throughout the month of October 1918. After hard fighting and serious casualties, the Americans were able to push the Germans out of the Champagne region.

After about eight days one of the big ones of Fritz hit to[o] close to me and knocked me quite aways and a [I?] lay for a few minutes taking into my lungs all the "nice" phosgene that was near in the air.[13] I came to soon and stayed on the job till that evening and then from the reports of the men that cared for me, I went completely nutty, a crying maniac, and was sent to the first aid station and marked "gassed and psycho-neurosis". From there I went to the field hospital and then immediately into another ambulance and to an evacuation hospital. I was awake by the time that I had arrived there. Had a nice cup of chocolate fro[m] the hands of a real American girl. Was carried to the hospital train by Boche prisoners. Was surprised to find that one of them spoke good English— he asked me if I were riding all right. When I replied no he set me down and moved me on the stretcher until his body didn't touch me as he walked.

For two days we rode on a French hospital train, arriving finally at Blois.[14] Spent two weeks in the BH there. The unit in charge was from Georgia. Certainly knew how to treat a man that was all bruised up and hadent [sic] had a night in a real bed or a real meal in several days. I was classified B-2 or unfit for line duty temporarily on account of my lungs.

I was assigned to duty with the S.O.S. and sent to this station as assistant to the Zone Major. Am located in view of the Chateau occupied by General Pershing.[15] Am 2 km from GHQ. Personally I live in the Chateau that was the hunting club of Louis XV in this district. It is owned

13. Phosgene, a colorless gas, was extremely dangerous. It was responsible for around 85,000 deaths during the war.

14. Blois, a city of around 24,000, was far to the west of the front lines, about 120 miles southwest of Paris.

15. John Joseph ("Black Jack") Pershing (1860–1948), a West Point graduate (1886) and already an experienced army officer, was chosen by Secretary Baker and President Wilson to command the American Expeditionary Forces. Throughout the war he resisted attempts to incorporate Americans into French or British commands, insisting that American troops would remain a single unit under his command. See his own account, *My Experiences in the First World War* (1931).

and occupied by Marquise Tisserande de Lazier. Nice place to live in but I prefer the one room that I had in the S[igma].N[u] house in Norman and will be glad when I can get back there.

My new address is below and should you or any of the other Sooners desire to write, I will be pleased to hear from you.

Sincerely,

Joe C. Creager
1st Lt Inf
Asst Zone Major
20th Zone

Chamarandes Haute Marne
Via A.P.O. 706
Amer Ex Forces
France

Mutilate this before showing to any one for I never was a literary genius—not in my line as I am one of the "rough engineers"

Hughes B. Davis

Co. "C", 335th Bn. Tank Corps,
Noidant le Chatenoy, France[1]
A.P.O. 714, American E.F.
December 10th, 1918

Dr. Stratton D. Brooks,
President University of Oklahoma,
Norman, Okla.

Dear President and friend:

In reply to your letter of a short time ago, asking for our experiences since entering the war, works rather a hardship on some of us coming after the censorship has been lifted. Before the censorship was lifted we could hint at all kinds of excitement, which we, of course, were unable to give in detail because of the strict censorship rules. Now we must adhere to facts, and facts regarding the life forty miles behind the front are not very exciting. I believe every man who entered the service and was fortunate enough to serve through the war has been benefited by his experience.

Since entering the service I have been stationed at several different places and have found Oklahoma University men everywhere I have

---

Hughes B. Davis (1889–1948) was born in Tennessee and came to Oklahoma with his family in 1896. He graduated from the University in 1917 and was assistant high school inspector until his enlistment. He returned to Norman after service as a captain in the tank corps and taught briefly in the College of Education. He was also superintendent of schools in Duncan. In 1926, he began working for the Cities Service Oil Company in Bartlesville and remained with the company until his retirement. Davis was prominent in the state's American Legion organization and served as its state commander. This letter was published in the *Norman Transcript* on January 24, 1919.

1. Noidant le Chatenoy is a tiny village in the Haute-Marne district of northeastern France, about 125 miles south of Verdun and 160 miles southeast of Chateau Thierry.

gone and they have been considered among the best. The first company I was in was made up largely of Cleveland County boys. I had the pleasure there of doing "K. P." with Professor Alonzo H. Stang[2], and he was just as careful and efficient in handling the pots and pans in the kitchen as he was the finest equipped [equipment?] in the "lab" at school. In fact I believe it was our good work at "K. P." that kept both of us out of the awkward squad.[3] I went from there to the field artillery. Found several O. U. boys in my battery. Anytime there I desired to be remi[n]ded of a freshman being ridden on a board I only had to take a look at Roy U. Woods astride a big wheel horse at a fast trot.[4] In the training camp a goodly percent were Oklahoma University boys, and almost without exception they secured commissions. I went from the training camp to the Tank Corps, Gettysburg, Pa., where again I found several O.U. boys. The Camp at Gettysburg is situated on the old battlefield, and my quarters were located in the old peach orchard famous in Pickett's Charge.[5]

2. Davis meant *Ambrose* Henry Stang (1889–1972). Born in Pennsylvania, Stang earned a PhD in Physics from the University of Michigan (1916) and took a job at the University of Oklahoma as a professor of Physics. At the end of the war, he worked at the National Bureau of Standards in Washington, D.C., and after returning to Norman briefly, he went back to Washington and rejoined the bureau, where he remained until 1949. He published numerous scientific papers and received several national awards for his work. After retirement, he and his wife moved to a farm in Prattsville, Virginia.

3. The "awkward squad" is a term, used especially in military slang, to describe a group of incompetents.

4. Roy Ulysses Woods (1887–1953) was born in Colorado, but moved with his parents to Verden, Oklahoma, in 1907. He received his degree from the University of Oklahoma in 1911. Woods was a sergeant in the Field Artillery. After the war he returned to Verden and was a dairy farmer and stockman there for the rest of his life. A wheel horse in the artillery was attached to a gun carriage and pulled the weapon into place.

5. Pickett's Charge was a key moment at the Battle of Gettysburg, when, on July 3, 1863, a Confederate infantry advance of 12,500 men was repulsed by Union troops, with the attackers suffering great losses. The defeat marked the end of Robert E. Lee's invasion of the North.

I stayed at Camp Colt so long handling recruits that I think I will be able to go back after it is all over here and act as a battlefield guide.

I came over on the steamship Leviathan, the old "Vaterland". On board I met Lieutenant Jones, formerly with Wissie at the Varsity shop.[6] On board I was Police Officer and I found my former experience on "K. P." served me in good stead. We spent a few days in England, and several of the boys said that they had always been of the opinion that the people of England spoke English, but found when they began to converse with the natives that they were badly mistaken. We crossed the Channel in a "tub" and many of those who boasted about crossing the Atlantic without getting seasick were strangely silent the next morning. I was no exception to the rule. The trip across France by train was very interesting. The cars were marked "Capacity 8 horses or 40 men" (8 chevaux 40 hommes). I am now stationed about 50 miles from Alsace down near the Swiss border. Our nearest town of much size is Langres.[7] This town is very interesting. It dates back to the time of Caesar and is fortified by moats, walls, etc. Many of the roads here were built by Caesar. The source of the Marne and the Cave where Sabinus, Chief of the Gauls, lived for seven years with his wife[8] is about a mile from Camp. I am billeted in a little French village and have my quarters in an old French chateau.

One feature of the soldier is that he is never satisfied and always wants a change and as sure after every change he jumps out of the frying pan into the fire. I have heard them rave over sunny France one day that it

6. The Varsity Shop was a popular general store near the University campus. It opened in 1912, and it sold "everything the Sooner wants," from books and fountain pens to candy, tobacco, and toiletries.

7. The ancient town of Langres, formerly called Lingones, contains, as Davis notes, many artifacts from the days of Roman occupation.

8. Julius Sabinus was a Gaul who became a Roman officer. He attempted a rebellion against Rome in 69 AD, and after his defeat, was hidden by his wife Epponina. Nine years later they were both apprehended and taken to Rome, where both were executed.

was like Southern California and that the French women were the prettiest in the world, and the next day he will probably be saying that the sun never shines in France and that it is as cold a[s] Northern Labrador and that the women were good looking at a distance, the greater the distance the more in her favor. As a fighter he is highly respected by the French, English and especially the Germans. I certainly believe that Chateau Thierry was the Gettysburg of this war and the sudden end of the war was due in great measure to America.

I received the University News Letter regularly and always find it very interesting.

With best wishes to the University, I am

Sincerely,

Hugh B Davis

Capt T.C. USA

Co C 335th Bn Tank Corps

A. E. F.

James Hubert Finley

Company G 126th Infantry

Ober Hummerich, Germany[1]

Dec. 25, 1918

President Stratton D. Brooks

Norman, Oklahoma

Dear Sir:

Your letter of N[o]vember 6th, has been received, and I was indeed glad to receive it as it was a letter from America, and any news from there is always welcome.

I cannot comply with your request to give my experiences in detail, for they have been too numerous in the last few months. However, I will give you a general outline of the movements of this company since it left the United States.

We left Hoboken on Feb. 19th 1918 and landed at Brest France on March 4th. The journey across was without accident except on March 1st about 4 o' clock in the afternoon a submarine appeared on the port side of the ship I was on. Several shots were fired at it but I cannot say if any of them were hits. When the alarm was sounded there was an awful rush among the men to get to the life boats and rafts. None committed suicide by shooting themselves or jumping overboard, and with

James Hubert Finley (1889–1955) had come to the University from New Bloomfield, Missouri, and had just graduated from the law school and gained admission to the bar when the war broke out. He went to training camp in May 1917. Finley was wounded twice, once at the Second Battle of the Marne and again at the Battle of the Meuse-Argonne. He was in several other skirmishes before being sent into Germany with the Army of Occupation. He was a captain by the end of the war. He later practiced law in Ardmore before moving to Muskogee to take up a position as an official of the Indian Agency there.

1. Hummerich is about 13 miles east of the Rhine River and 40 miles southeast of Cologne.

the exception of a few weak knee stevedores every one on the ship gave a good account of himself.

We remained at Brest only one day. From there we went to St. Nazaire where we remained for three weeks when this regiment was ordered to Champlit[t]e.[2] There we trained for three or four weeks and then were sent over in Alsace where on May 12th. we went into the trenches[.] After a stay of forty days in the trenches in Alsace near the towns of Hecken, Gildwiller, Falkwiller, Soppe Le Bas, and a few others[3] we were sent to Chateau Thierry where we were engaged for the first time in a real fight. This company was in the front line there for eleven days. We made the attack at the Qurcq river and from there we drove the Huns back to the Vesle river where they made a desperate stand. After some severe fighting we drove them across the Vesle. During that time this battalion, which is the second battalion of the 126th infantry, lost 75% of its men and all of its officers except four in killed, wounded, and missing. I was wounded in that battle. Got a slight wound in the left shoulder from a high explosive. This division (32nd) was relieved by the 77th division. We went back about four miles behind the front lines and there remained for about two weeks when we were sent up near Soissons and there fought the battle of Juvigny. There this company was six days on the line. By the front line I mean the leading element of the attack. Our losses there were about 60% of our strength. I forgot to mention that we received replacements after the battle of the Marne. From Juvigny we went to Osne Le Val[4] where we

2. The ancient town of St. Nazaire, on the west coast of France was, like Brest, one of the chief destinations for American troops. The U.S. Naval Base was established there in June 1917, and immediately began to receive both men and supplies. Champlitte, a city near Dijon and close to the Swiss border, was a journey of 450 miles eastward from St. Nazaire.

3. These towns, in far eastern France, were less than 50 miles from Basel, Switzerland.

4. The Battle of Juvigny, part of the Meuse-Argonne offensive, was a five-day struggle (August 27 to September 2) against five German divisions. The cost in American casualties was heavy. Osne-le-Val was about 230 miles north of Juvigny.

stayed for two weeks. There we again received replacements. On September 22 we left Osne Le Val and went up in the Verdun sector and there took part in the battle of the Argonne Forest. That is said to be the biggest battle of history. It certainly was the biggest fight this company ever had. We were twenty two days on the front line. I was again wounded there. Got a machine gun bullet in the left hip. I was also promoted at that battle. This division was relieved by the 89th division, a national army division from Missouri and Kansas. It probably will be of great interest to you to know that the 90th division from Oklahoma and Texas was engaged by the side of this division in that battle and they did WONDERFUL fighting. We went in the lines again on Nov. 9th. and were in the front when the armistic[e] took effect. I had a man seriously wounded at 10:45 p.m.[5] We were at Breheville[,] a small town just north of Verdun when the fighting ceased. This division was among those selected to go to the Rhine. The following is our route of march: Breheville-Jametz- Noers-Longwy-Selange-Keispelt Kodange-Osweiler-Meckel-Huttingen-Grosslittgen-Daun-Weleherath-Mayen-Ober Mendig-Miesenheim-(crossed the Rhine Dec. 13th.) Gladbach-Ober Hummerich. That route of march took us through parts of four foreign countries; France, Belgium, Luxembourg, and Germany.

You asked that I give my impressions during my service in the war. I can only mention in a general way the things that have made the greatest impressions on me. In the first place I was very favorably impressed by the sight of land, just any land, after we had been on the water for sixteen days and had been subjected to several attacks of seasickness and one or two of submarines.

In France as in America there was but one aim and that was to win this war. They had decided to hold out to the last, and unlike America,

5. Probably Finley means 10:45 a.m., only 15 minutes before the end of hostilities.

France has no slackers,[6] here every man, woman, and child plays his or her part. The men between the ages of eighteen and fifty are at the front while old men, the women, and the children do the work.

I have seen only a small part of Germany but if the part I have seen represents what they call "Kultur" then I thank God America is not infested with "Kultur."[7] We have not been here long enough to form any opinions as to the condition of the present German government.

I hope that I have in some measure answered your questions and I hope in the future to be able to answer more fully any questions you may care to ask.

With best wishes, and appreciating any news from America, I am

Sincerely yours

James H. Finley

Captain 126th, Infantry

O.K.

Capt. Jas H Finley

Co G 126 Inf

A.E.F. Via NY City

6. The term "slacker" was widely used during the war years to denote and condemn those who were not doing their patriotic duty, whether by avoiding military service or in other ways failing to support the war effort.

7. A term meaning German civilization. Americans used the word disparagingly to indicate their distaste for that country's militarism, authoritarianism, and boasts of superiority.

Fay Lester Garton

Bourges, (Cher) France[1]
P.E.S. A.P.O. 902
May 14 1919.

Mr. Stratton D. Brooks, president
The University of Oklahoma

Dear sir:

After months of delay I have received your letter asking that I, with the other Oklahoma men, contribute a page in our Universities history in France; and I will have to admit it occurs to me over and over again what can such a little cog in such a large machine know about a war that concerned millions of men and thousands of miles. And yet I believe there was something in that little part that would do to tell. And so I will tell of a little experience that although it does not mean war and desolation or dying pal or marching troops, yet it happened in the midst of all of these things, in the time when things were happening each day that made men realize our nation, that brought to the surface the thrilling realization that we are Americans—all Americans.

It was my fate to be one of the first in that most notorious camp, St. Aignan.[2] We were there the first of March 1918 (casuals, a mere

---

Fay Lester Garton (1894–1942) was born in Illinois, but moved to Blackwell, Oklahoma, at an early age. He played on the football team and graduated from the University in 1915. He was married on September 17, 1917, and entered the army (infantry) on October 3. He served for fourteen months in France. Gorton returned to Blackwell where he became the assistant postmaster.

1. Bourges, the capital city of the Cher department, is located near the geographic center of France.

2. Located in the Cher department, the camp at St. Aignan was a "replacement camp" where soldiers were assigned to take the place of those wounded or killed in combat. The camp also contained a hospital for wounded soldiers. The place was nicknamed "Camp Agony" because of the overcrowded and unsanitary conditions. The camp was built to house 1,500, but was occupied by as many as 25,000.

handful of us) before there was a building at the classification camp, and during the next five months grew up with it. Historically St. Aignan was on the road of the American line of supplies and train loads of everything (everything that it took to send Huns to Hades) trailed by like links on an endless chain. Coming and going there was about one train every five minutes of the day and night.

To the Americans the small cars and high wheels and most of all the "peanut roaster" engines were a source of humor, and the everlastingly shrill t-t-t-t-t-t-tooting was something that it took a long time to which to become accustomed. Perhaps we noticed it more than others because we were billeted only a few yards from the track itself.

Those were the smileless days, when the Huns had broken through and the British lines had given way. Day by day we watched the growing indentations toward Paris and night by night we lay and listened to the rain and breathed the fog, until it seemed that the very dampness in sympathy had soaked into us. On one of those heavy drizzly nights for which this part of France is famous, we lay in our bunks and courted sleep. Taps had blown two hours before and everything was quiet, when out of the darkness came the voice of a new arrival, the Woo—Woo—W'Woooooooah of a heavy grumbling freight.

Would that I could tell how thrilling it was. To us it was the call of the wild wild west, and it brought back all of those things we had begun to forget. Some way it was a part of us, an American engine, an American engineer and greatest of all a whistle, whistled a la Yank. Cooties were forgotten, the entire billet came to life and we gave vent to our penned up energy, and from the bottom of our hearts we yelled, every one of us. Here was the language of home in a land of strangers. Two minutes later it came again softer and low like an echo. Another cog in the great machine, maybe a casual too, and it spoke American.

Those of us who heard it then and later saw gradually more and more of them and then on November the 11th saw the swarming "Buddies" (two millions of them) perhaps now realize more than some of the others what a symbol the first Yank engine was to the old war song "The Yanks are coming."[3]

Just to relate this I thank you very much and I remain,

Yours very truly,

Cpl F. L. Garton '15

3. A line from the patriotic American song "Over There," by the celebrated songwriter and vaudevillian George M. Cohan.

Lee Burwell Goff

APO 778
Dec 27, 1918

My dear Dr. Brooks:

It is certainly a pleasure to answer your thoughtful letter of Christmas, and to thank you for remembering the boys who have gone out from the University.

I have been fortunate in meeting quite a number of Oklahoma University men over here and we all join in the universal wish to return to the University as it was before the war.

Yours sincerely
Lee Goff

Lee Burwell Goff (1896–1987) was from Oklahoma City. He enrolled at the University in the fall of 1915, and enlisted on April 9, 1917, a week after war was declared. He was commissioned a second lieutenant with the Field Artillery in August 1918. He spent twelve months in France, fought at Chateau Thierry, and was part of the Army of Occupation after the armistice. He ended his military career as a first lieutenant. Goff returned to school after the war and was listed as a junior in the College of Arts and Science in 1920. After the war, he worked as a car and truck salesman, and eventually moved to Monterey, California, where he died.

Mark Blandell Grimes

AMERICAN RED CROSS
ON ACTIVE SERVICE
WITH THE
AMERICAN EXPEDITIONARY FORCE

Province of Lorraine
Toul, France 1/3 1919.

Dr. Stratton D. Brooks
Norman Okla

My dear Dr. Brooks:

I hope that you will not consider it improper if I should write you a fine [few?] lines concerning myself (a former student in the University) on the morning of my evacuation from the hospital.

If you remember I delivered an original oration of my own in chapel in your presence, and if you recall, I said some very strong things and I am writing you that to the last I fought for those principles and the ideals which I cherish. I was wounded in the right leg in the great fight at St. Michel, and I am proud now forever that I had an opportunity to have had a part, humble tho it was, in this great and final enterprise of humanity. And, Mr. President, I intend to come back to the University, and I should like very much to arrange an interview with you, and I contemplate some forensic work when I get back and I should like very much to secure such aid as you can give me.

I am, Mr. President,

Yours very sincerely,
Mark B. Grimes

Mark Blandell Grimes (1898–1981), from Stuttgart, Arkansas, graduated from Stanford University and earned a law degree at the University of Oklahoma. He served in the Arkansas legislature before joining the Rock Island Railroad legal department and moving to Shawnee, Oklahoma, in 1927.

Arthur Edmund Haage

YMCA
WITH THE COLORS

Yuma Camp
Yuma, Ariz, Jan. 9, 1919

President Stratton D. Brooks and Members of the Faculty and Student Body present and past:

In response to your request for letters and for the benefit of those who may be interested, I shall add an account of my experience in the service of the Army Y.M.C.A.

On August 1st, 1918 after a three-weeks course in the Y.M.C.A. War Work Training School at Camp Travis,[1] I was assigned to the position of Educational Secretary at Yuma. In spite of the reports of exceedingly high temperatures here[,] the spirit for service practically every man who left the school had and the belief that I could go wherever our soldiers were sent, helped me to face the plains of Texas and the desert of New Mexico and Arizona.

August 2nd, the day before I arrived, was the hottest day in years, the thermometer registering 126° F in the shade. The next day was nearly as bad, but a sand storm that night and frequent showers modified the temperature for the next two weeks. Then the heat was very trying

---

Arthur Edmund Haage (1883–1935) was born in Keokuk, Iowa. He was a member of the class of 1916 at the University. After his work with the YMCA during the war, he stayed in Arizona and became a schoolteacher and, eventually, a justice of the peace in Peoria, a small town near Phoenix.

1. Camp Travis was located in San Antonio, Texas, attached to Camp Sam Houston. It began its operations in July 1917 as a mobilization and training facility. It was capable of handling 43,000 men, most of whom were from Texas and Oklahoma. By the time Haage was there, Camp Travis was a major induction and replacement center.

through September and until October 5th. By Thanksgiving the nights [were] so penetrably cold that much bedding was required under one as well as three or four blankets to cover with. While the heat of summer is intense and of long duration, the winter is most pleasant.

When I came here there were two companies of the 35th Infantry and a detachment of the Hospital Corps, about five hundred men, with two [YMCA] secretaries to serve them. There was no opportunity for educational work as the soldiers were anxiously awaiting their reported early removal. Before they were all gone, I was left in charge of the "Y" and have been alone from August 24th until the present. Two companies of the 25th Infantry (Colored) arriving from the Hawaiian Islands on August 29th, my services have been almost entirely with another race.[2]

Being alone my duties among these men have been varied indeed. I had to keep the house in order, provide stationery, ice water, and reading matter. On Sundays I arranged for a religious meeting and taught a Bible Class three nights in the week. I operated a moving picture machine. During the quarantine on account of the influenza epidemic the building was open to the soldiers for reading, writing and amusing themselves with the phonograph or the piano[,] but no meetings were permitted to be held. We made the quarantine less irksome by hanging a screen outside and showing pictures five times a week. I carried mail, sold stamps, cared for the library and went on all kinds of errands even to selling Liberty Bonds, buying money orders, depositing money in the banks and assisting to secure [a] marriage license and the services of a minister.

Every two weeks a guard detail of 18 men was sent to Andrade, California, a point on the Mexican border, to protect the customs house and the intake of the Imperial Irrigation Canal. Another detail of eight men went

2. For the story of African American soldiers in the war and their rigidly segregated units, see Arthur E. Barbeau and Florette Henri, *The Unknown Soldiers: Black American Troops in World War I* (Philadelphia: Temple University Press, 1974).

to the Laguna Dam thirteen miles up the Colorado River to guard the intake of the canal for the Yuma Irrigation Project.[3] It was a part of my work to visit these outposts occasionally. Besides taking stationery, reading matter and athletic goods to these men at times I was able to get some ladies of the town to go along to sing and play a folding organ. Thanks to the Y.M.C.A. "Ford" that made it possible to reach and serve these men.

In the afternoon of November 21st the camp was almost completely destroyed by fire. A high wind carried the flames[,] some burning refuse in the rear of the camp[,] to the thatch shades which covered the tents running the full length of the company streets. These were made of arrow weed, an oily plant, that had become thoroughly dried and burned as paper. Only a few of the men saved their lockers and rifles. Extra clothing, bedding, and personal effects, such as toilet articles, souvenirs from the Hawaiian Islands, photographs and in some cases Liberty Bonds and money to the value of several hundred dollars were lost. The U.S. Reclamation Service provided quilts and men slept wherever they could the first night, some finding shelter in the Y.M.C.A. For the next week until tents were received, quarters and kitchen and dining accommodations were provided at the Yuma Indian School across the river.

The men were re-established in camp and routine activities resumed for less than a month when orders came to join the regiment at Nogales, Ariz. On January 1st the two companies departed leaving a permanent guard of sixteen men and three members of the Hospital Corps at Andrade and a detail of thirty-five men to police the camp and ship the property. Sixteen of these men are quartered in the Y.M.C.A. building and I am waiting for instructions for the disposition of the property. The camp is being abandoned as there is no immediate need [for] a large guard here.

3. These were two major irrigation projects begun in the early twentieth century by the U.S. Bureau of Reclamation (established in 1902) to provide water from the Colorado River for California's Imperial Valley and Arizona's Yuma Valley.

In this old regular colored regiment are men who have seen active service in the Spanish-American War and in the Philippines. Two men I know of have nearly twenty-nine years service to their credit in the army. Many of them enlisted about the time war was declared and old and young alike were anxious to get to Europe. It does seem rather unfair that men who had chosen fighting as a vocation should be denied the privilege of participating in the greatest war in history. In general they are a lot of manly fellows who would have dealt terror to the enemy, if the opportunity had been given.

I consider it a privilege to have labored among them. The Y.M.C.A. has sought to assist in the war by helping the individual soldier regardless of race or color, to be cleaner, better informed, in closer touch with home and more contented with the new conditions of the army. By keeping in mind the purpose of the organization, I have heard many expressions of appreciation of services rendered.

On account of demobilization many have been allowed to leave the Y.M.C.A. so it was a surprise to me to be requested to take charge of the educational work in a new building at Douglas, Arizona. After the property is disposed of here I shall take the car across the desert for some border post farther east.

Most sincerely yours,

Arthur E. Haage '16

Tellus Bert Hendrick

Proven, Belgium[1]

Dec. 26, 1918

Mr. Stratton D Brooks
President University of Okla.
  Norman Oklahoma.

Dear Sir:

Your letter of November 6, 1918, after a considerable bit of travel to American camps, has reached me here in Belgium. It is indeed a pleasure to know that yourself and the University has not forgotten the boys that were forced to leave the "Old Varsity" for the time, to do their bit in France. And if any thing in my experiences in this war will be of interest to the students and faculty I am more than glad to relate them.

My experience in Brief has been this. On friday June 1, 1917 I took my last examination for the year[']s work in school. The next Saturday I applied for enlistment at Oklahoma City and on the following monday I took the oath in the United States Army at Fort Logan, Denver Colorado. It seems now that the rookey [sic] days at this fort are several times farther back in time than in reality. However, there is one thing that will always be fresh in my memory and that was the fine Spirit shown by the men from the first day.

The Summer of 1917 I was sent from Logan to [Fort] Riley and assigned to the 18th Ambulance. In August of 1917 I was transferred to Camp

---

Tellus Bert Hendrick (1896–1970) was born in Indian Territory and had been in the University's class of 1920, but enlisted on June 2, 1917. He was a sergeant with the Medical Corps in France and Belgium for ten months. He then was part of the Army of Occupation. He spent the rest of his life in Oklahoma City, working at various jobs, including credit manager in the grocery business.

1. Proven is a small village in West Flanders, Belgium, about 88 miles west of Brussels.

Lewis,[2] with the rank of a Corporal, to help with the first draft.[3] After ten months of training at Camp Lewis I sailed with the 362nd Ambulance Company of the 91st Division, for active service in the A. E. F. Crossing the ocean I was very fortunate in being sent on the SS Olympic[4] and as I am a Non-Commissioned above the grade of seventeen Sergeant first class, Med. Dept., I had a very good state room and the best of food and companions for the trip. During the night of July 18, 1918 our ship docked at the White Star pier South Hampton, England.[5]

The next night I crossed the English Channel on the Prince Edward, landing at Cherbourg, France.[6] Four days in an English rest camp was sufficient to convince we Americans that the English were in dire straights [sic] as far as food was concerned. The bravery of the smile of the tommy[7] at this camp during those crucial hours was the beginning of our respect for our Ally that became fast friendship when we took our place on the fighting front by their side.

From Cherbourg we traveled by rail to St Nazzaire [sic], for a month of intensive training. Our next move took us into the thickest

2. Camp Lewis was a brand-new training facility of 43,000 acres, located south of Tacoma, Washington.

3. When it was clearly realized that the United States could not rely entirely on volunteers to fight a war of such magnitude (six weeks after war was declared, only 73,000 men had volunteered), Congress enacted the Selective Service Act of 1917, and it was signed into law by President Wilson on May 18, 1917. By the war's end, around 2 million men had volunteered and 2.8 million were drafted.

4. The *Olympic* was a British ocean liner of the White Star Line (and a sister ship of the *Titanic*). The *Olympic* was used as a troop transport during the war and then was returned to its owners once the war was over.

5. Southampton is a port city on the English Channel. It was an important embarkation point for troops heading to France. Its population at the time was close to 160,000.

6. Cherbourg, on the northernmost tip of the Cotentin Peninsula, is located close to the southern coast of England. The city was a principal landing place for ships coming from England with troops and supplies. During the war Cherbourg had a population of around 40,000.

7. "Tom" or "tommy" was a common nickname for the British soldier.

of thick action that allowed us no rest until after the signing of the armistice.

Our Division took its place in the line in [the] M[e]use sector. By night marches we went to the St Mihiel sector where we acted as the first Reserve. More night marches and Auto trips brought us into the first lines of the Argonne forest. Sept 26, 1918 we went over the top and kept going for ten days. Any one who would tell the truth about any drive in which he has been in will have subject enough for a book. In that ten days I lived several years. Twice I almost decided I never would be able to see Oklahoma again. I with others of my Company went thru a Machine Gun barrage, shelling and gas. I can also testify to the daring of German snipers for our stretcher bearers found them quite a menace. The German's Prussian Guard seemed to have a passion for shelling wounded and dressing stations.

A very few days rest and my division was ordered to action in Belgium. We detrained near Ypres, Belgium on October 19, 1918. A week in shelter halves out in the worst bit of the devastated battle ground perhaps the world ever has seen,[8] found us ready for fighting. Our drive in Belgium was begun at the Lys river near Oyghem. The English on our left[,] the French on our right flank and the King of Belgium as Corps commander we felt proud to carry an equal part of the battle that cleared Belgium of Germans from the Lys to ten kilometers past the Schelt.[9] On the 11th of November at eleven oclock my Company was doing their best to keep in touch with the fighting. But our "dough Boys" were following the Bosch so fast that we jumped our station twice in one day

8. Before American entry, Ypres, in West Flanders, Belgium, had been the scene of two horrific battles (October–November 1914 and April–May 1915). The casualties were staggering on both sides and the destruction in every section of the city was massive.

9. The action Hendrick describes took place in West Flanders, about 50 miles west of Brussels. The Schelt River flows from northern France into western Belgium, and then on to the Netherlands and the North Sea.

by Motor and then were behind. Very few men were wounded in the last days of fighting.

After almost six months in the A.E.F. my record shows twenty-two days of fighting and traveling that covers a large part of France and not a little of Belgium.

Throughout my experience I have been conscious of the fact that America is not [now?] realizing her hold on Europ[e]. People high and low, the rich and poor, the learned and ignorant are looking forward to a visit to the United States. Their belief in our abilities is akin to the respect a big boy shows for an older brother. Our mobility and energy is a wonder to all. But does this lesson [*sic*] our duty toward these nations?

Not all future history depends upon our action, but the better part of our national history depends upon our individual attitude toward these people. We may follow an arrogant attitude which will kill the love of these splendid people for us. They have for a fact many ideas of living that is not common in the United States, yet we cannot say we are superior to them. Our materials and machinery are recognized as excellent but they do not excel as greatly as we some times make our selves believe. The roadways of Europ[e] if transferred to America would open unthought of opportunities for advancement. The french or belgian farmer would feed a family on our turning rows and fence corners. If we in the States would follow the European plan of planting trees along our roadways and streams we would be able to laugh at the deforestation scare of the Economist. The Sammies[10] in the A. E. F are learning lots of splendid ideas in these Countries and in return are taking back with them equally as many plans for improvement. The question is can they leaven the whole lump?

We fellows in a large measure have lost our opportunity for preparing our selves by a finished college education for our life[']s work.[11] We will

10. "Sammies" was a nickname for American soldiers fighting in World War I.
11. This was Hendrick's way of saying that he would not be coming back to continue his education at the University.

start our civilian life with the knowledge of life as it has come to us thru a hard task master. But to you, the faculty and students who will study and develop the new economic ideas as they are brought back by the soldiers in A.E.F. You stood back of us in the fight for life and now we are looking for you to help us carry on in the living of our national and individual life. We men over here are looking for the leaders in life that should come from our University halls to join hands with us in maintaining the friendly relations of our allies that now exists.

A friend and former student,

Tellus B. Hendrick
Sgt. First Class

David Elsworth Hilles

University of Cincinnati
Cincinnati, Ohio
November 19, 1918.

My dear President Brooks:

It has been my intention to write you ever since I have been in the service but because of so many things that a fellow has to do in the Army he sometimes forgets to do the things that he doesn't have to do. I have owed you and the University a debt that I can never repay. I believe every man that went to Sheridan[1] last summer as representatives of The University of Oklahoma feel that to yourself and the other members of the committee we owe a great debt for any little success we might have attained in this game of military.

You have asked me to relate my experiences in the war. Well, that will be easy for me for I am one of those unfortunates who has not been able to sniff the smoke of battle or who is not able to relate his exploits in "no mans land". My war experiences end with the feeling that I have been IN; that I have had the desire to do whether I did or not; that what I have tried to do I have done in a conscientious way; and, that whatever I have done for Uncle Sam and this great country of ours I have done in the best spirit and the best way I knew how.

David Elsworth Hilles (1897–1961), from Sapulpa, Oklahoma, was elected president of his freshman class in 1916. He enlisted on July 17, 1918 (infantry), and was commissioned a second lieutenant on September 16, 1918. He helped train engineers at the University of Cincinnati. After the war, he returned to Norman and is listed as a junior in 1920 in the College of Arts and Sciences. Afterward he settled in Stillwater, Oklahoma, and held several jobs there, including U.S. marshal.

1. Camp Sheridan, in Montgomery, Alabama, was created when the war began. Thousands of men were trained there, starting with 30,000 from Ohio. The American writer F. Scott Fitzgerald was among those stationed at the camp.

Of course, I have responsibility, having two hundred and nineteen of the finest bunch of Engineers that ever went to The University of Cincinnati, to look after and hold in line, but at that I realize that I have missed the great experience of leading men to battle, to suffer and to even die for the greatest old country that ever existed. It has been a pleasure to teach these men what I know and what they do not know about how to do the military, but I have missed the satisfaction of finding out how much they have learned would help them if they ever came in line of the Hun's guns. There is a certain regret that all of the men in the service in this country feel that the war didn't last long enough so that we might have all had a chance to get a crack at the dirty Hun. I feel that I have missed the greatest opportunity of my life to really do a great service for Humanity. To fight for the principles that were involved in this war and to even die if needs be, is the greatest opportunity that can come to a man, in my mind.

But now that it is over, we can look only to the future, forward to peace, to the time when we will all be back at the old Alma Mater again. And she is indeed a great school. Until a fellow gets away he little realizes what a school he is from. Oklahoma University should be proud of what she has done for the war and I am sure every Sooner is proud of his school. The men from Oklahoma, I know, were up to and a way above the standard at Sheridan and I know they were wherever they were in Camp or in France.

With best wishes for your self, and highest hopes for our University, for the future, I am,

Sincerely,
David E. Hilles

Herbert Christopher Hoover

Camp Sheridan, Ala.
Dec. 4, 1918

Pres. Brooks

My Dear sir:

Some one has said, "The hardest thing about going 'over the top' is the waiting" and <u>waiting</u> to be discharged from the military service, after peace has been declared, is, and will be the hardest duty the American Soldier will be called upon to perform. Not a murmur upon being taken into the service, for every red-blooded American is anxious to do his part; not a kick at the long hard hours of drill, for he realizes that he must be prepared to meet "Fritz"; but when it is "Over Over There" he will immediately feel that he must get back to the loved ones, to the farm, to the office, to the shop, to the mines. Back to the business will be, and is, his one consuming desire. While the American people will not stand for any foolishness from King, Kaiser, or "Kultur," they love Peace and Liberty.

When the "Homing bird" of peace comes in from across the troubled waters and the battle-torn fields of the earth, she will be no less welcome in the dear old U.S.A., than in the lands of greatest sorrow. Then the mothers, fathers, sisters, young wives and sweethearts, who only a few months ago said, "Go it is your duty," will chafe under the suspense: they too, will have to wait. Loved ones at home will be more anxious for the soldiers['] return from the chill fields of American Camps than they were from the battle fields of Europe. But we soldiers must wait and the loved ones at home must wait and be patient. Four million men cannot be sent

Herbert Christopher Hoover (1898–1972) was born in Fort Smith, Arkansas, and moved with his family to Hobart, Oklahoma, as a child. He was a freshman when he enlisted. He returned to the University after the war and in 1923 earned a degree in electrical engineering. He moved to various locations in and around the District of Columbia, working as an independent consulting engineer. He eventually settled in Pennsylvania.

home in a day, in a month or in a year. Two or three years may be required to accomplish this task. Even those now in camp in the United States cannot be mustered out for months after the peace treaty has been signed, for much less work is required in placing a man's name upon the roll of the Army than is required in the process of turning him back into civil life.

What then shall be the duty of this nation to her citizen soldiers during the demobilizing period? Shall they be allowed to loaf in the camps and Adjacent Cities subject to the temptations that appeal to idle hands and idle brains? No, these men must be kept at work and at drill and at study for "An idle brain is the devil's workshop" and unused muscles soon become unfit for hard physical toil. Further-more, they must be supplied with good wholesome entertainment, amusements and moral training such as are furnished by the Army & Navy Service Clubs, Y.M.C.A. and like organizations, especially the camp library. This particular work will become much more necessary after peace has been declared than it has been during the period of the war. Military authorities can and will look after the drill and physical training, but it is absolutely essential that the people at home, throughout this great country, provide the necessary means with which to carry on the other features of this great work.

This great war has been a national asset, patriotism has been intensified, selfishness is dying, "Man's inhumanity to man" is passing, whiskey has the delirium tremens[1] and we are going to come back home better men than when we answered our country's call. But this can only be accomplished with the con[tinuous?] effort of every one now in civil life, helping each soldier all that he can, as Bennie[2] says "Everybody help somebody else."

1. Hoover refers to the tidal wave of sentiment on behalf of the prohibition of alcoholic liquors during the war. That sentiment culminated in the Eighteenth Amendment, proposed by Congress in December 1917 and ratified, with overwhelming national support, by 46 out of 48 of the states, on January 16, 1919.

2. Hoover invokes the name of the legendary University of Oklahoma football coach Benjamin ("Bennie") Gilbert Owen (1875–1970), for whom the playing field in the University's stadium is named.

Your letter of recent date asking for a letter from me was most welcomed by me.

Hoping to be back HOME and among my old friends at the University sometime in the near future. I am,

Sincerely yours,
Herbert Hoover
Co "A." 209 F.S. Bn.
Camp Sheridan
Ala.

Richard Lee Huntington

Chinon France[1]
December 13 1918

President Stratton D. Brooks
University of Oklahoma
Norman, Oklahoma

My dear sir:

I was very glad to receive your letter, last week, asking me to write letters from time to time of my personal experiences of interest during the war. No doubt the accounts from men who have seen service in the front line trenches will be the most thrilling ones, but since I have been in the S. O. S (Service of Supplies area) during my stay in France I shall tell you, in several letters, some of the happenings I underwent as a soldier behind the lines.

The Ocean Voyage

A Water Detail of eight chemists were selected from a casual medical company at Ft Riley Kansas on September 12, 1917, and sent to Camp

---

Richard Lee Huntington (1896–1972) was born in Blackwell, Oklahoma. In 1917 he graduated from the University of Oklahoma with a bachelor's degree in Chemistry. After enlisting on August 10, he served first in the Medical Department and then in the Chemical Warfare Service. He was in France for 14 months. During the war he joined a water supply regiment but soon became an expert in chemical warfare research. Huntington would go on to earn an MA and PhD from the University of Michigan in 1933 and 1934. After a decade working for private oil and gas companies in Tulsa, he joined the faculty at the University of Oklahoma, and from 1933 to 1955, he served as chair of the School of Chemical Engineering. He was an expert on the chemistry of oil and gas, and published a book and around 50 papers on the subject. He retired from the University in 1966.

1. Chinon is a picturesque medieval village in the Loire Valley, about 200 miles southwest of Paris.

Dix New Jersey[2] from whence we found we were soon to leave with the 26th Engineers for service in France. One Saturday, late in October as I lay feverish-like in bed after my sixth shot of typhoid vaccine, of the day before, the half-way expected news came that we were to leave Camp Dix the next evening, just after dark for a destination unknown! I was out of bed in short order, for none of us cared to endure the monotonous cantonment life any longer. Our luggage and equipment was heavy. Into our barracks bag, which was about the size of an ordinary gunney-sack, we crammed an unnecessarily large supply of clothing and personal property. In our horse-shoe pack we carried over our left shoulder, were three blankets and a compact which the Red Cross had given us. Soon after dark Sunday evening (everything was kept as secret as possible) we "fell in" and our top sergeant gave us the command "squads right—March" which started us on our way to our "unknown destination". The next morning, I woke up—really I had not slept much due to the cold—and found that the train was standing in the Jersey City terminus which is on the bank of the Hudson River. We were issued a breakfast of hot coffee and sandwiches & then loaded on a ferry boat. Soon we were moving up the noisy Hudson as it always is on such a cold misty morning as it was on that day, for the ferry boats are so thick that they need to let forth a shrill whistle to let the rest of the river know that they are hurrying laborers to and from their work.

All of us were wondering as to which would be our transport to ferry us across when suddenly the ferry boat pulled up between two gray monsters. The Leviathan and the Agamemnon which previously belonged to Germany under the names of Der Vaterland and Kaiser Wilhelm II respectively.[3] Soon we were embarking on (much to our disappointment) the Agamemnon.

2. For Fort Riley, see the letter of Charles Brake, note 1, above. Fort Dix, near Trenton, New Jersey, was brand new. Constructed in 1917, it served as a training and embarkation facility.

3. For the *Leviathan,* see the letter of Andrew Nimrod Boatman, note 4, above. The smaller (19,000-ton) SS *Kaiser Wilhelm II* was renamed the *Agamemnon,* also

For a life time native of Oklahoma, like myself[,] it was a new experience and a very interesting one, just to roam over the boat the several days we were docked there in Hoboken before setting sail. Our 'state room' consisted of triple deckers on the fourth deck down at the forward end of the ship.[4] I called it the 'front end' at the time; and the air was very hot & close. However as the French express it—C'est la guerre.[5] October 31st was Hal[l]oween night but we did not celebrate. Instead of that we slowly slipped out of our dock in the middle of the afternoon and much to our surprise started up the Hudson but as soon as the fast falling darkness hid our steel gray ship from sight, the Agamemnon turned around and steamed full speed down the river. We were allowed to go on deck & take a last look at the Manhattan shore, but absolute quiet was the order given out so even when our lightless ship passed by a ferry boat whose passengers were noisily yelling good-bye to us, we constrained ourselves so as to not talk above a whisper. Soon after we glided down into the harbor and passed the Statue of Liberty which we watched for an hour or so until it fell from sight beneath the horizon of the dark sea. The next morning was bright and sunshiny & the sea was only slightly choppy. Then the routine daily life of our eleven days of sailing which were to follow, began. Mess was served to the five thousand men in a large hall. Breakfast from 7 to 9 A.M. Dinner from 11 A.M. to 1 P.M. & Supper from 4 P.M. to 6 P.M.

The eats proved to be very good during the whole journey and it's lucky they were for the salty air gave us wonderful appetites. Guard details were assigned. It was my duty to be on submarine watch for an hour at a time three times a day: at 10 A.M. 6 P.M. and 2 A.M. respectively. This was, with the possible exception of an occasional fire drill, the most exciting part of the voyage. To stand and gaze intently over a

---

in 1917. The *Agamemnon* transported around 38,000 men to Europe during the course of the war.

4. Triple deckers were bunk beds, stacked three high.

5. A French expression meaning "That's war."

small sector of the sea was no easy thing to do. I was equipped with a pair of field glasses thru which I looked about one third of the time, and a megaphone thru which to report to the bridge the sighting of any floating object. Everything went nicely for nine days as we took our zig-zag course, on somewhat of a southern route, across the Atlantic viz. the Bermuda Islands & then northward to Brest France.

Our convoy consisted of four large troop ships which sailed abreast the greater part of the time and ahead of us were our trustworthy leaders and guardians—the battleship North Carolina[6] & two speedy destroyers.

The greatest task we had was to keep out of the road of the dreaded submarines yet each boat, even amongst the transports, was ready at any moment to give battle to a nest of submarines. But as usual the unexpected happened—no submarines came near us. Nevertheless, the ninth night out from New York City when our convoy was in the vicinity of the Catalina Islands,[7] came very close to spelling catastrophe for the Van [sic] Steuben,[8] an old German ship, which had been sailing to our port side, and our ship, the Agamemnon. November the ninth had been a rainy day and at four o clock the officer of the day had ordered all smoking lamps out, in readiness for our usual nightly plunge through the ghastly darkness which indeed meant uncertainty on this night for we were getting into the 'danger zone'. A Mr. Kanable who stood guard (or lookout) with me, and I had eaten supper early so as to be ready as usual for the six to seven o clock watch, but no sooner had we taken our posts on the port side and had just begun to fasten our gaze on our assigned

6. Actually, the *North Carolina* was an armored cruiser.

7. There are no "Catalina Islands" in the Atlantic. Perhaps Huntington meant the Azores or the Canary Islands.

8. The *Von Steuben* was another German ship seized by the Americans after the outbreak of the war. Originally named the *Kronprinz Wilhelm* by the Germans, it was renamed after Friedrich Wilhelm von Steuben, the German hero of the American Revolutionary War,

sector of the rapidly darkening sky-line than our attention was drawn away from our gaze forward by the alarmingly shrill cries of the men all along our port side. Kanable & I were at the forward end of the ship. The Van Steuben had been keeping well to the rear of us during the afternoon and just before dark had come up abreast with us, however it was easily three-quarters of a mile, as one would gage distances on the sea, to our port side. Suddenly for unseen reason, shortly after six o'clock when our trusty flag-ship the North Carolina was going straight ahead, the Van Steuben turned her course and headed full speed thru the dusk of the evening right toward us (midships). The captain of our boat fortunately had noticed this strange maneuvre and had begun to swing our boat around so that when we heard the cries of the men, we turned around & saw the monster ship racing alongsides and towards us. Our men ran toward starboard and no sooner had I gotten away from my post than the Van Steuben's prow crashed into our forward well deck (port side) tearing a small hole above the water level in our strong ship. The two ships then rocked away from each other; then came the second crash as the Van Steuben's star-board side smashed against our boat tearing to splinters all of our life boats on our port side. The men quickly prepared to abandon ship and all were so terror stricken that not a word was said. Then the piercing siren blew and every one [believed?] that it surely meant that it was time to be getting into the sea. The swift destroyers of our convoy were soon around us, throwing search lights against the sides of our ship. Many men were converted in that short time—some men ran around calmly stating that if they ever got to land again they would always be good. In our anxious waiting to find out whether the ships had been seriously damaged the time passed only slowly. Soon our nerves were eased by the lights going out and our ships steaming forward with the assuring news that all was well. Even at that the men slept very little that night. The next day at nine o'clock we caught up with the other ships which had gone ahead according to the rules of the convoy, when we had had the accident the evening before. The Van Steuben had a large hole torn in her prow, thru which much water poured, but by constant pumping she kept going alright.[9] Two long days passed as we sped northward thru the danger zone; and then on Monday morning we saw land which all believed to be England. At ten oclock that morning we found out that our convoy was in Brest harbor. What a good feeling of security it was to step on real old mother earth again two days later and get into a "Hommes 40 Chevaux 8" stock car for shipment to eastern France.

Shall tell of my trip across France in a box car when I write my next letter.

Your friend
R. L. Huntington
Chemical Warfare Service Laboratory
A.P.O. 703. A.E.F. in France.

9. The collision between the *Von Steuben* and the *Agamemnon* occurred around 6:00 p.m. on November 9, 1917. The *Von Steuben,* carrying 1,223 men, was on its first voyage under the American flag. The accident was more serious than Huntington indicates. Both ships lost men overboard, and men on both ships sustained injuries.

Neil Robert Johnson

Letters rec'd state news Armistice was signed. I rec'd this at 2:20 a.m, Nov 11, while it was not signed here until 11 a.m Nov 11. Makes us feel we are a long ways from home.

AMERICAN YMCA
ON ACTIVE SERVICE
WITH THE
AMERICAN EXPEDITIONARY FORCE

Dec. 8 1918

My dear Pres. Brooks:

Thanks to armistice and the removal of certain obnoxious censorship regulation, I can at least, in response to your letter of Nov. 6/18 tell you that I am at present, resting at Blanc Fontaine one Kilometer from Stenay.[1]

Stenay is on the Meuse, some distance from Verdun. It was extremely honored in having the Ex Crown Prince of Germany occupy one of its beautiful chateaus for two years. The inhabitants had one thing against

---

Neil Robert Johnson (1893–1970) was born in Indian Territory. His father was Chickasaw, and Neil was an enrolled member of the Chickasaw Nation. He graduated from the University in 1915, and was quarterback and captain of the University's football team. He had been president of his freshman class, president of his law class, and president of the Business Opportunity Club. He enlisted on April 9, 1917 (cavalry), and rose to the rank of captain. He served nine months in France. Johnson was involved in ranching and later wrote *The Chickasaw Rancher* (1960). He moved back to Norman and became an important citizen there, serving as president of the Board of Governors of the University's Memorial Union, president of the Norman Chamber of Commerce, and president of the Norman Board of Education.

1. Stenay is in the Lorraine region of northeastern France, where some of the fiercest fighting of the war took place. Located 30 miles north of Verdun and 30 miles northeast of the Argonne Forest, Stenay was (as Johnson notes) the last town taken from the Germans by American troops on the morning of the armistice.

him, which was the killing of all the family cats with six large hounds that followed him at all times.

Stenay is the last town taken by the 90th Division, which is made up of Oklahoma and Texas men. To distinguish them from all others, every man has a red ⊤⊙ on his left shoulder. All vehicles are also marked with this distinctive sign. The fighting part of this Division is at present marching in German Territory to be part of the army of occupation.

We are engaged [in] moving the Ammunition forward by Truck, and will soon have the pleasure of treading on enemy territory.

Fortunately or unfortunately the Horsed Battalion has been with the Artillery all of the time, which was unable to be equipped, consequently have never seen any real fighting.

Just a little to[o] late all the time although we have been kept busy carrying out their numerous wishes.

We are called a "Horsed Battalion," not much in a name after all, because we have over five hundred jar headed mules, purchased from all corners of the globe, not a single horse; so just picture, if you can[,] one hundred four mule teams hitched to the U.S.A. escort wagon moving down the road with all officers and non commissioned officers mounted on mules, that will be our solemn entry into Germany.

A long eared mule looks fine under an English flat saddle, as one officer stated, "He felt like Christ entering Jerusalem."

Now and then an old grenade or mine goes off or they fire an ammunition dump which shakes the plaster from the walls, which causes a stampede among the dignified staff, because it sounds as if a shell has passed through the roof.

Pictures are unknown things in our young lives, while at La Corneau, which is near Bordeaux,[2] we had great difficulty in getting pictures for our Identification cards. It is enough to say, it was near the sea, sand six inches deep, full of filth, which had accumulated during the training of

2. Johnson probably means La Corneu, which is about 50 miles east of Bordeaux.

French, Italians and Russians. The last started an insurrection and over one thousand graves show the efficiency of modern machine guns let loose.

After fighting the "Spanish Flu["], and cleaning the place, we were moved to a little inland town called Cirey les Mareilles.[3] There we had our first experiences of Billets.[4] Our opinion of the high flying French, which we had received at Bordeaux and Aracachon [sic] disappeared.[5] These were the true people of France: polite, courteous, working night and day, doing everything possible for us, and really adopting us into the family.

As is the custom, when we started to leave, they submitted claims for things which our men were supposed to have broken, but in reality [were] broken in 1871 when the Germans occupied the village.[6] Their distinguished mayor, who looked like a tramp in the week, but a lord on Sunday, dressed in high silk hat and everything, was Mayor in 1871. Most all of them had relatives either killed or captured. Many prisoners returned while we were there, so we obtained very good information on conditions beyond the Rhine.

From Verdun up the Meuse, nothing but crumbled stone, where villages stood, barbed wire, trenches, shell holes, dug outs, which resemble a prairie dog town.

The Germans in their hasty retreat left most of Stenay in tact, we are using German coal, hay, oats, flour, furniture, pianos and real German "Liberty Cabbage".[7] Helmets are everywhere as well as machine guns, gas masks, ammunition, but so far from railroad that they object to

3. Cirey les Marsielles is a village in northeastern France, about 140 miles from the German border.
4. Arcachon was a resort area on the Atlantic, about 40 miles west of Bordeaux. It had a population during the war of around 10,000.
5. Billets are private homes that are ordered to house military personnel.
6. Johnson refers to the Franco-Prussian War of 1870–71, when the Germans decisively defeated the French and took Lorraine.
7. Sauerkraut.

sending it. All supplies are extremely scarce; trucks in running condition, short, railheads very far away.

The civil population is returning very fast; they are showing excellent qualities of "getting things while Getting is good". Each morning they come in droves with baskets on their back and a cane in their hand to scratch. Just like a bunch of chickens, never overlooking a thing, yet each morning they return to Stenay loaded.

Slowly they collect these things, beg everything they can; then they start a store. Of course some are destitute, but all are cared for by the French military authorities.

A bicycle in France is sought for just as much as a fine passenger touring car in the States; at the present time [they] cost as much as a Ford. As these people return to their homes, sketches and rules are brought forth and they start digging;[8] as we were cleaning the area around our stables, we had the pleasure of watching a Frenchman dig up nearly 1,000,000 francs. This morning at Dun Sur Meuse;[9] a well dressed woman was superintending the digging of four ex French soldiers. First they found the Bank Books and were after the money when I left. One thing a Frenchman is thorough; makes few mistakes. Women are just as efficient and work just the same as the men. False modesty which has been created between men and women in America does not exist. It is disappearing rapidly here between the men and what few American women we meet. It is more a basis of comrade or friend. A free and frank discussion as between man and man.

The nurses, Y.M.C.A. entertainers and canteen workers are living the life of a soldier and are undergoing all of the hardships of campaign. That is those that are following the armies. Nothing grand or spectacular for them, as one nurse told me she was "Just a common army nurse".

8. In preparation for the German invasion, many French families hid or buried valued possessions, and now, after the cessation of hostilities, they were returning to their homes and attempting to recover their belongings.
9. Dun-sur-Meuse is about 9 miles south of Stenay.

I was in one hospital for a day. There were about two thousand patients, one nurse, but I feel sure that has been changed by this time.

The American soldier is a great individual[.] [E]ach day brings something new and entirely different; they adapt themselves to these conditions, just as rapidly as they come.

Although filled with men from all parts of the country, even some of Villa's Mexicans,[10] they are all good soldiers. More like a bunch of boys, we are the instructors to keep them straight.

To give my experiences in detail would take the volume, because the experiences are numerous and different each day. May this suffice for the time being, and when I have wandered to the Rhine, decided that the Canadian [River] is good enough for me, I trust that I may have the pleasure or returning across a quiet sea from whence I came, and relating my trials and tribulations.

Sincerely yours,
Neil R. Johnson
Hq. Hs. Bn. 31
American E. F.
Trn Amm[unitio]n

When I get an envelope for this, the Lord only knows. Then it will be mailed. OK.   Neil R. Johnson Capt. USA

First Paper in two weeks just arrived. Also envelopes. Great Day.

[This letter] To be put in Volume, but please do not publish anything. Just prejudiced that's all.

10. Followers of Pancho Villa (1878–1923), the notorious Mexican general who helped depose Porfirio Diaz in 1911.

Richard Bowie Knight

AMERICAN YMCA
ON ACTIVE SERVICE
WITH THE
AMERICAN EXPEDITIONARY FORCE

Jan. 15, 1919
Donnemarie, France[1]

Pres. Stratton D. Brooks,
State University,
Norman, Okla.

Dear Sir:

Several days ago I received a letter from you requesting a letter from me, as a Soldier of the A. E. F., relating my experiences.

It would take me a long time to give in detail an account of what I have seen and heard during the past eight months that I have spent in the service of my country. Therefore, I shall write the experiences that are most vivid and the ones that I can never forget.

I was planning to enter the Summer School at O.U. last June and continue my course there until this Spring when I would have finished the necessary work for an A.B. degree. But the country needed me, and I was called to the colors May 25, 1918. I was sent to camp Bowie, Ft. Worth, Texas, where many other Okla. Boys were sent at that time to

Richard Bowie Knight (1893–1985) was born in Texas and moved to Bokchito, Oklahoma, a small town in Bryan Country. After the war he returned to the University and in June 1920 received his bachelor's degree from the College of Arts and Sciences. He became a school administrator and a county commissioner in Holdenville (Hughes County). The last four years of his long life were spent in Florida, where he died. He is buried, however, in Holdenville.

1. Donnemarie is a medieval village about 60 miles southeast of Paris.

fill up the 36th Division for overseas duty. We were kept in a Detention Camp for three weeks under quarantine. It was in the detention camp that I learned my first lesson of Army life. I learned the mysteries of the Soldiers Mess Kit, and how to line up for chow.

From the Detention Camp I was assigned to Co. L. 142nd Inf. I remained with this Co. one week and was sent to the hospital for an operation. I was in the hospital four weeks, and was sent from the hospital to Camp Mills, New York.[2] The Division left while I was in the hospital, so I was assigned to the Casualty bunch of the Division. We numbered about 850.

On Aug. 3, 1918, we steamed out from the harbor at Hoboken New Jersey. We were on the Leviathan, the largest boat afloat. I could not help but feel glad, yet sad we passed the Statue of Liberty. It was an impressive moment of my life. The Band was playing "We Won't Come Back Until It Is Over Over There!" Every Sammie was yelling and waving to the large crowd on the docks.

We were seven and one half days coming across the Atlantic. My!! How glad we were to see land again. We landed at Brest Aug. 11, just three months to an hour before the Armistice was signed.

We marched out from Brest about 4 Kls and began to soldier by stretching our "pup" tents. While at Brest we were amused by the strange ways the French do things. We could not understand their two wheel wagons, their stone houses with out any windows, their rock walls around the small farm and house, and all the ancient looking streets. Everything is so different from America.

We were loaded on boxcars Aug. 18, and the train pulled out for we knew not where. We were on the train for five days and nights, forty two of us to the boxcar. And they are not more than half as large as a boxcar of the States. At Bar Sur Aube we were ordered off the train, and marched

2. Camp Mills, located on Long Island, was an embarkation post where as many as 40,000 recruits could be trained and prepared for the journey to France.

out into the country 14 Kls to Sulane, a little isolated village.[3] Here we were assigned to various Companies of the 143rd Inf. I was assigned to Co. A. There was only one boy of the entire Company I knew. But it did not take me long to get acquainted.

We were put to training for six weeks, and there was no play, it was all the week thru, Sunday the same as any other day.

One Sat. Afternoon in Sept. we were ordered to roll packs with all of our equipment. We were glad to get a chance to move, and we were anxious to go toward the front. We were loaded on boxcars again and shipped by night to Epernay. Here we could hear the big guns and see the airplanes fighting. Each night we were marched a little closer until Oct. 9 we passed under shell fire and relieved the Second Division.

The first Battalion of the 143rd was in reserve, until Oct. 11. We went over the top. Well, I can't describe my feeling as we chased the Huns and the shrapnel and machine gun bullets whistled around me. For three days we chased them and could not get close enough to see them. We drove them across the Aisne River, and there they dug in. Eighteen days we were on the front. Our Company went over the top twice, and did not lose a single man. I went on one patrol the night before we were relieved. We went very close to the enemy and gained some information necessary for our safety.

Naturally we were glad to get back where we could walk around in the day light without being in danger of the shells. We came back to a rest camp and was there when the Armistice was signed. Again, I can't express my feelings as I expressed them the morning of Nov. 11.

Soon after the Armistice was signed we started on our march back from the front to the area we are now located in. We marched eleven days and my! How proud we were to reach our destination.

3. Perhaps Knight means Maisons-les-Soulaines, which is around 12 kilometers (about 7.5 miles) from Bar-sur-Aube.

Dec. 28. I was selected as a military police and sent to this city where a new Co. of M.P.s were being organized. We are enjoying ourselves very well. Our fondest ambition is to cross the Atlantic again. And my greatest desire is to get back in school.

I do not know when we are to return, but I hope it will be in time for me to attend the Summer 1919 term at O.U.

Sincerely yours,
Richard B. Knight
36th. Div. M.P. Co
A.P.O. 796. A. E. F

Joshua Bryan Lee

AMERICAN Y.M.C.A.
ON ACTIVE SERVICE
WITH THE
AMERICAN EXPEDITIONARY FORCE

July 12, 1919

Dear Dr. Brooks:

I enclose a copy of the paper that published my essay.[1]

It was an A E F essay contest conducted by the Comrades in Service, and the Sec[retary]. wrote to me saying that 260 essays were submitted.

It seems impossible for me to get away from the Army. I am promised and fed on promises until I'm "nuts." "I want to go home" I have even engraved on my mess kit lid. When the last A.E.F. steps on board I'm going to yell "me next!"

My last stand off in the way of a promise is that if I'll just stay with the troop and play for one more week, then I may go home. Oh, no, I'm

Joshua Bryan Lee (1892–1967) graduated from the University of Oklahoma in 1917 with a reputation for eloquence. In 1916, he had won the national collegiate oratorical championship. He was with the 135th Infantry in France and was tasked with providing entertainment and raising morale among the troops. After serving 14 months in the war, he returned to OU as chair of the Public Speech Department, a position he held until his successful bid for the U.S. House of Representatives in 1934. He was elected to the Senate in 1937 as a loyal FDR-supporting Democrat, and was sometimes mentioned as a possible vice-presidential candidate in 1940. In 1942, he was defeated as a Senate candidate by Robert S. Kerr. He ended his career practicing law in Norman. Lee published a performance piece in 1919 entitled "The Battle of Cognac," as well as two collections of poetry that focused on the war.

1. Lee had finished second in an essay contest for soldiers. The essay was printed as "We Will Make Our Dreams Come True," a patriotic declaration of American soldiers' determination to realize their hopes and ambitions once the war was over. The newspaper is unknown.

not a bit excited over it, for I've already celebrated my release to go home three times.

I say [saw?] Miss Pickering in Paris the Day after the Peace was signed. I saw Herold Ditzlar [*sic*][2] in Romorantin just before I came here.

Very truly

Josh Lee

P.S. We are now playing here in Bourges.

2. Miss Pickering is unknown. Harold Ditzler (1894–1982) was a Norman resident. He was a marine sergeant during the war and then lived in Oklahoma City, where he worked for Southwestern Bell. Lee encountered him in Romorantin, a town about 120 miles south of Paris.

David Matthew Logan

SCHOOL FOR AERIAL OBSERVERS
POST FIELD
FORT SILL, OKLAHOMA

Nov. 15, 1918

From: David M. Logan, 2nd Lt. C.A.C. Att. Q.S.A.

To: Stratton D. Brooks, President University of Oklahoma, Norman, Okla.

Subject: The Battle of Fort Sill

I have been thinking of writing to you for a long time, but kept putting it off because my respect for your time outweighed my inclination to write. Now that you have asked for letters I want to file one alongside those from the battle field [*sic*]. However mine is not a narration of stirring events, but is the first of a life long series of explanations as to why I didn't get into the World War.

I don't think I have written to you, nor seen you, since I passed through Norman last spring so I shall begin back there and sketch over what I have been doing since that time.

I left Seattle May 15 and after stopping in Norman a day and Tahlequah a couple of days[,] I reported at Langley Field, Va.[1] May 25 to take the airplane observers course. The first two weeks were spent on ground

David Matthew Logan (1894–1983), from Tahlequah, Oklahoma, graduated from the University in 1916, a prominent figure in campus life and president of his senior class. A year later, he was placed in charge of Mechanical Drawing in the College of Engineering. He enlisted on August 25, 1917, and was commissioned a second lieutenant in November. Logan was stationed as an instructor in Air Observation at Fort Sill, Oklahoma. He was discharged on February 1, 1919, and entered graduate school in the fall. Logan moved to Okmulgee, where he worked in the oil industry.

1. Tahlequah, in northeastern Oklahoma, is the capital of the Cherokee Nation. Fort Langley, in Hampton, Virginia (near Newport News), was created as a training camp, primarily for the Air Corps, in 1916.

work; radio practice, machine-gunnery, miniature range, and interpreting aerial photographs. The remaining five weeks were used in flying; or rather we would fly a half day and attend lectures or study the rest of the day. During the first flying I drew sketches and took photographs, and during the latter part of the course I observed fire for a "smoke puff" battery. However not all the flying time was used on prescribed work for many are the times I would go off on an aerial acrobatic party before returning to the aerodome [sic].

I completed the observers course July 13 and was then given five days leave before reporting to an advanced school of aerial machine gunnery at Selfridge Field, Mount Clemens, Mich.[2] I spent the leave in Washington and Niagara Falls. While in Washington I stopped with Whittemore, who now has charge of all the materials testing at the Bureau of Standards.[3] If we could have gotten together the former instructors in the engineering college who were in the city at that time it would have resembled a faculty meeting. Besides Whittemore and myself there were Bozell, Morrow, Tom Sorey, and er! Abraham Press.[4]

2. Like Langley, Selfridge Field was opened in 1916 as a center for aerial combat training.

3. Herbert Lucius Whittemore (1876–1954), who earned his BA at the University of Wisconsin (1903) and MA in Engineering there in 1910, had been appointed assistant professor of Mechanics in the College of Engineering at the University of Oklahoma in 1916. He resigned in January 1919 to become head of the War Materials Testing Laboratory at the Bureau of Standards in Washington, D.C. Whittemore wrote several books and articles about the strength and properties of steel and other materials. See Tom J. Love, Jr., *The University of Oklahoma College of Engineering: The First 70 Years* (Norman: self-pub., 2008?), C 3–6, for Whittemore's charming reminiscence of early days at the College.

4. Harold Veach Bozell (1886–1972), a pioneering figure in the College of Engineering, was the head of Electrical Engineering. In 1916, he left for the Army Signal Corps School at Yale. He returned to his former position after the war and served as secretary of the College of Engineering for many years. Thomas Lester Sorey (1895–1958), from Oklahoma City, was a junior in Engineering in 1917. He was appointed an assistant professor of Mechanical Drawing. Whittemore (see previous note) brought him to the Bureau of Standards in 1917. When the war ended, Sorey

The school at Selfridge Field lasted only three weeks. During the first week I learned everything there was to know about a Lewis machine gun;[5] and I used up a few thousand rounds firing on ground ranges and from a high-power motor boat. Most of the last two weeks was spent in flying. On the first flights instead of having a machine gun to fire, I had a piece of machinery the same weight and appearance as a Lewis machine gun. In place of pumping lead it shot pictures. Films were loaded in a magazine instead of cartridges, and when the trigger was pulled there was a "snap shot" instead of a lead shot. A pull on the "charging handle," the cocking piece, would turn the next exposure. Two planes equipped with these guns would be sent up to meet each other in an aerial combat at a certain altitude. Each observer tried to get a properly aimed picture of his opponent, and it counted against the pilot if he let the observer in the opposing plane shoot him. I am attaching a print of a shot I made. All of this was very interesting work and had more sportsmanship to it than anything I have ever experienced. You may imagine the acrobatic maneuvers that the plane would go through in such an engagement. Following this I had target practice from the plane at all kinds of targets, including airplane silhouettes on the ground, trenches

---

returned to Oklahoma City as a draftsman for an architectural firm. He was then asked to come back to the University as head of Engineering Drawing. While teaching, he completed his BA, receiving his degree from the College of Arts and Sciences in 1920. After making several important innovations, Sorey resigned in 1923 and entered private practice as an architect. He and his firm built the University's Memorial Union and half a dozen other buildings on the campus. See Love, *College of Engineering*, 47. Lester William Wallace Morrow (1888–1942) was a professor of Electrical Engineering, becoming director of the department in 1916. Two years later, with the war on, he took a leave to teach at the Army Signal Corps School, where Bozell was already teaching. Morrow did not return to the University. Abraham Press (b. 1887) was a Russian immigrant who taught Electrical Engineering for one year (1916–17) before leaving the University.

5. The Lewis machine gun was developed in the United States but used primarily by British and French troops. It could be employed both by infantry units and from airplanes.

(for sweeping fire), targets towed by a motor boat, and aerial targets towed by another plane.

The course in machine gunnery ended August 10, and everyone in my class was given a ten days leave to visit home before going over-seas. Our over-seas orders, we were told, would be telegraphed to us at our various leave stations. After I had told everyone in my native village that I was on my way "over-there", I got a telegram ordering me back to Langley Field, Va. I couldn't understand it until I got back to the observers' school and found I had been returned as an instructor. Of the forty-four to finish in my class at the gunnery school, forty got their over-seas orders, and I was one of the four to be returned as an instructor. We were the sorest quartet I ever saw. It was the second time I had gotten left, for my regiment went across two weeks after I left it for the air service.

I saw I was stuck for a few months, so put in for a transfer back to the artillery. The C.O. wouldn't listen to it, so in desperation I filed a resignation of my commission Aug. 30 so that I might enlist as a private in some organization at the port of embarkation. The resignation came back disapproved. Then for the first time in my life I wished I was married.

In September the director of the observers' school at Post Field, Fort Sill[,] wrote our school for an exchange of instructors; following out an old college practice. I heard of the letter so asked our school director to get in on the exchange, and for the first time the C.O. granted my wish—I guess he was glad to get rid of me. I left Langley Field Oct. 5 (with no regrets). I stopped off in Norman a day on my way here. I did not make my presence known to you, because I did not want to embarrass the treasurer of the United States, who was with you at the time,[6] by having you turn your attentions from him in order to entertain me.

I have been down here more than a month now and I like the place very much. This school is about as efficient as a training school could

6. The treasurer of the United States in 1918 was John Burke (1859–1937), a former governor of North Dakota.

be. In fact, there is no comparison between the work done at Langley and the work here.

I have been instructing in the "laision["] [*sic*] department which includes all artillery observation, the puff batteries, and the infantry contact patrol training. This week I have been assigning planes to the observers out on the field.

I like the flying game more every day. In fact, I am now hoping to become an aeronautical engineer some day. I have been trying to get authorized instruction in piloting, but so far my experience in handling a plane has been limited to a few trips in a dual control machine when the pilot would give me the stick.

I can not help but feel enthusiastic over the future of the airplane industry when incidents like the following happen. The commanding officer here wanted to go to Dallas in a hurry one day last week. He got one of the pilots here to take him down in a DeHaviland [*sic*] (Liberty motor) plane.[7] They left at 10:am and the pilot brought the plane back by 6:pm; and he laid over in Dallas nearly three hours before starting back. Another instance: last week an officer got a telegram at 4:pm ordering him to arrive at another station by a certain time. He would have had to leave on a 3:30 pm train in order to get to his destination on time. At 4:30pm he left the ground in an airplane, overtook and boarded the train at Chickasha. The pilot brought the plane back to the field before dark.

Prof. Davis[8] was down here for two or three days the past week. He is very enthusiastic about his proposed course in airplane mechanics, and I think he enjoyed his visit very much, especially his flight. The major in

7. The airplane mentioned here was a biplane designed by the pioneering English aircraft designer Geoffrey DeHavilland (1882–1965). He had been making and flying planes since 1910. During the war DeHavilland worked as a designer and test pilot for the Aircraft Manufacturing Company. In September 1920 he formed the famous DeHavilland Aircraft Company, which, over the years, introduced numerous innovations in the industry.

8. James Christopher Davis (1889–1937) earned his Bachelor of Science degree at Purdue University in 1903, and master's degree in Engineering at the University

charge of the engineering department and I are going to see if we can get a cross-country flight to Norman—of course, just for the necessity of showing Davis' class what a real machine and motor look like. And of course I have to go in order to give a lecture on artillery observation to Dr. Reeves[']⁹ class. Really, if the University would like to have a couple of planes fly up from here sometimes I would be glad to cooperate with you in getting them.

I am planning to do some Masonic work in Guthrie next week¹⁰ and if I do, I shall come down to Norman Saturday.

I want to thank the University for the copies of "Sooners and War Service" that I have been getting. I now wait the announcement of the big reunion when I can gather with my former class mates and listen to "what I did" and explain "what I didn't."

David M. Logan

---

of Oklahoma in 1914. Three years later, he became an associate professor of Mechanics. He remained at the University until his death in 1937.

9. Probably Samuel Watson Reaves (1875–1950), an important figure in the history of the University of Oklahoma. He was hired to teach mathematics in 1905, and he taught that subject for the next forty years. He was perhaps best known as the popular dean of the College of Arts and Sciences from 1923 to 1940. He made numerous contributions to the University and the city of Norman.

10. Guthrie, Oklahoma, the former seat of the Territorial government of Oklahoma and the first capital of the state, was the center of Scottish Rite Masonry and the site of the Masonic fraternity's temple (1908). The building is renowned for its architectural beauty.

Leonard Marion Logan Jr.

AMERICAN YMCA
ON ACTIVE SERVICE
WITH THE
AMERICAN EXPEDITIONARY FORCE

12/7/1918

Pres. Stratton D. Brooks,
   Norman, Okla.

My dear Pres. Brooks:

It was very encouraging indeed to receive your interesting letter. Letters from friends back in the States are as encouraging and as highly appreciated as money from home in the good old days when I was back in O.U.

I am receiving the News Letter regularly. Through its medium I have been enabled to get in touch with many of my friends whom I would never have reached otherwise.

I have been in France seven months now and have seen a great deal of it. At present I am in the Q.M. depot in Marseilles. For awhile we were billeted in some university buildings. I was in the Natural Science building. The classic designs on the building served in quite a contrast to the

---

Leonard Marion Logan Jr. (1891–1974) was the elder brother of David Logan (see the previous letter). Leonard graduated from the University in 1914 as president of his class. He enlisted on January 10, 1918, as a sergeant and was discharged on February 11, 1919. In 1923, Logan joined the faculty as a professor of Economics and, later, of Sociology. He was an expert on city planning and founded what later became the University's Department of Urban and Regional Studies. He taught in Norman for 38 years, retiring in 1961. In 1972, he and his wife moved to Okmulgee.

O[live].D[rab]. uniforms on the "campus" which was nothing more than an open court.

For awhile I was assigned to duty down at the docks. Just a little way out across the bay was the Chateau d'if where Monte Christo served his days of confinement.[1] Prisoners of war are kept out there now and visitors are not permitted to land on the little island.

I like France but give me America first, last, and always. The French are more artistic but lack the pep of the Americans. They have borne the brunt of the war bravely and have a special place in their hearts for the Americans. The war has been cruel indeed. But to us who have seen a little more of it than the folks back home, see the benefits of it. It has brought humanity to its senses, the shock has purified the atmosphere of civilization. German universities were the home ports of German propaganda. The war has proven that the Hun idea of civilization is a failure. It was based too much on the intellectual. They left God out of the question and "Gott" licked.

My war experiences have been some what limited. I have loaded ships, worked in ware houses and convoyed train loads up the line. I have never been over the top nor seen no man's land.[2] There are fewer Americans over here who have had that experience than those who haven't.

From the present outlook it doesn't appear that our outfit will get back very soon.

I am willing to keep in touch with my Alma Mater but, President[,] don't let any of my letters appear in print. I don't care for publicity.

1. The Chateau d'if had been built as an offshore fortress at Marseilles, but became a prison, made famous by Alexandre Dumas' setting of *The Count of Monte Cristo* (1844) there.
2. In World War I, "no man's land" was the open ground between the opposing armies' trenches.

I will be delighted to get an Oklahoma Daily[3] now and then if you send any to the boys in France.

With best wishes to you and for the welfare of O. U. I am,

Yours sincerely,

Leonard Logan, Jr.

Sgt. Q.M.C. A.P.O. 752

Amer. E. F. France

---

3. The *Oklahoma Daily* was the student newspaper. It was founded two years earlier, in 1916. Logan did not realize that the paper had been suspended since May 1918 because of student enlistments and the draft. It would not resume until January 1919.

Front page of the student newspaper, April 12, 1917, a week after America entered World War I. Courtesy of the Oklahoma Historical Society.

Stratton D. Brooks (1869–1949), third president of the University of Oklahoma. Courtesy of the Stratton Brooks Collection, Box 1, Western History Collections, Special Research Collections, University of Oklahoma Libraries.

Wartime secretarial staff in Evans Hall. Courtesy of the Stratton Brooks Collection, Box 1, Western History Collections, Special Research Collections, University of Oklahoma Libraries.

FOREWORD

A wonderful time to live in, when all the world's afire! Men in their prime have left the campus for the battlefields of Europe. It is the humble aim of the 1918 Sooner to commemorate and keep fresh the memory of these men who have so gallantly offered their lives to their country.

"Foreword" from the 1918 *Sooner Yearbook.*

Posters urging enlistment. Courtesy of the Library of Congress.

University of Oklahoma students in uniform, members of the Company "B" student regiment. Courtesy of the Stratton Brooks Collection, Box 1, Western History Collections, Special Research Collections, University of Oklahoma Libraries.

One of the dreaded German U-boats. Courtesy of the Library of Congress.

The USS *Leviathan*, the largest ship afloat, was commandeered from Germany and used to transport thousands of American troops to France. Courtesy of the Library of Congress.

Two professors in uniform: Walter S. Campbell (Stanley Vestal) (*left*) and John O. Mosely (*right*). Courtesy of the Stratton Brooks Collection, Box 1, Western History Collections, Special Research Collections, University of Oklahoma Libraries.

Letter from Abraham Lincoln Blesh to President Brooks, November 25, 1918. Courtesy of the Stratton Brooks Collection, Box 1, Western History Collections, Special Research Collections, University of Oklahoma Libraries.

YMCA poster, 1918. The YMCA, as many of the letters in this volume attest, provided important and multifaceted services to American servicemen during the war. Courtesy of the Library of Congress.

Front page of the *Daily Oklahoman* announcing the armistice, November 12, 1918. Courtesy of *The Daily Oklahoman* digital archives.

In Memoriam

Fred Allen, '08	R. E. Alexander, '14
James D. Avery, '22	E. Hardin Davis, '18
Dick B. Breeding, '16	Eloise Eagleton, '18
Walter Drew, '18	Benj. G. Jones, '17
Lewis Isle, '19	Lonnie L. Lyon, '18
John M. Kates, '12	S. J. McAdams, '21
Charles Milam, '15	Wakefield Revelle, '19
Arnold Rasmussen, '20	Louis B. Southerland, '20
Homer G. Stocking, '18	Henry G. Adams, '15
Wesley F. Grube, '19	Charles S. Price, '18
George R. Anderson, '16	Robt. L. Hull, (Faculty)
Meade Frierson, Jr. (Faculty)	F. B. Sorgatz, (Faculty)

A tribute to those Sooners who lost their lives in the war, from the 1919 *Sooner Yearbook*.

Herman Patrick McCrimmon

U.S. NAVAL RESERVE TRAINING
LOS ANGELES HARBOR
SAN PEDRO, CALIF.

Nov 25, 1918

President Stratton D. Brooks

Dear Friend:

I was very much pleased at receiving your letter and appreciated it very much.

Boys from O.U. are rather scarce in this camp, in fact I have met only one.

I am sending a view of part of the camp.[1] On the extreme left is Russell Hall where the boys can read and study. In the back ground are the San Pedro ship yards. Here is where the new "Camouflages" are built.[2] The rocky cliff is Dead Man's Island, the island mentioned in the book, "Two years before the Mast".[3] In the back ground between the ship yards and the island is Long Beach, California. The picture was made just before Saturday morning inspection. The two small picture[s] are of the parade

Herman Patrick McCrimmon (1897–1989), from Norman, enlisted early in his college career. He was part of the U.S. Naval Reserve, stationed in San Pedro, California. He attained the rank of captain. McCrimmon resumed his education, enrolling in 1919–20 at the University and graduating from the School of Medicine in 1925. He practiced medicine in Illinois, Minnesota, and New York, maintaining his connection with the U.S. Navy for more than thirty years. He retired to San Antonio, Texas.

1. McCrimmon sent some photographs of the navy's training camp at San Pedro, the harbor for Los Angeles. The camp was one of those created in the 12th Naval District.

2. "Camouflages" were ships painted to obscure detection by the enemy or to confuse the vessel's distance or size.

3. Richard Henry Dana's classic memoir of 1840, exposing the cruelty and harsh conditions endured by American seamen.

the sailors in camp put on the day peace was declared. The flags of all the allies were carried by sailors who were held on the shoulders of other sailors. The other is where they are standing at attention to the "Marseilles". The ship is the McCullough, a revenue cutter, which was rammed by the Governor.[4] The picture was taken just before she left on her last cruise. The other is the same ship sinking.

The influenza quarantine was lifted this week. We have been quarantined eight weeks. This seems bad yet it was the very best thing for us, for we never lost a man from influenza. Since this camp was established June 14, 1917 there has only been four deaths, three from pneumonia and one on the operating table. One of the "Flu" patient[']s temperature went to 108 degrees, but by faithful work and staying on the job we managed to pull him through. So you see this has been a busy place.

A fellow gets some wonderful experience in the navy. I will never forget how we used to be disturbed at five thirty in the morning with the thundering sound of, "Rise and Shine", "Hit the Decks". I believe the most popular song in the navy is "Oh! How I hate to get up in the morning".[5] I am in the Hospital Corps. The boys here are certainly disappointed at not seeing foreign service. Ten corp[s] men left the other day for Va. on their way to France, but I was not quite old enough in the service to be one of the lucky ten. If any one does not believe the fellows wanted to go across all he has to do is to go to the Personal [*sic*] Office and look at the applications stacked up asking to be put on the next boat going out. But anyway I am glad that it is over and peace is here, though I got no farther than San Pedro, California. Now I hope to soon be back in school.

Sincerely,

Herman P. McCrimmon.

4. On June 13, 1917, the Coast Guard cutter *McCulloch* collided with the passenger ship SS *Governor* off the coast of Point Conception. The *McCulloch* was sunk, but all hands were saved.

5. The popular 1918 song was written by Irving Berlin, shortly after he was drafted into the army.

Charles Harold McNeese

Norman, Okla.
March 29 1919

President Stratton D. Brooks,
University of Oklahoma

Dear Sir:

Some time ago, I received a letter requesting me to write to the University regarding my military experience. As this letter was sent to the 16th. Infantry, it was forwarded to me only to find me discharged from the army and again enrolled in the University. But even at this late date, my mind is still vivid with the memories of my military career, and I consider it an honor to be able to contribute to such a collection as you intend to compile. From my date of enlistment to my date of discharge, my service in the army has varied from the border of Mexico to the border of Alsace-Lorraine. When the Mexican situation became intense in June, 1916,[1] I enlisted as a private in the Co. "M" 1st Okla. Infantry. The middle of

---

Charles Harold McNeese (1892–1955) was born in Bellaire, Ohio. He moved to Oklahoma City and entered the University of Oklahoma in September 1913. His career as a student was interrupted when he enlisted for military service on the Mexican-Texas border (see note 1) and by subsequent service in World War I. He suffered a gas injury on November 5, 1917, and was wounded on July 18, 1918, at Soisson. He fought in the Battle of Cantigny and the Second Battle of the Marne, and was commissioned a second lieutenant in the infantry, August 15, 1917, and afterward a captain. (McNeese would later serve as a colonel in the Army Reserve during World War II.) He returned to Norman in January 1919 and received his bachelor's degree in Geology on June 8, 1920. He and his wife moved to Ponca City in 1925, where he was employed by the Continental Oil Company. He was transferred to Houston in 1951.

1. A series of incidents on the border between the United States and Mexico (including a raid into New Mexico by Pancho Villa in March 1916) led to ever-worsening relations and troop buildups on both sides. McNeese refers to a major skirmish at Carrizal on June 21, 1916. It was only the threatening situation in Europe that prevented President Wilson from asking for a declaration of war against Mexico.

July, the same year, found us debarking at San Benito, Texas, about 25 miles from the Mexican Border. In Sept. our company was placed in guard of the Santa Marie and La Faria pump stations on the Rio Grande. In August 1916 I was promoted to Corporal and was mustered out as such on March 1 1917.

My civilian life at this time was destined to be short however, and on April 1 1917, [I] was again called into federal service.[2] A short time after this second call, I was promoted to the rank of Sergeant, and on May 22, 1917 was sent from my company to the First Reserve Officers Training Camp, located at Leon Springs, Texas.[3] On August 15 1917, after three months of hard work, I received my commission as First Lieutenant, Infantry Section, U.S.R., and on the same date, I also received my orders to report to the Commanding General, Port of Embarkation, Hoboken, N.J. equipped for extended field service.

Of course the officers who received such an assignment were all smiles for it meant that they would be among the first to "get over", but little did they think of the true meaning of these orders. True it meant that they would get over in good time, but it also meant that there would be many of them, who, sailing out of the harbor, would wave a goodbye to the Statue of Liberty never to see her again, and such was the fate of a great many of these officers who went with this first contingent.

It was about the first of Sept. that we set sail from Hoboken on the USS Dekalb, formerly the famous German raider, Prince Eitle Freidrick [*sic*],[4] and about the middle of the month, landed in France at the now

2. This was five days before the formal declaration of war by Congress.

3. The 17,000-acre training camp at Leon Springs, Texas, had been in operation for about a decade. The Reserve Officers Training Corps (ROTC) program, designed to produce officers in 90 days (the so-called 90-day wonders), was begun in May 1917, and McNeese was a member of the first graduating class in August.

4. The *Prinz Eitel Friedrich*, originally a German mail carrier, was converted by Germany to military purposes at the start of the war. It was interned by the United States in 1917 and renamed the USS *DeKalb*, after General Baron Johan Dekalb. (Like the *Von Steuben*, it was renamed for a Revolutionary War foreign-born

famous port of St. Nazaire—known as the first place that the American soldiers set foot on French soil.

From this place, the officers were sent to various French and British schools. Our contingent consisting of thirty five officers were sent to the First British Army School, Hardelot, Pas de Calais, France.[5] Here we were to receive instruction from English and Canadian officers who had spent a considerable time in the front line. With us at this school, were about one hundred English and Canadian officers, and about seventy-five non-commissioned officers, whose divisions were in the [front] line and who had been sent there for a similar course of instruction.

After a course of five weeks in this school, we were allowed to go back with these officers for a week[']s tour of the line as their guests. My lot fell with the 38th Division, which held a sector in the line in advance of Armentieres. Upon arriving at the divisional Headquarters, near Stenewer[c]k, I was assigned to visit the 10th Bat. South Wales Borders.[6] Upon my initial entry into the line, I was given a reception by the Boche that I will never forget.

Brigade Headquarters was as far as we could ride, and from there, started on foot to the headquarters of the 10th. It was a walk of about five miles, and the way led through the town of Armentieres. At dark, the earliest time we could leave Brigade HQ, I was furnished a guide to take

---

hero.) The *DeKalb* became a transport ship and was to convey more than 11,000 fighting men across the Atlantic Ocean.

5. The British army established its headquarters in France in the Calais region, directly across the English Channel from Dover. As part of the sprawling complex, a military school was established at Neutchatel-Hardelot, southwest of the village of Calais and on the shore of the channel.

6. Stenewerck, where the British had set up a divisional headquarters, is a small village a few miles to the west of the battlefield at Armentières. That town, located on the Belgian border, had experienced a notable battle back in 1914, when, early in the war, British and German forces "raced to the sea." But four years later, in April 1918, the Germans launched a notorious mustard gas attack on Armentières, forcing the British to withdraw. The town was probably just as well known for the popular and bawdy British song "Mademoiselle from Armentières."

me to Battalion HQ and to vouch for my identity in case we were stopped by any Military Police. Before we started I had adjusted my gas mask in the alert position, put on my "Carnegie Derby", and strapped my pistol to my Sam Browne belt.[7] As we walked along I tried to converse with my guide, but being unable to understand his dialect, found it necessary to keep my thoughts to myself. We walked along in silence, a drizzling rain was falling, the night was dark and the silence was so intense that I could almost feel it. The big guns were unusually quiet and only occasionally broke the silence with a dull distant boom that grew more notic[e]able as we approached the line. At a distance we could see the star shells burst over NO-MANS LAND and turn that inky blackness into daylight in hopes of finding some careless patrol that is out after information. Now and then the silence would be broken by the rat-tat-tat of the machine gun as it spread its death dealing shower over some point in the enemy line.

We were well into the town when the first signs of war became apparent. We were walking through the town with intense silence all about us when suddenly we heard the sound of an enemy shell. The boche had begun a bombardment on the artillery and soon the air seemed full of whizzing shells. We kept on, dodging to the side of the road when an occasional shell would come in our vicinity. After what seemed to me to be hours, we reached our destination.

Being tired from the long walk, I decided to retire early. It was then that I missed the soft bunk that I had been used to in camp. My bed consisted of a box frame over which had been stretched some few pieces of chicken wire. My mat[t]ress was made up of a few sand bags placed upon the wire to keep it from making an imprint upon my body. My covers consisted of two blankets that had seen better days. I was not permitted to take off any of my clothing except my shoes and coat. That much satisfied me as I was tired and much in need of rest.

7. A Sam Browne belt consists of a wide belt at the waist, attached to a narrower strap that goes over the right shoulder. There were attempts to confine its use to commissioned officers, but others adopted the design.

As I lay there on my bunk listening to the shells making their mournful sound as they traveled overhead, I noticed that they seemed to have a different sound than the ones I had first heard. My worst fears were soon realized as a head was thrust into the dugout and a cry of "GAS" caused me to jump for my mask and adjust it immediately. After five hours of suffering with that instrument of torture, I was told that the attack was over and the remainder of the night was spent in comfort and sound sleep.[8]

The next morning, I awoke with a sickening sensation, a head ache and exceedingly sore eyes. Some how or other I had inhaled a little of the gas and its presence in the dugout had burned my eyes. As time went on I seemed to get worse, but would not go to a hospital as there was nothing to do but to let it wear off. In a few days I was ordered to join the 16th Infantry of the First American Division, where I arrived a few days later but in no condition to do any work. After about three weeks of doctoring, I finally regained my voice which the gas had taken away and was able to assume my new duties as Regimental Signal Officer.

My regiment was at this time stationed at Demange-aux-eau[x]. (Meuse),[9] where we remained in training until January 19, 1918. On this date, our regiment started the relief of the French in the Montsec sector about 10 miles east of St. Mihiel. This was what is known as a quiet sector, and there was nothing much of interest connected with it except that it was the first sector in any part of the line to be occupied by Americans under American command.

The first division occupied this sector until about the middle of April when it was relieved and we were sent in the vicinity of Montdidier in the face of the great German offensive that had reached great proportions.[10]

8. The German gas attack that temporarily disabled McNeese occurred on November 5, 1917.

9. Demange-aux-Eaux was about 55 miles from Verdun and 33 from Saint-Mihiel.

10. The German offensive had begun a month earlier, on March 21. The attack reached "great proportions" partly because the surrender of Russia enabled Germany to move thousands of troops to the French front. The Allies, bolstered by

Here conditions were very different than in the sector we had been occupying. There were no trenches, the Germans had been stopped there and it was up to us to dig in, consolidate our positions and hold the line. In order to best consolidate, we were forced to capture the town of Contigny, the story of which has been printed in our papers.[11] This was the first offensive ever attempted by any American troops. It was entirely successful from every standpoint and helped show the true spirit of the Americans. In this battle, the help of the artillery was invaluable. The machine-guns never worked better. The tanks and the aviation service were borrowed from the French.

We stayed in this sector seventy-six days and in the second week of July were relieved by the French, and went back of the line a few miles to wait until our entire division was assembled when we were put in trucks and hurried in the direction of Soisson[s] where we went over the top several times and made a touchdown each time.[12] We had traveled over night in trucks and by morning found ourselves in in [sic] a huge forest known as the Foret de Compiegne.[13]

---

increasing American arrivals and by transferring British troops from the Middle East, were able to stop the attack and launch a counterattack of their own by the beginning of August.

11. Contigny is a small village about 5 miles northwest of Montdidier. It is situated on a rise and was occupied by German soldiers. On the morning of May 28, 1918, some 3,500 Americans of McNeese's 1st Division charged across "no man's land" and, in the face of machine gun fire, through hand-to-hand combat, took the village from the enemy. The action, which was ordered by General Pershing and planned by young Lieutenant Colonel George C. Marshall, was the first test of American doughboys in the war.

12. The Battle of Soissons, July 18–22, 1918, was a tremendously costly operation. The town of about 14,000 was about 60 miles northeast of Paris. Hoping to blunt the German offensive, Allied supreme commander Ferdinand Foch ordered the Allies into a counteroffensive. The operation cost the Allies 125,000 casualties, with Americans sustaining 12,000 of them. The Germans suffered 168,000 casualties, and the Allies regained most of the territory that had been lost in the German offensive in May.

13. Foret de Compiègne, located about 30 miles due west of Soissons, consisted of more than 35,000 acres and is the third largest national forest in France. It was

We stayed in this place under cover that day, and that night started on foot toward the line. We could see the flashes and hear the distant boom of the big guns as we walked single file along the road that was all but blocked with heavy traffic. There were two streams of transportation moving in opposite directions. Going toward the line, were trucks of every description filled with ammunition of all kinds, strings of machine gun carts interrupted these, guns of every description and caliber from a 75mm. to a 320mm., and tanks, which crept along the road like some huge monster of fabled days.

The next day, we stayed in another woods to keep out of sight of the enemy airmen, and that night we went into the line and took up our formation for attack. Not a word was spoken above a whisper. We had laid aside all surplus equipment and were now carrying only guns, ammunition, and two days supply of food. Zero hour was 4:35 A.M. on that morning of July 18, and by a half hour before that time every man was in his place and ready to go. We watched our watches breathlessly, thinking of what was to come and praying, not that we might be spared and allowed to see our loved ones again, but that the Almighty Power might be with us, help us to give the best there was in us, and keep us from showing "yellow".

A few minutes before "zero" hour, the Boche spotted us and opened on us with his artillery. Strange to say, we suffered few casualties, and promptly at 4:35 our protective barrage opened up, and the infantry started to advance. I was just behind the first wave, and the sight I saw made an everlasting impression on my mind. The sun was just peeping over the horizon as the boys started forward toward it. They advanced in perfect line as straight as they ever did on the parade ground, and the sunbeams glancing from their fixed bayonets made them see like a wall of fire advancing over a pra[i]rie.

---

the staging area of Americans preparing for the Battle of Soissons (see preceding note). The place was to achieve special importance because the armistice that brought the war to an end in November was negotiated and signed in General Foch's railway car there.

All went well for a while, but soon the first wave began to thin out as the Boche machine guns played havoc with the advancing wave. As we approached[,] the bullets began to zip past us with a crack that reminded us of a mule-skinner as he laid the lash to his beasts, and all around me my comrades and friends would give a cry of agony and fall to the ground into eternity. But we kept advancing, little by little until by the end of the fifth day we were ten miles beyond our starting place. What was accomplished in tha[t] drive all the world knows, we not only demoralized the enemy but we established a place in armies of humanity for the Americans.

Upon being relieved from this place by the Royal Scots of the English Army, we went to the town of Danmartin[14] where we entrained for Toul and again went into the line in a quiet sector with a regiment reduced in fighting men from 3000 to about 800.

It was while we were in this sector that I received the order that sent me back to God[']s country to join a new division with the rank of Captain, train them and go back over with them. I never joined them, for the armistice was signed before we left Camp Dix, where we had been quarantined on account of the flu. Feeling that my use to my country was ended in a military way, I applied for discharge and received it a short time before Christmas, and in time to enter the University from which I had been absent so long.

With the greatest respect and hope of continued peace,

I remain,

Yours sincerely

Chas. H. McNeese

exCapt. Infantry U.S.A.

14. Perhaps McNeese means Dammartin, a town in the Seine-et-Marne department and on the outskirts of Paris.

John Ohleyer Moseley

Company "A" 107th. Supply Train,
MARIENHAUSEN, GERMANY[1]

19 January 1919

President S. D. Brooks,
University of Oklahoma,
Norman, Oklahoma.

Dear Dr. Brooks:

I am just in receipt of your letter of November 6th, and I appreciate greatly the good wishes and kind thoughts expressed in it. Of course, I comply gladly with your request to write of my "Impressions", over here, although I have not had time yet to work up any good impressions; and I fear that this letter will degenerate into a record of personal experiences common to all of us who have on this business sailed from some well known port in America to an equally well known port in France. After

---

John Ohleyer Moseley (1893–1955), the son of a Presbyterian minister, had earned a BA from Austin College in Sherman, Texas (1912). After teaching high school Latin in Durant, Oklahoma, he undertook graduate work at the University of Oklahoma, receiving an MA in English in 1916. Moseley was a Rhodes Scholar, earning two degrees in Oxford. He enlisted in May 1917, and was commissioned a second lieutenant in August. He was in France for 15 months and saw action at Chateau Thierry and the Argonne. He then was part of the Army of Occupation. After the war, Moseley earned a degree from the University of Oklahoma's law school and embarked upon a distinguished career. He taught Latin at the University for fifteen years. He later rose to the presidency of Central State College in Edmond (1935–39) and ended his career as president of the University of Nevada, Las Vegas. He was very active in his fraternity, Sigma Alpha Epsilon, and became its executive secretary after his retirement. See Joseph A. Brandt, "John O. Moseley," *Sooner Magazine* 7 (February 1935): 102–3; and George C. McGhee, "John Ohleyer Moseley (1893–1955)," *American Oxonian* 42 (1956), 27–29.

1. Marienhausen is located about 45 miles across the Rhine and 40 miles southeast of Bonn.

encountering world wonders continually the past twelve months, I am beginning to believe that impressions are better made by getting off somewhere and thinking of things than by seeing them. However, what is written must be written quickly for rumor in what seems to be its final and authentic form has just been around again, saying that within a very few days, we begin using the return part of our ticket, that event which everyone of us have looked forward to ever since losing sight of the lady in the harbor.

On September 11, 1917, I was sent to the 32d. Division composed of Wisconsin and Michigan Guards at Camp MacArthur, Waco Texas.[2] I found no troops and only a few Staff Officers there. By the end of the year under the great leadership of Major-General W. G. Haan,[3] the division was adjudged by army inspectors "Ready to Go". On January 31, 1918, the Division Headquarters sailed on the Adriatic.[4] We landed at Liverpool, and made the customary trip to Winchester, where we waited four days until at South Hampton [*sic*] they had unloaded the cattle from the boat which was to take us across the channel. From the train going to Winchester, I had one glimpse of "The Spires of Oxford.["]"[5] From

2. Camp MacArthur was only a few weeks old when Moseley (and 18,000 men from Wisconsin and Michigan) arrived. Located within the city of Waco, it accommodated 45,000 men during the war. In March 1919 the installation was closed and the land returned to the city of Waco.

3. William George Haan (1863–1924) was a West Point graduate who had seen service in Cuba and the Philippines. When the war broke out, he was promoted to brigadier general and assigned to Camp MacArthur. See Richard Kehrberg, "Haan, William George (1863–1924)," in Anne Cipriano Venzon, ed., *The United States in the First World War: An Encyclopedia* (New York: Garland, 1995), 267–68.

4. The British ship RMS *Adriatic* had been, since 1907, a luxury passenger ship that sailed between Southampton or Liverpool and New York City. During the war it was converted into a troop transport. Once the war was over, it resumed its normal route until its final run in 1928.

5. Winchester, located 25 miles from the disembarkation port of Southampton on the channel, was only 25 miles from the major port of Liverpool. Of course, for Moseley, as a former Rhodes Scholar, catching a glance at the spires of Oxford would have held special importance.

Havre we took the usual "Forty Hommes, Eight Chevaux" train to our training area, (No. Ten.) which was between Langres and Dijon, and comprised such towns as Prauthoy, Vaux-sous-Abigny, Montsaugeon and Champlette.[6] The people in this area had never seen Americans before; and here the boys of our division began a long and exhaustive study and experience of French language and customs. Here they first became acquainted with Vin Blanc and noted the difference in response given by it and its sister Champaigne or fuzzy water. Here they learned to recognize a man's wealth and social standing by the size of his straw pile at the back door—and all those whose letters I censored wrote this home as an original observation. Here they discovered that many English words happily expressed the same idea in French[,] among them "Promenade". And finally but primarily they decided that French Ideals and purposes so similar to their own were worth fighting for—and they learned to do the fighting.

In April came orders to move. We entered Alsace near Belfort,[7] and again were the first American Troops ever in that land. I came overland with the advance party and never will I forget the amazed looks of the people followed by waving and cheers, as they realized who we were. Many times along that Langres-Lure-Vesoul-Belfort road I saw mothers carry their little children and even babies out of the house and point toward the automobiles, so that they fifty years hence could tell the story to their grand-children.

This sector extended from north of Masevaux to the Swiss Border.[8] At first we held it with the French, but soon they moved out, and it became one of the first all-American sectors. Nothing transpired here except patrol fights, small raids, and spasmodic artillery exchange. A

6. This area in central and eastern France is about 330 miles southeast of Paris.
7. Belfort, about 250 miles east of Paris, is located near the Swiss and German borders at the southern edge of the disputed territory of Alsace.
8. Masevaux, a few miles north of Belfort, is in the heart of Alsace and about 40 miles from Basel, Switzerland.

most interesting point is that just before the Boche shelled a place the inhabitants could be seen leaving. There is, no doubt, that they were in communication with the Germans; and there are stories that the German inclined went thru secret passages with food and news to the German lines. Certainly it is true that during a bombardment the houses were the safest places to go, for the Germans wished to keep on friendly terms with the people and would not shell the towns.[9] I have heard that this was not the case in the latter days of the war, when the Germans realized that Alsace was lost to them. Boche planes came over frequently in broad day light with no opposition except for a few anti-aircraft batteries. No attention was paid to them for they never dropped anything. We were soon to experience a marked change in that respect.

On July 18th. Foch[10] began the offensive which turned the tide. In preparation for it the 32d. Division having been relieved by another American Division moved by rail just behind Chateau-Thierry. Again I was fortunate enough to be sent over land by way of Langres, Chaumont, Bar-sur-Aube and Senlis. The Division was stationed in Verberie, Pont-St-Maxience and the adjoining towns.[11] And one morning nearly a thousand French Trucks of every make, size and age, driven by Anamites [sic][12] lined up and our boys climbed on. They went into battle near Mezy just across the Marne from Chateau-Thierry, and drove the enemy in what experts declare the fiercest fighting of the war out of Jaulgonne

9. Historically a part of France, Alsace was taken by Germany in 1870, and after nearly a half-century of animosity, a large portion of the population spoke High German.

10. In response to a German attack (July 15, 1918), Ferdinand Foch (1851–1929), an experienced French soldier and now commander-in-chief of the Allied forces, ordered the counterattack on July 18 at Chateau Thierry.

11. Moselely's approach to the battlefield was from the southeast. Verberie and Pont-Sante-Maxence are about 45 miles to the west of Chateau-Thierry.

12. "Annamites" was the name given by the French to the Vietnamese. Vietnam was under French rule until 1954, and numerous Vietnamese resided in France for economic and educational reasons. As will be seen, Moseley mistakes the Vietnamese for "Chinamen," the traditional *enemies* of the Vietnamese.

across Reddy Farm capturing the town of Fismes.[13] For this work the division earned the name of Les-Terribles from the Poilus[14] and a two page citation from the French Army Headquarters, as well as being included in General Pershing's citation of all American Divisions, participating in the drive. Then we settled down for a so called rest, which will be remembered by me as one of the worst periods of time I ever spent—made so by the flies, to say nothing of air-raids and continuous artillery fire. The weather for the first time was hot and the flies were everywhere in great groups—active contenders for one's food. Everyone had the "Hoof and mouth disease", as we called it. The flies reminded me of King P[h]aroah's Troubles.[15]

Chateau-Thierry was the sight of the war to me. Never have I seen such wreckage. That at Verdun was more colossal but not as recent. The houses were literally ripped open and their contents exposed to view. Expensive furniture, clothing, table-ware, books and pictures were piled together and most pathetic of all usually the babies play-things would be there all broken and torn as in Field's "Boy Blue".[16] The Germans had stripped the finer houses of their valuables and had stored them in the churches. But they never got to Germany.

At Mezy some of our men who were sleeping on a hill side opened up their rifles on a low flying Boche Plane. They had been accustomed only to the ones in Alsace. But this fellow flew straight at them his machine gun popping like six boys "running a picket fence". The way those men gained the crest of that hill and then disappeared over the top sans shirt, sans pants, and almost sans everything else was one of the funniest sights I saw over here. After that they swore off even lighting a cigarette at night. It was at Mezy also that a plane dropped a bomb squarely on a Field

13. The fiercely contested advance from Mezy-moulins, across the Marne and to the village of Fismes, was about 25 miles.

14. "Poilus" is a common name for a French infantryman.

15. Exodus 8: 20–24.

16. Eugene Field's poem "Little Boy Blue" (1888) tells of the death of a young boy through the eyes of his abandoned toys.

Hospital erected that day; and then circling back he swooped down and emptied his machine gun into it. Fortunately there were no patients in it and the Doctors and American Girl Nurses got to their dug outs in time. This reminds me of another one that happened in one of our so called rest areas. The Division Q. M. needed a place to store bread. The only shed suitable had some sixteenth century machinery in it which the owner positively refused to move. Applying Military Law the shed was requisitioned[,] the machinery moved out and the bread moved in. My company was hauling the bread and just before dark the last load was put in. As we were leaving a Boche Plane was seen circling high in the clouds, evidently looking for the railhead. At random he let down his "Tail gate", and one bomb fell squarely on the shed. Bread flew around there for the next week. The machinery was not touched.

General Mangin[17] to whom had been entrusted the Soissons drive asked for one American division for his spear head, and expressed a preference for the 32d. Again we travelled in those 'one lung' sight seeing busses driven by the funny Chinaman, and stopped for a few days around Pierrefonds where is the famous castle of the Duc d'O[r]leans.[18] The 32d. with French Divisions on either sides "Went in" just above Vic-sur-Aisne, and "Went out" when Juvigny plateau was captured. This was a great cave country many of them large enough to accommodate a regiment, some even were electric lighted; and in this one sector dough boy and general eat and slept in the same room. At the mouth of one of these caves one day I saw two hundred prisoners starting out to do some work. A stray Boche shell fell among them killing twenty and wounding many more. The yelling and crying the rest of them put up would have done

17. Charles Mangin (1866–1925) was the unpopular French general in command at the Soissons advance. That battle (July 18–22) was the Second Battle of the Marne, part of the Allied counteroffensive to the spring offensive launched by Germany in March.
18. The medieval castle at Pierrefonds, about 55 miles northeast of Paris, was built at the end of the fourteenth century under the direction of Louis I, duc d'Orleans. It underwent an extensive restoration in the mid-nineteenth century.

credit to "Skeery Willyum" in the funny paper.[19] They thought that the American artillery had been turned on them.

The next sector was a "Bon sector"–the beautiful country south of St. Dizier.[20] Here we rested ten days. This part of France had never been in the hands of the Germans though continually threatened. The people regarded the Americans as their saviors and treated them like kings. Time was all too short here, and one bright morning the grinning Chinee and his bus appeared. The men mounted them brave and outward[ly] indifferent. We were all praying that this would be the last of such rides—and indeed it was. A picture that will go with me forever is the faces of those men as silently they marched out, and at the word of command entered those trucks, grim and resolute knowing full well by now the nature of this ride, and that a large per cent of them would never come back. After a few miles American spirit asserted itself; everything was funny; shouts and laughter were heard; and horseplay was seen on all the trucks. In every village men, women, children and dogs ensemble turned out. The people threw flowers to the boys and shouted encouragements at them; and they pinning the flowers to their caps called to them in our new language American-French. Both waved until the last truck had passed from view.

We stopped a few days in the woods near Fluery-sur-Aisne.[21] The Americans had here a large evacuation hospital and a railhead. Here we saw one of the wonders of the war. One day there rolled in an American passenger train—real coaches—sleeping car—American engine polished up like a Milwaukee Bar—a man's size whistle on the engine[—]dough boy engineer and fireman, and a sure enough negro waiter in the diner,

19. *Scary William* was a cartoon strip, published from 1906 to 1914, by H. H. Knerr (better known for his *Katzenjammer Kids*) and continued by Joe Doyle until June 1918.

20. Saint-Dizier is about 130 miles east of Paris.

21. The small village of Fleury, in the Aisne department in northeastern France, is about 60 miles northeast of Paris and less than 30 miles from Chateau-Thierry.

with a white coat and everything—and the train was full of American Officials, including the Secretary of War [Newton Baker]!!

After a few days of final preparation we went up into that Hell of all Hells Argonne Forest.[22] To even mention that place would take a book. The Germans had concentrated everything they had here, and they were making their last stand. Defeat in this sector would mean a collapse of their Army and retreat cut off. It seemed that all their guns and all their planes were called in and put here. But we had a few ourselves. On October 4th the Americans put over the greatest barrage of history called the "Million dollar Barrage".[23] All night there had been the usual exchange. About two hours before day break the American side quieted down. Gradually the Boche batteries slacked up also, throwing over only an occasional "Barrack Bag", or "Ash Can".[24] Just at day break an American Plane sailed over the lines; and after making the circuit opened up his machine gun. We heard the first rata-tat-tat, but the rest were drown[ed] out by what seemed the explosion of everything in the world. Every hill was red, and the earth rocked. And that kept up until we could have sworn that nothing was left of Germany. But a few days later came a sight that easily out-ranks everything in my experience or imagination. Late one afternoon we heard a great buzz of motors and looked up. An enormous fleet of planes larger than we had ever seen before was coming over in beautiful formation. They had a leader, scouts and flew in perfect order. The sky was black with them. And then

22. The journey from Fleury to the Argonne Forest was about 115 miles due east.

23. During the critical battle of the Argonne Forest, this intense artillery bombardment of the German positions dislodged the enemy and paved the way, a month later, to the German surrender. The episode also marks the ascendancy of field artillery as a decisive category of weaponry in modern warfare. See Justin G. Prince, *Million-Dollar Barrage: American Field Artillery in the Great War* (Norman: University of Oklahoma Press, 2021).

24. An "ash can" is a depth charge—a bomb that explodes underwater to destroy submarines.

to our amazement another fleet the same size followed behind them! After the third fleet every body refused to look. Nearly three hundred planes passed over within the half hour. Thank heaven they were Germany bound!

We stayed in this region a double shift. When our time came for relief there was no one to relieve us, so we stayed on. After we made the second advance, I had my company for fifteen days in the woods around Montfaucon.[25] We hauled food, ammunition, and wounded men. The company was most of the time in advance of the artillery and the shells from both sides passed over head day and night. I hope someone some day will write the truck driver's epic. They are exposed to danger all the time and they suffer every conceivable inconvenience of roads, weather, and machinery. The trains had the first and the last casualties in the Division. Three of my company were drowned with the Tuscania,[26] and one killed by shell fire on November 11th a few minutes before eleven o'clock.

Finally our relief was ordered. I shall never forget the night of the relief which was the last night of the war for me. The 89th Division was to take over the 32d Division position; and they came up over the Epionville road,[27] using in part the wonderful plank highway the Germans had built. At one hour after dark with the 89th still two hours on the road, and our division worn out and ready to go, the Boche launched one of the fiercest counter-attacks of the Argonne fight. I was with a machine gun battalion that night whose barrage stopped the attack. But it looked bad for awhile.

25. The Battle of Montfaucon (October 14–17, 1918) was one of the most significant of the Meuse-Argonne offensive. By the end of October, the Allies had gained 10 miles and controlled the Argonne Forest.

26. The Tuscania was another ocean liner that was converted to troop transport. On February 5, 1918, the ship was attacked by a German submarine, and it sank four hours later. Although many of the 2,400 aboard were rescued by other ships of the convoy, around 200 soldiers and 30 crew members were drowned.

27. Epionville was between two and three miles west of Montfaucon.

We were pulled back for a much needed rest and cleaning up. [E]very man was given a cootie bath[28]; and some leaves were granted. I received orders to go to school; but I was under the weather a bit and went to the hospital a week at Dijon. By that time the armistice had been signed. I went on to school at Decize[29]; but that school has no place in this narrative. After my escape from there I had the best time of my army life in rejoining the Division. I visited at Nevers, Gievres, and Tours[30]—where I saw General Harboard, commanding general, S.O.S., decorated with a Croix-de-Guerre[31]; and arrived in Paris in time to see President Wilson make his triumphal entry into the city. I stood in the Place de-Concorde. The historic surroundings, the enthusiastic crowd, and the collection of notables gave to me that day another great thrill and a lasting picture. From Paris I went to Toul where pleasantly I was held up a few days before getting a train to Metz. From there I went to Treves and Coblenz and then to my outfit once more.[32]

At the present writing we are comfortably settled in this little Rhine town waiting to go home. I forgot to mention that I came over with

28. "Cootie bath" refers to the use of insecticides to combat the troublesome insects.

29. Decize, on the Loire River, is about 170 miles south of Paris.

30. The three cities are in central France along a route of around 150 miles.

31. James Guthrie Harbord (1866–1947) had been in the army since 1889, and had served with Pershing during the Mexican campaign. During the European war, he served as Pershing's chief of staff, and was given command of troops at several crucial battles in mid-1918. In August he was placed in charge of the S.O.S. After the war, Harbord became the head of the Radio Corporation of America (RCA). See Charles A. Endress, "Harboard, James Guthrie (1866–1947)" in Venzon, ed., *The United States in the First World War*, 272–75.

32. Moseley's 32nd Division was part of the newly created Third Army sent to occupy Germany after the war. To recognize its extraordinary role in the battles leading to the German surrender, the 32nd was chosen to head the march into the Rhineland. Pausing at Treves (Trier, Germany), the Army of Occupation (250,000 men) took control of the territory around Coblenz, remaining until April 1919. Marienhausen, where Moseley was stationed, is about 25 miles north of Coblenz.

Division Headquarters; but when we began active operations I got into Company "F" 107th. Supply Train. Since my return I have been in command of Company "A". Many of the men in the company speak German so we get along well with the people. At first the people were not so cordial and seemed a little afraid; but now they are enthusiastic about the Americans and do anything in their power for them. The trouble is to keep the Americans from fraternizing with them.

This section of the country shows the effects of the war not much more I imagine than America does. Certainly they did not feel it a thousandth part of what France did. There is plenty to eat although certain articles are scarce. The people are well dressed and have plenty of money. In Puderbach a town of five hundred and fifty inhabitants,[33] the municipal store house had eight tons of flour and five tons of shredded oats used for forage which had been stored there two years. It also had five hundred bushels of rye, a quantity of oat-meal to be issued only to the sick, and about one thousand pounds of "Erstatz", coffee and other substitutes for cereals.

The people in this region know very little about the politics of the country. Many of them are indifferent and most of them uninformed, because of the scarcity of news-papers. The women now have a vote, but do not know how to use it. One man heard of the death of ex-president Roosevelt[34] and said that Germany had need of a strong man like him, possessing the confidence of the people, to lead them. In fact they all decry the lack of a strong leader and some wish for the Kaiser to return to tell them what to do. The people are strongly Catholic and fear that the approaching elections will result in a separation of church and state. They are prepared to combat that and hold town meetings—always by permission of the American authorities and a German speaking officer is present. Speakers at these meetings reiterate that Germany had been

33. Puderbach is about 6 miles from Marienhausen.
34. Former president Theodore Roosevelt had died two weeks earlier, on January 6, 1919, at Sagamore Hill, his home. He was sixty years old.

misled as to the causes of the war, and its entire conduct. Von Tirpitz[35] is blamed for bringing America into the war; and for deceiving the people as to the successes of the U-boat campaign.

A few villages from here is a man who was on the submarine which torpedoed the Tuscania. This interested my company especially for they were on the boat. He has picture[s] of it, also an excellent photo of the first American convoy to reach France. He says that the American convoys watched too closely for the submarine to do any good. The school teacher in this town was an aviator for three years. He doesn't look half as rough as I thought they did. Only a few recently demobilized soldiers have returned to this region. We hear that they are causing great trouble in the cities demanding food, refusing to work, saying that now they have earned an easy time.

According to discharged soldiers the morale of the [German] army is gone. The only idea of the soldier now is to get home unless he is a roiter [rioter?]. The fact that officers did not go into battles with [their] men is the greatest factor in this loss of morale. One soldier who has just returned said that before the armistice a story went through the army that the Kaiser and Royal Family had food stored up enough for seven years. This caused a great dissatisfaction. Another thing I have just heard although it has possibly been published in America is that our aviators dropped facsimiles of bread and meat tickets in the German towns causing great confusion. The school master at Shelters says that to help win the war school children were used in various ways. In the last year of the war, the school children of this town gathered eight thousand pounds of leaves and dried them for horse feed, collected

35. After a long career in the German navy, Alfred von Tirpitz (1849–1930) was named Grand Admiral in 1911. He is generally credited with both the buildup of the German fleet, which alarmed the British, and the policy of unrestricted submarine warfare, which compelled the United States to enter the war. See Patrick J. Kelly, *Tirpitz and the Imperial German Navy* (Bloomington: Indiana University Press, 2011).

pine knots for fuel, nettles for the making of clothes; and were employed in various other ways.

Money as usual is a problem here. Last month we [were] paid off in marks. At some places marks only are accepted and others Francs and at some both. The men in the company had great trouble in figuring out what they owed each other for the month before they had been paid in Francs. The people are compelled to accept Francs at the rate of one hundred sixty-six Marks per one hundred Francs, the German banks only give one hundred and forty-two marks for one hundred Francs. My company has been paid in dollars, pounds, francs and marks. By now they should be well up on financial matters, but we are all hoping that next time we will be paid off with the only real money there is.

I have visited Coblenz a number of times and it is quite a city. One of the Kaiser's numerous palaces is there. The thing that impresses me most is the great crowds of people in the cafes[,] restaurants and tea rooms eating and drinking. They have ice-cream and all kinds of fancy pastry, things we never saw in France. The people are well dressed and act as if there had never been a war. All railroad, postal and other official employees are required to salute officers, which they readily do. The civilians doff their hats of their own accord to all soldiers. In the little towns where we have had band concerts the children take off their hats when the Star Spangle[d] Banner is played.

I fear that I have written far to[o] much now. You must pardon me. If I had more time I could have made it shorter[36]; but I have rambled on jotting down a few of the things I have seen and heard, and I trust they will be of some interest to you. If I have consumed too much space you may abridge this letter as you see fit for better use in your book. I enclose a few snap shots. Those of interest may be used in any way you wish. I

36. Perhaps Moseley was intending to echo here the witticism often attributed to Mark Twain ("If I had more time, I would have written a shorter letter"). To date, scholars have failed to find the comment in any of Twain's writings, but they have discovered similar comments in writings by several other authors.

am very sorry but most of my pictures of general interest are stored with my other property in France or are not yet developed.

I appreciate greatly the contact which the University has kept with its alumni and have enjoyed and benefitted by all the news and letters of encouragement sent out. I am sure that the school can be justly proud of its part in this great emergency, and will move forward to greater heights of power for good and service to the state.

With kindest personal regards, I am,

Sincerely your friend,

John O. Mosely

Harry Stephen Oderman

WAR DEPARTMENT
OFFICE OF THE CONSTRUCTION DIVISION OF THE ARMY
WASHINGTON, D.C.

December 21, 1918

Stratton D. Brooks, Esq.
President of the University of Oklahoma
Norman, Okla.

Dear Sir:

The urgency of my duties has prevented me from replying to your letter of November 6th before this late date; however, before proceeding on my Christmas Leave, I want to take this occasion to thank you for your thoughtfulness and the University for its kindness during the days of the War.

Information has been requested relative to the nature of my activities. At the opening of the War, following the request of General Littell[1] to the packers for Refrigeration Engineers, I was selected from a corps of engineers and sent to Washington for work in connection with the first Meat and Ice Plant in France. This plant was designed for a capacity of

---

Harry Stephen Oderman (1891–1951), a 1916 graduate, enlisted in July 1917 and rose to the rank of captain of the Construction Division of the Quartermaster Corps. He was discharged on March 5, 1919. Drawing on his war experience, Oderman would go into the ice business, and rose to become president of the Detroit City Ice and Fuel Company. He died in Detroit, but was buried in Oklahoma City.

1. Brigadier General Isaac William Littell (1857–1924) was a West Point graduate (1883) from New Jersey. He transferred from the infantry to the Quartermaster's Corps, and in 1917 was placed in charge of the construction of all kinds of facilities for the U.S. Army (training camps, arsenals, warehouses, plants for making explosives, and so forth). After creating the Construction Division and building 16 army camps, Littell quarreled with Quartermaster General George Goethals and resigned his position after one year.

Letters from Sooner Doughboys   151

2000 tons of ice per day and a cold storage capacity for 2,000,000 pounds of frozen beef. I later worked on the inspection and expediting of mechanical equipment and structural materials for this project. Upon completion of the pioneer work on this plant, I was assigned to the Inspection Department of the Construction Division of the Army and shortly thereafter assigned as Officer in Charge of the Pittsburgh District. The duties of this office consist of supervising inspection and expediting of materials, investigations of claims and also some experience in the procurement and commandeering of materials. In this connection, it may be of interest to you to know of the magnitude of the activities of the Construction Division. I will not burden you with a lengthy discussion of this but will only select two items taken at random from the "Constructor", the semi-monthly publication of the Construction Division of the Army. These are as follows: "During the two weeks ending August 10th, there was mobilized by the Materials Branch of the Construction Division $11,753,949.15 worth of materials to be used on the various building operations for the army." "The "Construction Division of the Army has under way about 350 projects, aggregating something over $600,000,000." The activities of the Construction Division have been discussed in several technical journals and the work that this division has performed has been so marvelous that, although I regret deeply that I could not secure the opportunity of going overseas, I, nevertheless, feel proud to be a member of an organization such as this.

Again thanking you for all thoughtfulness shown and conveying to you and your official family my heartiest greetings of the season, I am,

Sincerely yours,

H. S. Oderman, '16

Captain, Quartermaster Corps

Clifford Carl Oster

AMERICAN YMCA
ON ACTIVE SERVICE
WITH THE
AMERICAN EXPEDITIONARY FORCE

Dannemoine,[1] France

December 9 1918

Dr. Stratton D. Brooks

Dear President:

I received your letter of November 6, asking me to write you a letter giving my experiences in detail and my impressions during my service in the war, but for lack of writing material I was unable to reply sooner. I fear that I will be unable to give my experiences in detail as I have had so much since I've been in the service, particularly the last four months which I've spent in France, so I will have to "hit the trail in high places" and leave the details for another letter.

I entered the service at Oklahoma City on May 31, 1918, and was sent to Camp Nicholls at New Orleans where I was given the final physical examination and a uniform. After five days I was transferred to Camp Logan at Houston Texas and was assigned to the 7th Recruit Co. of the 57th U.S. Infantry, but owing to my qualifications as a Signal Corps man I was immediately transferred to Camp Bowie, Texas, and was assigned

---

Clifford Carl Oster (1893–1957) was born in Missouri, but moved to Hobart, Oklahoma, as a child of four. He graduated from the University of Oklahoma in 1916, with a degree in Electrical Engineering. Upon enlistment, he was assigned to the Signal Corps. He served eight months in France and fought in the Battle of St. Mihiel. Oster worked in Oklahoma City for 41 years as an engineer for the Southwestern Bell Company.

1. Dannemoine is a small village in north-central France, about 120 miles southeast of Paris.

to Co. B. 111th Field Signal Battalion, in which I am at the present time. We remained at Camp Bowie only 10 days until the Division which is the Panther Division received orders to "partie" for France. We left Camp Bowie on July 8, and arrived in Hoboken on July 13, and were sent to Camp Mill[s] where we received our "over-seas" uniform and equipment and on July 17 we boarded the Antigone, an old German interned freighter, which had been remodeled for Transport service.[2] On July 18 we sailed out through New York harbor, passed the Statue of Liberty and bid Good Bye to the good old U.S.A. Our Convoy consisted of 12 transports, 3 destroyers, and the battleship South Dakota.[3]

We had a very pleasant voyage with plenty of excitement and arrived at Brest, France, on July 30. On July 31 we unloaded and hiked out to Camp Pantanezen which was about three miles from port. We rested here for 5 days and on August 4 we entrained at Brest for parts unknown on one of those French trains with which you are probably acquainted and traveled for 4 days arriving at Bar Sur Aube on Aug 8. We then hiked out to a little village by the name of Armentierres where we remained 7 weeks and received our finishing touches before going to the front. On September 26 we left Armentierres and after traveling via truck, train, and hob-nail[4] for 7 days we arrived at Suippes which was at that time only a short distance back of the line. On Oct 7 my division relieved the 2nd American division just north of Suippes and after five days of fierce fighting we forced the Germans to withdraw from their fortified position which was on the noted Hindenburg line back to the

2. Formerly the German immigrant transport *Neckar*, the ship was seized by American customs at the outbreak of war in April 1917. Renamed the *Antigone*, the ship transported more than 16,000 troops to France during the war and more than 22,000 back home when the war ended.

3. Built in San Francisco in 1902, the USS *South Dakota* was transferred to the Atlantic and escorted convoys to France. After transporting troops back home from Brest to New York when the war ended, the ship was returned to the Pacific.

4. "Hobnail" here means "on foot." Hobnails are the short nails on boots.

Aisne river, making an advance of about 18 miles, for which we receive[d] a citation from the French General. We then held the Germans at bay for 16 days when we were relieved by a French Division. On Oct. 28 we started our "to the rear" march and moved over near Verdun where we were to relieve the 1st American division in the Argonne forest and we were ready to strike our second blow when the Armistice was signed. I heard the last shots of the World War. On Nov. 17 my division started marching towards Troyes covering a distance of 150 miles in 10 days and arriving at Tonnerre on Nov. 28 which was one Thanksgiving Day I'll always remember.[5] The Signal Corps headquarters is at Dannemoine which is about 2 miles from Tonnerre.

In order to give you an idea of the work I performed while on the front I'll state in a brief way the duties of a Field Signal Battalion, which are the installation, operation and maintenance of telephone and telegraph lines between division headquarters and the front line. Practically all of our work was done under shell-fire and if I had words to express the feeling one has, when shells are flying and bursting over head and he is stumbling over dead men, while he is trying to locate line trouble in the dark with out the aid of a light I would do so, but for lack of words I'll leave it to your imagination. While on the front I was a combination lineman, trouble shooter, and switchboard operator so you see I had a taste of practically all the work—consequently of all the experiences. I realize that I did only a very small part but I did my bit as best I could and I'm more than pleased to have had a chance to do my bit. I think the dough-boy deserves the praise and when I get back in civilian life I'm going to shake hands with everyman I see who has seen service on the front with the doughboys.

Stinson has been with me since we entered the service and we are the only Okla University men in the Battalion. Stinson has written you too

5. Tonnerre, an ancient town of around 4,300, is located in north-central France.

and no doubt has told you the same story so one of our letters stands the chance of boring you. Here's hoping that you receive mine first.[6]

I've been receiving from time to time the war bulletins which contain much interesting news and I wish to give you my many thanks. We always appreciate news from home especially those concerning the Alumni and the University.

I am sorry that I have no camp kodak pictures to send you but we could not take pictures of scenes over here and I wasn't in a camp in the States long enough to obtain any pictures.

Hoping that I will hear from you again in the near future and wishing you a merry Xmas and a Happy New Year, I am

Yours truly
Pvt Clifford C. Oster
Co. B. 111th Field Signal Battalion
American Expeditionary Forces
A.P.O. No. 796.

6. See Robert Wilcox Stinson's letter, below, for interesting comparisons. The two men wrote their letters on the same day.

Samuel Hirsh Pogoloff

Jan 12 1919

My dear Dr. Brooks:

Accept my wishes for a Happy New Year and many of them.

My address has been changed so often since the armistice was signed that your letter dated Nov. 6 reached me on Jan 11. My Regiment has been on the move since Sept 12, date of the opening of St. Mihiel drive, chasing the Hun first from French soil and then still farther. At present we are in Hellisheim [sic] Germany,[1] that is doing the work of the Army of Occupation—indeed a monotonous work, but just as important as keeping our adversary from doing any harm.

Now in regard to the plan you have outlined I regret to say that I cannot very well help out in this matter. Perhaps if I have [sic] known of your wish while the war [was] still on I would have kept a note book or the like,—altho there would be difficulties of censorship, besides the Army order not to have such books while one is on the lines for fear of being captured. At present to relate my individual experiences would mean merely to tell things commonplace, stereotype[d].

It[']s true that I have seen things—I have seen so much, that I saw no more. The set of incidents was not recorded in my mind as separate anymore but as part of the big, terribly big world tragedy. Besides in this war the individual showed up but little—he was an infinitely small thing of the whole called an Army.

Samuel Hirsh Pogoloff (1893–1981) was born in Russia. He came to Norman to begin his medical studies at the University of Oklahoma. Pogoloff was assigned to the Medical Detachment of the 357th Infantry, and later was part of the Army of Occupation. After the war, he returned to the University and received his medical degree in 1923. He moved to Manville, New Jersey, and practiced medicine there for 56 years, until the age of 88.

1. Hillesheim is a town in far western Germany, less than 20 miles from the Belgian border.

As to the exceptional deeds, they can be told by the man in 3–4 words: "I captured a German with a machine gun": how it was done he cannot tell, for the man is in a state of stupor—his brain has only one single thought—to do the thing he is after, nothing else matters; he sees nothing and fears nothing. The man that extends himself on details of a heroic deed he [has] done on the lines, is either an exception or a liar, at least I doubt his words. Perhaps the last is a bold statement but such has been my experience.

To sum up I could hardly write of things gone through while at war which would be of interest as a distinct individual experience; the things every AEF soldier lived through are known—were told. Besides, to be frank, one wishes to forget that there was such a thing as this war; forget like a bad dream, a nightmare and return back to the good old U.S.A. The strain has been too big; we need relaxation [and] rest.

I shall probably return to our old Alma Mater as soon as possible and there perhaps relate to you orally what I failed to write.

Sincerely yours,

Pvt. Samuel H. Pogoloff

Med. Det. 357th Inf.

Jesse Lewis Powers

Camp Stuart
New Port News, Va
Dec. 6-1918

Dear Dr. Brooks:

I received your letter while in Camp Mills, Long Island, but have been unusually busy and, therefore, have not answered. I am indeed glad, along with all the other OU students and faculty members, of an opportunity to tell my experience in the Army.

I entrained at Chickasha Aug. 5, 1918 with forty-one other fellows from Grady Co[unty], bound for Camp Fremont, Menlo Park, Calif. The train gathered up units of drafts-men all along the road through Okla. until it carried a total of about six hundred. The general route we took was west to Amarillo Texas, Southwest to El Paso, west to Los Angeles and north along the coast to Fremont. Though it was a four-day trip, jolly making continued throughout and my duty as Captain of the Grady Co. group was easily executed.

I'll never forget the morning of Aug. 9, 1918 when we woke up to find ourselves in an environment all together new and different from that which we had been accustomed to. At an hour when we had been use[d] to enjoying a final dream, we looked out to find the land filled with

Jesse Lewis Powers (1890–1977) was born in Tennessee, but moved with his family to Thomas, Oklahoma. He played football at the University and graduated in 1917. Powers enlisted at Chickasha, Oklahoma, on August 5, 1918, and was discharged on January 20, 1919. He was part of a Machine Gun Company in Camp Fremont, California. After the war, he served as a longtime school principal and school board official in Oklahoma City.

soldiers—military police, guards, officers, and orderlies. All were busy and went about their duties with a quick and positive step. Soon there came columns of troops to the drill grounds from where could be heard commands, sharp and harsh as it seemed to us at that time.

We were soon told to assemble outside which we did in the civilian disorderly way. Physical examination preparatory to entrance into camp was given and we were placed in the casual camp.

It was another new phase of this new life to step into the tents and try to imagine them our homes. In the first place there was no selection of tents or tent-mates—the first six men were told to take one tent and the next six men the next tent etc. My five fellow-mates and I stepped into the dirt-floored, lampless canvas-enclosed space and thought "This is the war". We placed our suitcases on the ground and each sat down on the "bunk" he wished to occupy thereafter. We were tired and hungry (had not had breakfast yet) and probably some of us blue, but what of it? C'est la guerre.

After awhile the sound of the chow bell caught our ears for the first time. As fast as mess kits could be issued we stepped into line for "slum[.]"[1] We found the notorious slum to taste good. It is notorious in more than one phase. With the mess kit lid to hold the pudding or bread, the mess kit itself must hold the meat or meat stew (slum), gravy, cabbage, potatoes, soup and all and any other food which might be on the menu. Then the slum may have forgotten the salt or it may have come off the stove too soon. In this condition we call it slumy slum. Again, each food has its given name—given to it by soldiers. There's "glue" (pudding); "mush" (oats or cream of wheat), and "the drink" (water, lemonade, coffee or tea) etc.

Full physical examination, enlistment and inoculation began that afternoon and continued for three or four days before all were accepted or rejected. A quarantine was placed over us which confined us to company's street.

1. Short for "slumgullion," a stew made of various ingredients.

After being duly enlisted into the casual camp of the 8th division of the Regular Army, we were issued uniforms and began the initial steps of military drill. In parenthesis I might say that the uniforms were matchless and once in a while a fellow obtained a fit, and the shoes were of the hobnail trench type in sizes at least one number too big for the individual.

The first thing learned in the training was <u>at-ten-</u>tion, along with it, right- and left-face and then squads right and left. Our officers and non. coms. were unusually considerate in respect to being patient with rookies. They seemed to be glad to sit down at the noon hour and answer any question pertaining to a soldier's life.

Here we also came in contact with the Y.M.C.A. where sing-song and different amusements were prepared for us. In all my experience in the army I have found that the Red Cross and the YMCA have done more to help with the war than any other two factors outside of the force of the soldiers themselves. The Red Cross ladies seemed never to give up and the YMCA was always a friend of the soldier.[2]

There was only a week of casual camp life, as we were transferred to different permanent organizations. I landed in Co. F of the 13 Inf. Better conveniences greeted us here. Instead of dirt floors we went into plank floored tents, and instead of candle light we had electric lights. Bathing facilities were also better and the company commander bade us make use of it.

Now came the rub. Non. coms. seemed to delight in "bawling us out". It was no place for Sunday-school language. The language they used is unwritable. It was partly meant to harden us to military living but mostly because it is a soldier's mood [mode?] of life.

After a week's work in this regiment I was transferred to the Machine Gun Company of the 12 Inf. of which I am still a member. I had hoped

2. Perhaps as a result of his wartime experience, Powers remained involved with both the YMCA and the Red Cross after the war. He was active with the YMCA for 35 years, and a founder of the Oklahoma City Junior Red Cross.

to be placed into Chemistry work for which I had prepared myself in school, but the personnel board thought different. I then determined to work hard for a chance at the Officer's Training School.

In this Company I found a different class of fellows, mostly high school graduates, and part college men. They were all Americans too, so different from the letter companies. Here I also found the absence of unnecessary rough language although it was indulged in to some extent.

The drill with machine guns requires much less work than that of the rifle. We also did not have to do guard duty. As the life of a machine gunner is considered very short, the drill consisted to a great extent of "fall out one", "fall out two", "fall out one two three" etc. just as the case might be when the enemy's Artillery has found our implacements. Frequent lectures on "bands of fire", "indirect fire" etc., were given us. We also had to know the nomenclature of all the parts of the Browning, Vicoes and Colts Machine guns.

Some new and interesting things happened out on the range. I, with a few others (I had been made a runner) was once sent over the hill, on which targets were placed, to keep people off the danger zones. We scattered and took up separate positions. The bullets glanced over the hill and probably far over me but sometimes I felt they were glazing the grass over my head as I lay stretched out on the ground. They came too fast for me to wonder if the next one would hit me. If it was only possible I would have burried [sic] myself into the ground so close did I lie. Between bursts of fire I would take up my duty. But no sooner would firing begin again than I would drop to the ground.

The hand grenade range was also full of excitement. A fellow in one of the letter companies, an Italian, went through the counts to the last one when, instead of throwing the grenade, he handed it to the sergeant standing near and "beat it" around the corner of the trench. Another one went through all the counts but instead of turning it loose at the right time and in the right place, he struck the sergeant over the head with it, dropped it in the trench and "beat it" around the corner. The grenade then had to be picked up by an officer and hurled out before the five seconds were up, else his time on earth would have been up.

There was only one accident in the whole division. The day after the 12th MG Co was out, a recruit dropped the grenade and in an effort to get it out of the trench it exploded in his hand, blowing his arm off.

After being in the army the required time for admittance to the Officers Training School, I decided to put the question to the Company Commander. Having obtained permission from the 1st Sergeant to speak to him, I chance[d] to meet him on the Co[mpany]. street, clicked my heels together, saluted and said "Sir, private Powers has permission to speak to the Co Commander" "Yes, what is it?" came back. I told him my business. He informed me that he had had me in mind for some time and said he would send in a recommendation as soon as a chance permitted. That chance didn't come for it was but a short time afterward when all recommendations were canceled preparatory to going over seas.

About the middle of Oct. the division began moving to Camp Mills N.Y. The M.G. Co. 12 Inf left Fremont October 22 and landed in Hoboken N.J. Oct. 29. Another experience of being confined to one car and having one mess car to feed the whole train is still imminent in my memory. And had it not been for the Red Cross "hand outs" and the wonderful spirit of the people in the different towns we came through, the trip would have been irksome. As it was we enjoyed it as a whole.

We reached Camp Mill[s] l Oct 29. Dirt-floor tents and candle lights welcomed us again. That wasn't so bad this time because [we] were to start for France in a few days. All of the time was taken up in drawing equipment and supplies for the trip and for usage over there. On Nov. 2 we rolled our packs to be in readiness to leave at 3 oclock next morning. Orders came late in the evening, postponing the leaving 24 hours. Again it was postponed 24 hours and then indefinitely until Nov 11 when the inevitable came and our chance of going over vanished. Of course gladdened hearts were all through the Companies, still there was a regret that we didn't get over and into the fray.

Instead of letting up on drill it became more intensive. Close order drill with few rest periods was indulged in from daylight till dark. This was partly to keep up discipline no doubt. As long as the battle front wasn't very many weeks ahead of the soldiers the drill was a serious matter and every opportunity to learn and become fit was taken advantage of. But when news of the Armistice came drill became irksome and more so when no let up came.

On Nov 22 we left Camp Mills and came to Camp Stuart Va. where we are still located. As we made the trip on the transport we got a taste of what the boys received on their trip across the sea. To say the least we were glad when we landed. We are now here in the barracks with all the conveniences a soldier is allowed.

I have written of my experience but probably not enough of my impressions of the army life. One fact easily detected was that Sec. [Newton] Baker kept his word in rushing troops across to France. We were drilled intensively every day, realizing that the better fit we were the better chance we had.

As a whole the Officers were good and the Officers Training Camp a success. In some instances, however, it was plainly seen that commissions had been given through "pulls". The same idea seemed prevalent through out the whole system of the US Army.

Sanitation was usually well cared for. The camp was policed up from one to three times a day. Each company was responsible for its own streets, tents, and mess hall. Inspection of these occurred every day. I notice that I have made the above in the past tense. My mind runs back to the camp where the most intensive training took place and so I speak of it mostly.

Doctor's service wasn't valued very highly by the soldiers. It was claimed that a pill was all the medicine that they ever gave.

The thing that was hardest to contend with was quarantine. In this regiment we have been under quarantine or restriction three months out of the four. That makes one feel like he has been in the penitentiary so long.

As to Cooperation, the men seem to pull together. Although curses and rebukes of all description were exchanged at times, all were ready to fall in line as good sports and let the "dead burry its dead". All had one purpose—that of bringing the Kaiser to his knees and as I write these lines the paper states that England has demanded the person of Wilhelm II now interned in Holland.[3]

As for me I hope he pays the penalty to the utmost for the unforgivable sins he has committed.

Dr. Brooks, I hope this letter is not too bulksome. It is only a part of the experiences that have entered my life since enlisting in the army. My dearest hope now is to return soon to my wife and babe who are anxiously waiting for me.

With best wishes I am

Very resp. yours

Pvt Jesse L. Powers

3. The announcement of Kaiser Wilhelm's abdication occurred on November 9, and the actual abdication on the next day. He fled across the border to the Netherlands. There were some efforts to extradite him and put him on trial for war crimes, but the Netherlands refused to accede to those demands. Wilhelm died there in 1941.

Edward Henry Reeves

ARMY AND NAVY
YOUNG MEN'S CHRISTIAN ASSOCIATION
"WITH THE COLORS"

HEADQUARTERS COMPANY "H"
SEVENTH ENGINEER TRAINING REGIMENT
Camp A. A. Humphreys, Va.[1]

November 26, 1918

President Stratton D. Brooks:

Norman, Ok

Dear Dr. Brooks:

Since leaving Oklahoma University on May 26, 1918, I have been in continuous military service. While in Officer Training School at Camp Lee, Virginia, the course pursued was very thorough. It comprised study and field practice in Tactics, Pontoon Bridges, Fortification and Demolition, Wire Entanglements, School of Fire and Infantry Drill, the last mentioned comprised the major portion of the hard work

---

Edward Henry Reeves (1888–1970) was born in Texas. He enlisted upon receiving his degree in Mechanical Engineering in 1918, and was a lieutenant with the 7th Engineer Training Regiment stationed at camp A. A. Humphreys. After the war, he moved to New Haven, Connecticut, and worked as a consulting engineer and an engineer for the Connecticut state government.

1. Opened in 1917, on the Potomac River and on the site of a Fairfax County plantation, Camp A. A. Humphreys was the home of the Army Engineers training facility. It had been acquired by the federal government in 1910. During the course of the war, almost 18,000 military engineers passed through the facility. After the war, the site became a demobilization center.

which seemed the most difficult in which to see results develop; but every Engineer Officer was required to be "proficient'" in I.D.R.

Camp Lee became to[o] small to hold us so on August 10th the entire E[ngineering].O[fficers].T[raining].C[amp]. moved to Camp Humphreys, Virginia. We arrived at night along with a downpour of rain and found empty mess halls awaiting us, but as all good officer candidates are well skilled in K.P. (Kitchen police) we were soon fed and established[.] [A]fter a month[']s further training I was commissioned 2nd Lieutenant on September 12th and assigned to duty with Engineer Replacement troops here at Camp Humphreys.

My first duty was to help two other 2nd lieutenants organize a company of 240 men, ten days later I was the C.O. with no other officer in the company. [T]wo days later brought relief, three other officers were assigned to my company and I was transferred to Company "H" Seventh Regiment. All was easy sailing then for about a week, the schedule was drill[,] lectures etc. For two and one half hours each day we trained the men in the "Use of cutting tools". This sounds well, but it consisted in swinging the pick and shovel, digging trenches for water mains; cutting and sawing logs and sundry other such tasks of <u>Skill</u>.

Returning from week-end leave on October 20th I found my Captain on an order for transfer, so being next in command the company became "mine". No regular drill schedule has been followed during the recent [flu] epidemic as about 80 percent of the men were sick at the same time. Just now the whole regiment is being dissolved and transferred to other units here in camp.

As we are occupied with discharging and transferring the army of men, there seem[s] to be little chance of getting over seas now. This war has been a great game and the Engineers certainly had it down to a system here. This camp was a regular forest last January, but now it has paved roads, water and sewer lines throughout the whole three thousand acres and looks like a well organized city.

Army life is certainly busy and hustling[.] [O]ne has little time left after all the paper work and outside details are attended too [*sic*].

Best wishes for the continued success of Alma Matre [*sic*],

I am very truly

E. H. Reeves

(2nd. Lt. Engrs, U S Army)

Frank Magnus Rentfrow

Pond Creek Okla[1]

Aug 26 1919

Stratton D. Brooks

President University Oklahoma

Dear Sir:

I have your letter which followed me about this country and finally reached me in France several months ago. I am ashamed to answer it this late in the day but will do so to help make the personal records complete. The University had me traced to Eberts Field Ark; I was commissioned 2nd Lt. there May 21, 1918 and ordered to Camp Dick Dallas Tex. About July 20, 1918 I was ordered to an aerial gunnery school for pilots at Tallifero [sic] field Tex.[2] I went thru the course there and waited for my over seas orders which came Sept. 19. 1918. I had a 10 day delay enroute which time I spent at home and after reporting at Hoboken had 5 days before sailing.

I sailed Oct. 6. on the Adriatic and landed at Liverpool Oct. 17. after a pleasant passage. I with a number of other casual officers were rushed across England the same evening of the day we landed to South Hampton [sic]. The following night we took a cattle boat across the channel to Le Havre. From Le Havre I was sent to St. Maxient a classification camp

Frank Magnus Rentfrow (1894–1951) was born in Missouri, and moved with his farming family to Grant County, Oklahoma, when he was a child. He was a sophomore in the College of Engineering when the war broke out. He returned to the University after the war and was a junior in the College of Arts and Sciences in 1920. After the war, he moved to Houston, where he held various positions as a real estate appraiser and manager.

1. Pond Creek is a small town in north-central Oklahoma, about 30 miles from the Kansas border.
2. Eberts Field, in central Arkansas, was established in 1917 as an Air Service training facility. After training in Dallas, Rentfrow went to Camp Taliaferro, in Fort Worth, which offered a three-week course in aerial gunnery.

for aviators and was selected for a "chasse" pilot, so the next day started with other pilots for Issondun.[3]

While at St Maxient I met a University of Oklahoma boy, an observer[,] but cannot call his name right now. We were glad to see each other and had a nice visit.

Issondun was prob[a]bly the largest aviation training school in the world, it consisted of 14 different fields, field 13 being our well populated grave yard and the others all specialized flying fields. I went thru the course there as fast as possible, learning to fly the fast little single seated battal [sic] planes. I was almost finished when the armistice was signed. I went ahead and finished my course however so that in case every thing wasn[']t "jake" I would be ready for the fun.

I was sent to "St Jean de Monts" to ferry aeroplanes from there to Romarntin a distance of 350 miles.[4] The weather was rainy and cloudy which made flying both difficult and dangerous. I was lost a number of times in clouds but managed to get three planes there without crashing. It wouldn't have mattered if I had crashed them, for I am pretty sure that later they were burned.

The first of February 1919 I was attached to the 185 aero Squadron which was a night "chasse" sqdr. using Sop. camels with a mono su-pop motor.[5] While with the squadron I filed my application to attend an

3. The St. Maxient Replacement Barracks was an important center for American air operations in France. Initially a receiving station for personnel, the St. Maxient operation, by the time Rentfrow arrived, undertook the job of classifying pilots and sending them to replace losses in existing squadrons. The term "chasse pilot," taken over from the French, simply meant a combat pilot. Issondun, a town of around 10,000, became the center for American air operations during the war. At its height the town doubled in population and was the largest air base in the world.

4. St. Jean de Monts is a seaside town about 45 miles from Nantes; Romarntin, a town of around 7,500, in the heart of wine country, lies due east of St. Jean de Monts.

5. The Sopwith Camel was a British, single-seat biplane, first introduced in 1917. Its main innovation was that its attached machine gun was synchronized to fire through the propellor discs. It was equipped with a Monosoupape engine. It was one of the most effective aircrafts of the war. Readers of Charles Schultz's

English or French University. I was selected to attend The University of Nancy France,[6] which I did from the first part of March 1919 until the last of June 1919.

This was a privilege that I appreciate very highly for it enabled me to learn something of the French system of education, and to meet some of the <u>better class</u> of French people. I formed an entirely different impression of the French people while at this university. I lived with a French family for the four months and learned to speak and under-stand their language fairly well. I took an intensive course in French and also a course in aeronautics and radio telegraphy at the university.

Although the University of Nancy had been bombed and some of it destroyed, I found it wonderfully well equipped, especially for sciences. Students come from all over Europe to study sciences, especially medicine and chemistry.

I was general athletic manager for the American students at Nancy and we took an active part in athletics. The American students of the 14 French Universities organized inter-collegiate athletics and were very successful in their efforts. This gave the French a better idea of our university life, and at the same time encouraged better athletics in their universities.

I think there will be a lasting good come out of our American University men having attended French universities. The American students raised a scholarship fund of $14,000 for the purpose of sending 14 French students to American Universities for one year, and have organized a campaign to keep this up by popular subscriptions in the U.S.

If you talk to the men who went to the French universities you will soon see that they have a different impression of France and the French people than the average American soldier who served in France.

"Peanuts" cartoon strip will remember that Snoopy the beagle flew in a Sopwith Camel as he fought the Red Baron.

6. Located in the Lorraine region of northeastern France, the University of Nancy was founded in the sixteenth century.

This is only natural for it is not so easy to meet the better class of French people and so many never had the chance to meet any but the labouring or lower class, which class was more seriously demoralized by the war.

I found the French people to be a kind hearted and sympathetic people, at the same time a little selfish at heart. They are close in money matters but have to be in order to live. They are a hard people to under-stand. I was once sitting in a cafe with an Englishman. I said to him "I can[']t quite understand these French[.]" [H]e replied, "don[']t let that worry you. I have lived over here all my life and dont under-stand them. They dont under stand them-selves[."]

The French people have taken a great deal off of our soldiers more than we would have taken from a foreign soldier. They are a people who do not learn new ways quickly like we do, and do not appreciate it when our soldiers run rough shod over their customs. For all their short com-ings and old fashioned ways of doing things, I like them and have some good friends in France. In things artistic the[y] lead the world it seems to me after studying their buildings, homes, paintings, etc.

I have seen pretty well all of France, also Belgium. In Alsace and Lor-raine I found the cities cleaner and more modern. Strasbourg is a very rich and beautiful city, as well as historic and interesting. In Belgium the cities seemed more modern than in France and the country like a gar-den. I liked the Belgian people better after seeing their country. Brussels I found to be one of the most beautiful and interesting cities I had ever seen. The people love their (rather democratic) king and queen and seem satisfied with their government.[7] I think they will recover quickly from the war.

You asked me in your letter to give my impressions in detail, but I am afraid I am boring you with details so I will hurry thru.

7. King Alfred of Belgium (1875–1934) was the country's ruler from 1909 until his death. His wife was Queen Elizabeth of Bavaria (1876–1965).

I was given a diploma for my work in the University of Nancy. I am rather proud of it, not for what little work I did there, but because of my association with the university. The school closed for the Americans the last of June and I took a 10 day leave. I saw several days of the inter-allied games at Paris,[8] as well as some more of France on my leave.

I sailed from Brest the 19 of July 1919 on a German ship the "Zeppelin"[9] and 10 days later landed at Hoboken. I came home steerage with 1600 other officers, it was the worst 10 days of my life, quite a contrast to my excellent passage over, when there was a real emergency.

I took a 15 day leave at Garden City[10] and spent some time in the east and on the way home. I will have to say here that I find the people more hospitable in the south and west than in the east. I was discharged at camp Pike Ark[11] Aug 19,1919 and it was one of the hap[p]iest days of my life. On my way home I ran down to Norman and engaged a room for the coming school term. I have missed two years but those two years have not been lost for I have learned that which I could not have at the university.

I was in the army two years and 19 days and during that time have made friends from San Francisco Bay to Lake Geneva not to speak of the country I have seen, so I think I can come back to the university better fitted to absorb knowledge than before. Oklahoma University is not a large university but none the less did its bit well. I met University of Oklahoma men in the camps in this country and France and later on at the universities in France and England.

8. Between June 22 and July 6, 1919, male athletes from the Allied nations gathered outside of Paris for competitions in more than a dozen sports.

9. The *Zeppelin* was launched as a passenger ship in 1914. It was anchored at Bremen during the war and given as part of reparations first to England and then to the United States. The ship transported 16,000 American soldiers back home.

10. Garden City, New York, is on Long Island and was the location of Camp Mills.

11. Camp Pike was another facility created in 1917 as a training and replacement camp. When the war ended it became a demobilization center.

I hope this letter will not be to[o] great a bore to you and say again that I am sorry that I never kept in closer touch with the university while in the service. Hoping this letter finds things running smoothly at the university[,] I beg to remain, sincerely yours,

Frank M. Rentfrow

Wakefield Revelle

President Stratton D. Brooks

Norman

Oklahoma.

Dear Sir:

Your letter of the 6th of Nov., last addressed to my son Wakefield in France was returned to me yesterday unopened with a number of other letters to him.

He was killed by a French machine[2] on the 2nd of December last by being run into while he was carrying supplies to the front. I note your request of him & I take the liberty of sending you a copy of his last letter to me thinking this may serve your purpose.

It has been the greatest trial of my life to have to give up my boy—just when he was within a few months of graduating and looking forward to the time when he would begin to reap the fruits of 14 years of study & hard work, for he had worked his way partly through school and stood at the head of his class in Chemistry.

Truly yours

J. K. Revelle

Wakefield Revelle first enrolled at the University of Oklahoma in the fall of 1916. He enlisted in March 1918, and went overseas with the 656 Aero Squadron. On December 1, three weeks after the end of the war, he was stationed in Paris. When he and several other men were delivering supplies to the front lines, their vehicle was struck by another car in the heart of Paris. The other men suffered only minor injuries, but Revelle died seventeen hours later in a French hospital. He was buried in the American cemetery of Surenes, a suburb of Paris. The first letter presented here is by Wakefield's father, who wrote to President Brooks to inform him of his son's death; the second, by Wakefield himself, was written to his father just a week before he died.

1. Walters, Oklahoma, is a small agricultural and cattle town in Cotton County in southwestern Oklahoma. It is about 20 miles south of Lawton, and during the war had a population of around 3,000.
2. "Machine" in this case means "automobile."

Clichy, France[3] Nov. 26 1918.

Dear Papa:

One year ago today I held up my hand and said "I do" and now that the censorship is removed for this particular letter I will tell you briefly where I have been and what I have been doing.

We sailed from Hoboken on Jany., 15th last. We went to Halifax and lay in the harbor there a day or two while the convoy was forming. Saw no subs or anything interesting until we left the convoy off the Irish Coast, and morning broke with the hills of Scotland dimly visible through the mist. We landed in Glasgow and went by rail to Winchester. We lived on English rations for three days, and pulled for La [sic] Havre, rested a day & a half and left for Paris. Clichy is a suburb just outside the city walls and about 10 minutes ride on the tram from Paris proper. I have been working here since Feby. 7th. The squadron left here sometime last May, & left about 12 of us on detached service. For the most part I have been jug[g]ling boxes & making shipments for the front. Have been out of Paris only once & that was when I went on my leave to Rouen.[4] I know this city better than lots of the French who have been here all their lives. Right now every one is asking "when are we going home" so I will leave the details until I get home which seems to be not so far distant as usual.

For the last two or three days I have been pushing a typewriter, & from present indications they will have me at it until the depot closes down.

Hero stuff is entirely out of my line. The only chance I have had to show bravery was one night when I was caught down town in an air raid. It was one of the biggest we have had. The Subways were of course out of commission until after it was over so I had to walk home. The cops

3. Clichy is a suburb northwest of Paris and on the Seine River.
4. Rouen is the famous cathedral city on the Seine in Normandy, about halfway between Le Havre and Paris.

were asking us to go down in the [*illegible word*] but we were brave. A little thing like an air raid was nothing for us. All the search lights were up & one of the heaviest barrages that I have ever heard. Shrapnel was an occasional close visitor but somehow we found the camp in the time allotted for that purpose.

This is about the sum of what your hero khaki boy has been up to. Hope you are all well. Write to me often

Affectionately

Wakefield Revelle

A.P.O. 702. A.S.S.D #1. A.E.F.

France

P.S. 11-29–Forgot to mention Big Bertha.[5] We were under fire from her off & on (mostly off) from March 24th, to sometime in September. We could time her shots & generally tell where the next one would light. Used to go out on the roof of the building & try to see the next one light. I never had that pleasure although some of the others did. King George[6] was in town yesterday. I excused myself from his company because there was an entertainment going on at the Palais DeGlace[,][7] the Y.M.C.A. entertainment center in Paris.

5. Big Bertha was the name given to a class of huge Krupp-designed howitzers. They could fire immense shells (420mm) as far as nine miles and were used to destroy Allied towns and emplacements.

6. England's King George V (1865–1936) reigned from 1910 until his death. He spent a week in Paris to congratulate President Poincare in person on the end of the war. See *New York Times*, November 25, 1918, 2.

7. Built in 1876 as a grand concert and entertainment center on the Rue du Faubourg du Temple in Paris, the Palais des Glaces is open to this day.

Leander Armistead Riely

AMERICAN RED CROSS
U.S. GENERAL HOSPITAL No. 14
FORT OGLETHORPE, GA.

Dr. Stratton D. Brooks

Dear Sir:

Your query a few days ago as to the alumnus & person[n]el of the faculty in khaki came to me here in Chickamauga Park.[1]

I was sent here July 14 1918 to take a basic course in Military discipline and customs. I must say that I was very much pleased with that introduction into army life as I had to learn it from the very first having never had any military experience in my life. This is a wonderful place for training physicians and the only one in existence at that time since Fort Riley was just closed.

We were taught how to march & drill & go through the discipline of the enlisted man. We were temporarily shorn of our rank while undergoing this training. Men of international reputation were doing menial jobs with the rest of us and no distinction shown.

Leander Armistead Riely (1874–1959) was one of Oklahoma's pioneers in medical practice and was highly respected among his colleagues (see "Era Ends: 'Doc' Riely Is Retiring," *DO*, May 31, 1951, 1–2). He earned his medical degree at the University of Louisville. After a year's internship at Louisville, he arrived in Oklahoma in May 1899 to launch his practice. At his retirement in 1951, he was the longest-serving physician in Oklahoma City. He was also a professor of Clinical Medicine at the School of Medicine until 1940.

1. On the border between Tennessee and Georgia, Fort Oglethorpe, Georgia, had been a military base (under another name until 1902) since the Civil War. It is adjacent to Chickamauga Park, commemorating the historic Battle of Chickamauga, which was fought in September 1863, and led to the Union Army taking the important nearby city of Chattanooga, Tennessee.

After two weeks of this work I was ordered to Camp Forrest[2] to superintend a tubercular and cardiovascular survey of 15[,]000 Engineer recruits.

This was wonderful experience as it enabled me to study the normal body of man such [as] I would never be able to do in civil life. It gave me a chance to better study Ethnology as this number of boys were recruited from among all the nations of the earth and that not far removed from their native haunts in many instances.

I was surprised to know how many boys of foreign born parents could not speak the English language and can see what an educational advantage this mixing of these boys will give to them. The Y.M.C.A. has classes in English, Mathematics, Geography and any thing these boys want and has been a most wonderful educational as well as social and home influence among them and has certainly done more than anything else in helping out the idea of the melting pot.

After six weeks of that work I was brought as assistant to the Medical Chief of General Hospital #14.

My duties are entirely professional and that of a consultant on medical cases. If I had the choice of my work in the Hospital I should choose the one I have because I get to see all the interesting and intricate medical cases in this hospital as well as borderline cases in surgical wards. So you see 1 have quite a responsible place of it here but since my work is so interesting and instructive I do not care about the hard work and responsibility. I have all [the] help I need in the way of instruments of precision, X ray, men in the various specialties of medicine, laboratories of great magnitude and willing to help and cooperate with any delicate test desired in a diagnosis.

I have never met a finer lot of men than [it] has been my pleasure to meet here in this Hospital and in the Army.

2. Camp Forrest (named for Confederate general Nathan Bedford Forrest) was part of the Fort Oglethorpe military base. It was devoted to the training of engineers, infantry, and machine gunners.

We are all in for one purpose and that purpose having been so successfully accomplished we are now just as anxious to get back home to our old businesses.

To give you a conception of the enormity of this hospital [I] would say that today we have 1421 patients in it.

We have taken care of over 1800 cases of pneumonia during the past two months.

It is one of the biggest United States General Hospitals in this country and is a permanent affair so that it will be a rehabilitation hospital for boys invalided back from Europe.

It has no architectural splendor as it is made of <u>many</u> buildings of various types of architecture and made to meet the exigencies of the occasion. So [I] could not send you a picture of it.

I trust Oklahoma University is prospering this year and that all of your faculty will be back ere long. We do not know when we will get home and from all appearances the medical men will be the last demobilized.

We have a school of Military Medicine with which I am connected here and help to instruct the men who are assigned to that course.

We can get out of the army if they need us bad enough at home. We are given charge [chance?] of resigning on three different conditions

1st   Immediate discharge
2nd   Prompt discharge with commission in Officers Reserve Corps.
3.   Application for commission in Regular Army

Since I have never been out of Chickamauga Park I cannot relate any war stories but have worked just as hard and as willingly as if I had had a hand in whipping the Kaiser "<u>over there</u>".

Yours sincerely

Lea A. Riely

Capt MC

201 Fairview Av.

Chattanooga Tenn.

Grover Garfield Rumley

AMERICAN Y.M.C.A.
ON ACTIVE SERVICE
WITH THE
U.S. NAVAL FORCES OPERATING IN
EUROPEAN WATERS

Feb. 10 1919

President Brooks,
University of Oklahoma

Dear Sir:

Your letters received containing statement of my attendance in The University of Oklahoma and requesting kodak pictures etc.

I wish to thank you very much for the statement of attendance for when I return to the states it will be of great value to me in securing discharge to return to school next fall. I was unable to return to school this spring because they are holding us to take the Submarine Chasers back to the states, which has been delayed owing to their small size and the stormy waters of the Atlantic during the winter months.

Our base is to be given back to the English Merchant Marine and we have orders to sail for the states February 15th. The men here not attached to boats are being sent to Germany for the German Merchant Fleet to transport soldiers back home.

I am very anxious to return to the University and finish my course in Chemical Engineering but my experiences have been invaluable

Grover Garfield Rumley (1895–1967) was born in Keota, Indian Territory. After the war, he returned to the University as a senior in Arts and Sciences and completed his bachelor's degree in Chemistry in June 1920. He later moved to Dallas, Texas, and worked for various companies, including Firestone and Shell Oil.

since leaving school. [I] spent my training period in Harvard University Naval Radio School. Since then I have been with the Mosquito Fleet of U.S. Submarine Chasers[1] operating in the English Channel and off the coast of Ireland with base at Plymouth England. Our Ship was credited with one German Submarine on September 13th, probably the last U boat sunk in the English Channel. Chasing Submarines is pleasant work when the sea is smooth, but a storm in the English Channel with this type of boat 110 feet long is far from a nice yachting voyage.

We have been very warmly welcomed by the better class of English people. They realize we came in a time of need and have tried to show their appreciations.

The members of the Rotary Club in London opened their homes to us Christmas, and a week of home life in London while our own president was there[2] was surely enjoyed by those of us who were fortunate enough to get it.

The American Red Cross and Y.M.C.A. have been the chief factors in our recreations while not actually on duty, and deserve much credit for their work.

The Naval authorities have been very lenient in giving leaves at this base since the armistice was signed, and I have been able to see a good part of England and France including Paris, which none of us miss if we can get there.

I am enclosing a few pictures, including some snaps of the surrendered U boats, one very interesting but a very poor picture of the U 161, which

1. In World War I, the "Mosquito Fleet" was a collection of converted yachts used to guard against German U-boats. They were employed mainly to protect convoys coming into Brest, but Rumley's group patrolled farther north.
2. President Wilson was in England December 26–31, 1918, prior to attending the Paris Peace Conference.

is supposed, by the Admiralty, to be the German Submarine which sank the Lusitania.[3]

Sincerely yours

G. G. Rumley, Electrician 2C)R)

U.S.S[ubmarine].C[haser]. 41

c/o Post Master New York

3. The *Lusitania*, a British luxury liner launched by the Cunard line in 1906, was attacked and sunk by a German U-boat on May 7, 1915. The deed, killing nearly 1,200 people, including 128 Americans, sparked outrage among Americans and angry demands that the United States immediately declare war on Germany. President Wilson resisted those demands and attempted to maintain "neutrality," but two years later, in April 1917, he was driven to ask for a declaration of war when Germany refused to abandon unrestricted submarine warfare. See Erik Larson, *Dead Wake: The Last Crossing of the Lusitania* (New York: Crown Publishing, 2015).

Luther Russell

Paris, France,
American Red Cross Headquarters,
Missions Anglo-Americaine,
December 16, 1918

President Strat[t]on D. Brooks
Norman, Oklahoma

Dear President:

Not only did I appreciate the spirit of your letter of November 6 but also the publication, "Sooners and War Service" both of which have just come to my desk. The path of duty as well as individual choice has led me to the scene of many historical places and events of peculiar interest to me since leaving the Sooner State where I was just entering upon my duties in the history department as teacher of American history at East Central State Normal.[1]

The architectural designs, modes of travel, streets and public places as well as the language and customs afford a great deal of material for thought, study and <u>amusement</u> during leisure times. One is able to

---

Luther Russell (1896–1925), from McCloud, Oklahoma, was a senior in 1917 and a prominent figure on the campus. He was one of the founders of the *Oklahoma Daily*, a member of various literary and oratorical clubs, and on the staff of the *Sooner Yearbook*. He played intermural football and basketball and ran track. Upon graduation, he served as superintendent of schools in Paden, Oklahoma. He enlisted on May 28, 1918, and spent a full year in France. He was the state High School Inspector after the war. Russell died in 1925, at age 28, by a self-inflicted gunshot wound, determined to be "accidental" by the coroner.

1. East Central State Normal in Ada, Oklahoma (since 1985, East Central University), is part of the regional normal schools created in 1909. It now teaches around 4,000 students in a broad range of subjects and maintains several branches.

picture numerous very vivid and at times shocking contrasts when thinking of Philadelphia, New York—where I spent some time prior to sailing—and some of the Metropolitan French cities where my work has led me from time to time. I have come to think that the work I did on the Oklahoma Daily during the <u>wee hours</u> of the night in '16–'17 was a very good preparation from at least two points of view for duties on this side.

It seems that I have had particularly good opportunities to study the effects of a system wherein every able bodied man spends at least three years of his life in some barracks. It appeals [appears?] to me that whether or not such an institution is wholly to blame, it at least creates an environment at such a time as to encourage the spreading of certain noxious and demoralizing habits too well known to those of us who have been more or less intimately associated with military camps. Personally, I feel very strongly that we may well congratulate ourselves on being able to claim a native land where there is an absence of any such institution.

Apparently the people in the states are rather justly congratulating themselves over a great military victory which naturally enough affords an abundance of "filler" for the radical newspapers which should have been permitted to send one of their editorial correspondents, who in arguing their sternest convictions were <u>less</u> afraid of public opinion than of a regiment of field artillery, to "scoop" a description of some of the things to be seen around a railway station through which pass all the wounded from some sector of the front enroute to some base hospital which in all probability is already full beyond capacity. I deem it scarcely necessary along with this to picture a scene where the outstanding improvements are some shiny trenches ranging from near the surface to twenty five or thirty feet deep, a mass of tangled barb wire, numerous shell holes, a few splinters and myriads of broken pieces of tile formerly used for roofing—all present to tell a story in terms more easily read than any that could have been penned by the hand of man.

Our work would grow very monotonous and far more wearisome were it not for the frequent expressions of heartfelt gratitude which we hear as we pass among the French people, some of whom have lost their all, delivering our message not so much in words as in the satisfaction of absolute human necessities which would go unsupplied were it not for us.

At present my company is stationed in a camp in the midst of a vast green meadow on a French Military reservation near the largest forest in France and not far distant from the Swiss border in sight of the Juras and Mount Blanc which I hope to climb when an opportunity presents. I am anticipating a trip to Marseille, Nice and other points on the Mediterranean during the Christmas season.

For a time I have been in a hospital and am now convalescing from an operation on a crushed left hand which the surgeon assures me will be all well and good in time with the complete loss of merely the little finger.[2] The pain could scarcely be borne for a time after coming out from under the effects of the anesthetic but has quieted to a very great extent now. I hope to be ready for full duty again in three or four weeks and back in Les Etats-Unis by another Christmas time.

Sincerely your friend,
Luther Russell
A.B. '17

2. The cause of Russell's injury is unknown.

Lewis Spencer Salter

YMCA
RAINBOW DIVISION
AMERICAN ARMY OF OCCUPATION
IN GERMANY

Neuenahr, (Rhineland), Ger.[1] Jan. 15, 1919

Dr. Stratton D. Brooks
University of Oklahoma
Norman, Okla.

Dear Sir:

Greetings from Neuenahr in the beautiful Ahr valley where the 42nd Division is stationed. It was my good fortune to be transferred to this famous division[2] recently, arriving in Coblenz on Christmas eve. I came as a replacement to the 141st F.A. band. I am playing tenor saxophone. I broke into the music side of the army just before we left the States being transferred to our regimental band (136th Inf) [as?] accompanist.

Lewis Spencer Salter (1891–1965) earned a bachelor's degree from the University of Oklahoma in 1912. But even before graduating he was appointed as an assistant piano teacher in the School of Music. Upon graduation he was immediately hired as an instructor. By the time the war began, Salter was an associate professor of Piano and Music Theory. He enlisted on June 19, 1918, and served in the Army of Occupation. After the war he returned to Norman to teach, and in 1926 became a full professor of Music. He received a master's degree from Columbia University in 1922. Salter was to become the director of the School of Music from 1936 to 1946, and dean of the College of Fine Arts from 1936 to 1947. During the last years of his service, he was also the music librarian at the University. He was a member of the faculty for 50 years. Salter wrote two letters in response to President Brooks's letter, both of which appear below.

1. Bad Neuenahr is a spa town in eastern Germany, about forty miles from Coblenz.
2. The 42nd was the Rainbow Division. See the letter from William Corkill (note 6), above.

Neuenahr is a summer and health resort and we are all billeted in villas and hotels. Jim Brill and Evon M. Barbour are here (167th Am. Co.) [.]³ Soldiering under these conditions is not so bad, but now that it is all over but the shouting we are anxious to get home.

I hope to be back at least in time for the fall term.

With best regards to all my University friends.

Sincerely yours

Lewis S. Salter

151st F.A. Band

A.P.O. 715

Am. Ex. F

AMERICAN YMCA
ON ACTIVE SERVICE
WITH THE
AMERICAN EXPEDITIONARY FORCE

Neuenahr, Ger. April 2, 1919

Registrar, Uni of Okla⁴
    Norman Okla.

April 1,1919

Dear Sir:

In accordance with Pres. Brook's [sic] request I send a brief "history" of my war experiences.

I left Norman June 24, 1918 in a draft contingent for Camp Cody, Deming, N.M. After five weeks training I was assigned to Co. A, 136 Inf.

3. For James Brill, see his letter, above. Evon Marion Barbour (1894–1972), a 1916 graduate, served as a private in a Field Hospital, with the 42nd (Rainbow) Division. After the war, he moved to New Mexico and became a teacher.

4. The Registrar of the University, since 1919, was George Ernest Wadsack (1895–1977). He would remain in that office until his retirement in 1964.

Shortly after the division (the 34th) left for the embarkation camp at Camp Dix, N.J. There I was transferred to the Band, H.Q. Co. 136th Inf. We had a serious Spanish Influenza epidemic which delayed the sailing of the division until Oct. 13, 1918. Our division became a replacement division and we were at Le Mans, France[5] at a large forwarding camp on Nov. 11. Our band was kept in tact and we were assigned to Base Hospital No. 84 at Perigreux, Dodorgue, France.

Dec. 18 I was transferred to the Third Army or Army of Occupation and became a member of the 151st F. A. Band, 42nd (Rainbow) Division. We have been here in Neuenahr, Rhineland, for three months and are just on the verge of departure back to the United States. This will give me about 10 months service of which six were spent overseas.

Sincerely yours,

Mus[i]c[ian]. Lewis S. Salter

57 F. A. Band

A.P.O. 715

5. Le Mans is an ancient city in northeastern France, best known today for its annual 24-hour sports car races, which started in 1923. During the war, its population was around 70,000.

Fenton Mercer Sanger

U.S. Army General Hospital 27
Ft. Douglas. Salt Lake, Utah
Nov. 7, 1918

Mr. Emil R. Kraettli[1]
Norman, Okla.

Dear Sir:

I wish to thank you for the number of the "Sooners and War Service" for October 15. It was forwarded to me from Ft. Snelling, Minn. at which place I was chief of the Orthopedic Surgery Service.

I came over here latter part of September and have been made Chief of the Surgical Service of this hospital.

The government has converted this entire post into a reconstruction hospital of 3000 beds. I am enjoying my work very much. Uncle Sam is

---

Fenton Mercer Sanger (1868–1951) was born in Enterprise, Arkansas. He graduated from Vanderbilt University. After teaching for a few years, he enrolled at the University of Oklahoma School of Medicine and earned his MD in 1907. During the war, he served with the Army Medical Corps and was discharged as a major. He returned to practice in Oklahoma City, and taught Gynecology at the medical school. Dr. Sanger wrote the first of the two letters presented here before he received President Brooks's November 6 letter. The second is in response to the president's letter.

1. Emil Rudolph Kraettli (1890–1979) was assistant secretary of the University and about to embark on a legendary career as secretary, serving in that office until his retirement in 1969, an illustrious tenure of 50 years.

sparing no money and service to give our boys the best of care and service in every branch of the Army.

Yours truly,

Fenton M. Sanger (M.D. '07)

Capt. M.C. U.S.A.

My best regards to President Brooks.

⁂

ARMY AND NAVY
YOUNG MEN'S CHRISTIAN ASSOCIATION
"WITH THE COLORS"

U.S.A. General Hospital 27.

Ft. Douglas.

Salt Lake City, Utah

Dec. 8, 1918

Dr. Stratton D. Brooks
Norman, Okla.

Dear Doctor Brooks:

Your letter was duly received several days ago.

You asked for some of my army impressions and experiences. I am afraid if I wrote all my experiences, I might be adjudged "A.W.O.L." and not "L.O.D."[2]

I have been in the service now nineteen months. I have had many pleasant experiences, [and] am, if possible, a better patriot than when I went into the service. I can say that the dear old flag that has never been

---

2. A.W.O.L. is "absent without leave." The website "Acronym Finder" lists 88 possible meanings for L.O.D., and it is hard to know what Sanger means here, but perhaps "line of duty."

in the wrong nor beaten, is dearer and has a purer meaning to me than when I donned the khaki.

In my ministrations to those entrusted to my care I believe I have done my duty. I believe I have the respect of all those with whom I have associated in the service.

It has not all been flowers or most pleasant in the service. We've had to do many things that wouldn't be tolerated in civil life.

I have applied for immediate discharge and expect to get back home soon.

Yours very truly,
Fenton M. Sanger
Capt. M.C.
Chief of the Surgical Service

Robert Mitchell Sayre

The Grunewald

BEST HOTEL SOUTH

New Orleans, Dec. 8, 1918

Dr. Stratton D. Brooks
President, University of Oklahoma.

Dear Sir:

I am taking this opportunity to reply to your letter of November 6, 1918. I would have written sooner but I have been on continuous duty on the waters of the Gulf of Mexico ever since I joined the Navy. As you are probably aware I joined the Navy on April 27 1917 here at New Orleans in the United States Naval Reserve Force. Two weeks later I was sent to sea on a patrol boat and since then I have done duty on a Torpedo Boat, an Oil Tanker, and two Submarine Chasers.

On February the first I received my first rate as a Petty Officer. This rate was third class Quartermaster. The Quartermaster ratings in the Navy are different from the Quartermaster department in the Army. A Quartermaster in the Navy is a line petty officer of the seaman branch who has charge of the signaling, steering and bridge of a ship.

After working this rate I was detailed aboard Sub Chaser #150, and went to Pensacola Florida where besides our submarine Patrol, we did seaplane duty. About May, the first, I took an examination for Ensign which I passed but was unable to receive as I was not then twenty one years of age. However I was promised a commission when I reached that age.

Robert Mitchell Sayre (1897–1984) was born in Pennsylvania and moved to Ardmore, Oklahoma. He was a sophomore in Engineering at the University of Oklahoma when he enlisted in 1917. After the war he returned to the University. He joined the Gob's Club, an organization of former navy men. Sayre received a bachelor's degree in 1920. He lived in various places in Missouri and Texas, and worked at various jobs. He was living in Austin, Texas, when he died.

On August, the first, I was rated Chief Quartermaster and transferred to Sub Chaser #157 as Executive Officer. On this vessel I received much experience in navigation and seamanship as we weathered a few hurricanes which I did not believe a sub chaser would be able to live in. I am enclosing a few Kodak pictures taken while I was on this vessel somewhere in the Gulf. They are not so good but as they are all I have they will have to do until I can get some more.

When the history of this war is written I believe much will be said about the American Submarine Chaser[.] Not so much of the Chasers on this side [of the Atlantic] although we have had our trials, storms to weather, the ceaseless patrols in all kinds of weather and for those who were fortunate an occasional encounter with an enemy submarine; but of the Chasers in the North Sea and War zone who were responsible for our success against the submarine.

I am waiting now for a commission of Ensign which as it has been promised me, I expect any day. I intend to come back to college either next semester or the Fall of 1919. In the meantime I expect I will do some more sea duty on a transport or merchant ship. My experiences have been very valuable to me and on the whole I have enjoyed them.

Thanking you for your interest in me I remain,

Sincerely yours,

Robert M. Sayre

R.M. Sayre, Chief Quartermaster

Receiving Ship, New Orleans, La.

Charles Robert Stephens

U.S. NAVAL FORCES EASTERN MEDITERRANEAN
U.S. NAVAL PORT OFFICE, TRIESTE

TELEPHONE 4402

ADDRESS "NAPORTUS"

LLOYD BUILDING CABLE

TRIESTE

March, 27, 1919

Mr Stratton D. Brooks
President of Oklahoma State University [sic]
Norman, Oklahoma

Dear "Sooner of Sooners":

I just received your letter of last November asking me to write of some of my experiences in connection with the service during the war. Your letter was addressed to me at the Norfolk naval hospital. From there it was forwarded to U.S. Receiving Ship at Philadelphia and from there to the following places: U.S.S. "Leonidas," U.S. Naval base #25, U.S.S. C #94, S.M.S. "Rodetzky" U.S. Naval Post Office at Cattaro in Northern Montenegro, and finally to me at my present address, US. Naval Port Office at Triest [sic].[1] Triest is alternately in Austria and Italy.[2] At present it is

Charles Robert Stephens (1897–1970) was a junior from Norman who enlisted on April 8, 1917, hours after the war was declared. He spent the war in the Mediterranean as a submarine chaser. As he predicts in this letter, he returned to school in 1919–1920 to receive his degree from the College of Arts and Sciences in June 1920. After the war he lived in Oklahoma City and worked for Southwestern Bell for 38 years. He retired in 1959 and moved to Okmulgee, Oklahoma.

1. The Leonidas, launched in 1898, was a collier for the navy until the war began. During the war, the ship did submarine patrols in the Caribbean and then went to the Mediterranean as a base ship for submarine chasers. The Rodetzky was built for Austria-Hungary in 1909. Close to the end of the war, the ship was surrendered to American submarine chasers.

2. The city of Trieste was long part of the Austrian Empire. As a result of the treaty between the defeated Austrians and the Italians (September 10, 1919), the city was now joined to the Kingdom of Italy.

considered in Italy. Of course I don[']t expect civilians to believe all I write about [the path of] that letter but "Doughboys", "Leathernecks", and "Gobs"[3] will believe it and others don[']t make much difference.

To start at the beginning, I enlisted April 6th 1917, and as is the custom of most "rookies" and "rubber boots" I was transferred to U.S Naval Training Station at Great Lakes. By a little extra effort and a long "line" I got out of there in short order, being transferred to Norfolk where I remained until last June 20th, when I was transferred into foreign service.

I came across on the U.S.S. Leviathan, the largest ship afloat. I met several old O.U. men aboard her coming across. We landed in Brest on July 15th. Then came the experience of experiences, my trip across France and Italy to Corfou [sic], Greece. I saw every town of any size in France except Paris so as you see I never saw France according to all of the "doughboys".

I haven't the heart to tell any one about U.S. Naval base 25 at Corfou. It is the awfullest "dump" of an island on which humanity may or may not be found. I had the "Flu" there and was back in the states for twelve days, being out of my head and expected to "kick in" during all of that time. Needless to say when I left there I could sing the following song, a parody on a "rag" that was modern when I left the states

I hate to lose you Dear Corfu, Greece,
Would rather be back home with the N.Y. Police
Those dear little honey bees
Will miss us, so will the flees [sic]
They'll hate to lose us they've gotten used to us now.

I hate to lose you, Dear Base 25
But I'll excuse you for not being dry,
I'm finished with my last hitch

3. Slang terms for army, marine, and navy personnel.

Finished with the Spigotty itch
I'll hate to lose it, I've gotten used to it now.

We'll soon be leaving the house on the hill
Those Navy beans and Old Canned Bill
The Spick who gathers our pay
Will go broke when we sail away
He'll hate to lose us, He's gotten used to us now.

When we get back home and look for work
It won[']t come off in the bath.
I has been there a month and a half.
We'll hate to lose it, we've gotten used to it now.

That was written by "Rube" Gans, boilermaker, from New York. I've got some others but I haven't the time or patients [*sic*] to copy them.

While at Base 25 I did first aid work with a unit of Chasers spending most of my time aboard U.S.S.C. #349. I was aboard her one day when we <u>heard</u> a submarine. An aeroplane spotted it for us by dropping a torch in the water. It was almost dark when our first "ash can" went off, but it was light enough to see the oil and splinters come up from that poor submarine. We were getting along nicely after a second one when a "lima"[4] troller ran across our bow and dropped an ash can dead ahead of us. I was down in the midship magazine handing up "ash cans" when that "lima" ash can went off underneath us. I felt the ship come up out of the water and then go back down. Oh boy! No I wasn't scared but I was sure curious. I stuck my head out of the hatch just as our own "Y" gun went off and the oil in the breach of it caught fire and blazed out almost in my face. I thought the Chaser was afire and came out of that hole "a flyin." Then I got the straight of it and got back on the job before anyone noticed my fright. Our engines were badly damaged by the explosion of

4. . Slang for "British" (i.e., "limey").

that lima ash can or we would have got the other "sub". Shortly after that incident came the "flu" and after my own recovery I was kept busy in the hospital at the base for some time, being a hospital corpsman.

Then came the day of the armistice and since that day I've been so homesick that I've been miserable all of the time.

Since then most of my work has been with the food Commission[5] and many are the times I have heard Jugo Slavs cry out "Vive La America" and "God bless you Americans". There's something about it that makes you love Old Glory even more than fighting for her. A true American cannot help being proud of the fact that this is the first time any nation has ever fed her defeated enemies.

I put in my request for discharge a few days ago and if possible I will be at O.U. next fall. I may even beat this letter back. I have sent most of my Photographs of things over here, back home. I will try to get some souveniers for the university trophy case. We fellows over here see so many souveniers that we don[']t care much for any of them.

I must close for this time with best wishes for Sooners and Soonerland.

I am

Your friend,
Chas. R. Stephens

5. Under the guidance and inspiration of the future president, Herbert Hoover (1874–1964), the American Relief Administration undertook the task of feeding millions of people in central and eastern Europe after the war. Millions of tons of food were transported and distributed to desperate people regardless of their wartime allegiance or politics.

Robert Wilcox Stinson

AMERICAN Y.M.C.A.

ON ACTIVE SERVICE

WITH THE

AMERICAN EXPEDITIONARY FORCE

Dec 9 1918

Pres Brooks:

Your letter of Nov 6 was received some few days ago but lack of time and writing facilities has delayed my answer. I am sorry that I could not have written while on the front for then perhaps my letter might have been more interesting[,] but since your letter was written only a short time before the signing of the armistice this was quite impossible and if my letter lacks interest place the blame on the boys of the A.E.F. for bringing the war to such an abrupt close.

I entered the service on May 31 and in rapid succession was transferred from Camp Nicholls, La. to Jackson barracks, to Camp Logan, Tex, and from there to Camp Bowie where I was assigned to the 111 Field Signal Bn. of the 36 (Panther) division. On the 18th of July we boarded the good ship Antigone at New York and with 12 transports in our convoy sailed for Sunny France. We debarked at Brests [*sic*] on Aug. 1st and from there were sent to Bar-sur-Aube in the state of Aube which was to be our home for the ensuing 7 weeks and also the scene of many maneuvers. On the first of Oct. we were moved via trucks, trains and hobnails to Suippes where we relieved the 2nd Div on the Champagne front directly north of Chalons. We entered the front line

Robert Wilcox Stinson (1893–1978) was from Mountain View, Oklahoma. He graduated from the University in 1915. In the 1930s, Stinson lived in Oklahoma City and worked for the Works Progress Administration (WPA) and then for the U.S. Bureau of the Census.

trenches on the night of October 6 and 7 and in five days had driven the enemy back from Somme Py to the river Aisne a distance of approx. 18 miles. Here we were forced to dig in and wait for the French on our right and left to catch up. On the night of October 22 we crossed the Aisne and captured many prisoners. We were relieved after the counter attacks had been repulsed and sent to a rest camp.[1] When we entered the trenches the front was on the old Hindenburg line and it was only after terrific fighting that we forced our way thru. The German fortifications and systems of wire entanglements and trenches on this sector was even beyond my wildest imagination and even now it seems impossible that they could be taken. The ground for miles was pitted with shell craters, so many in fact that they would over lap each other and not a wall was left standing at Somme Py, or Sovain which is a good testimonial of the destructive ability of high explosives shells. Credit is surely due the boys of the 36th especially the doughboys and I[']m proud that I was with them. We received citations for our work and are of course very proud of them.

We were at Condi-in Barrios near Verdun when the armistice was signed and were in reserve for an American div. on the St Mihiel sector. The news of the signing of the armistice brought beaucoup joy and a number of the boys, (I won[']t be personal) imbibed to[o] freely of the fastly becoming famous Cognac which, I might add, is neither stronger nor weaker than alcohol and has a soothing effect on the throat very distinctly reminding one of liquid fire and has a nice soft downy "kick" similar to that of an ostrich or an elephant stomping your anatomy shod

1. The battle Stinson describes took place during the month of October 1918. The German offensive (its last of the war) having been stopped in July, French and American troops began to drive the Germans back. The places mentioned in this letter (Suippes, Chalons, Somme Py) are neighboring villages in the war-torn Marne district. The distance from Suippes to Somme Py (known today as Sommepy-Tahure) is less than 10 miles. The German defeat and retreat led directly to the armistice two weeks later on November 11th.

with a velvety cushioned pair of our regulation hobnails. Shortly after the signing of the armistice we were moved inland to Tonnerre and are billeted there at present.

The front is very much as the papers have represented it to be and there is little that I can add. I have had quite a few rather exciting experiences in line of duty while on the front but it[']s hard to tell of them in an interesting way when my mind is so occupied with thoughts of going home. I shall never forget the whistle of the G 2 cans and whiz bangs as they passed over our heads nor the swishing sound of the big French 75 as they sailed by, bound for Germany. The first shell that sang by me scared me so bad that I forgot to move until the explosion came[,] but in a short time I had acquired the rapidity and grace of a dog in getting into a hole and should there be no hole I could put a steam shovel to shame in digging one. To me tho there is nothing that can bring the fear that the rapid fire pops of a machine gun does.

My Btn's duty was as the name implies to furnish lines of communication from the trenches to the division hdqs. The work was exciting and at times very unpleasant. If a line was blown into by a shell it had to be repaired at once[.] It rains all the time over here and as the shelling was done mostly at night we did the repair work at night, in the rain, without a light, and always it seemed to me in the face of shell fire. It[']s any thing but pleasant at the front, lots of times there would be nothing to eat for years it seemed and no time to sleep, but the excitement would keep one up and going for a long time and physical discomforts would be forgotten until they were over.

Since we were relieved from the front I have been assigned to a battery truck with two gas motor driven generators used to charge the storage batteries for our wireless and amplifier equipment and a 5 K[ilo]. W[att]. generator for furnishing Div and Btn Hdqs with electric lights.

I have of course seen quite a bit of France and am well impressed with the country which is very beautiful and with the people who are as hospitable and entertaining as their very limited means will afford. "But" I want to go back home. We are far ahead of them in every way with the possible exception of conservation.

The only Okla U man with me is C. C. Oster '16 E.E.[2] and we both send our thanks for the bulletins which have come regular and enabled us to keep in touch with many of our old O.U. friends. We both hope to be at the Alumni reunion this spring.

Sincerely

R. W. Stinson E.E.

Pvt RWStinson

Hdqs Co 111 Field Sig Btn

A.P.O. 796 Am E. F.

2. See Clifford Carl Oster's letter, above.

Thomas Earl Sullenger

U.S. Naval Med. Detach

St. Elizabeth[']s Hospital

Washington D.C.

Jan. 3 1919

Pres. Stratton D. Brooks
  Norman Okla

Dear Sir:

I received your letter stating my standing in "O.U." I have had it filed with my application for release from the Navy. I certainly appreciate your kindness in sending it to me.

As this is the first time I have written to you, I am going to make a few statements in regard to my naval life.

I enlisted the same week I withdrew from the University last May. I enlisted on May 4th and was assigned to duty as an assistant medical examiner in the Navy recruiting station at Louisville Kentucky. I worked in the office until the later part of June, then was assigned a territory in west-central Kentucky. I was to go from town to town, make talks in the interest of the Navy and secure applicants for enlistment in the service. I examined the applicants and sent them to Louisville for final examination. I found this work real interesting and at some time[s] very beneficial.

On August 8th all recruiting was suspended and of course I was called back to Louisville to await orders. As I had always been exceedingly

Thomas Earl Sullenger (1893–1977) came to the University of Oklahoma from Hurricane, Kentucky. His quest for a bachelor's degree was interrupted by his enlisting. He returned to the University to finish his degree and went on to earn a master's degree in Sociology in June 1920. Sullenger was elected president of his Graduate School class and was also president of the Sociology Club and the "Gob's Club." He later became a professor of Sociology at the University of Omaha and the founder of the Bureau of Social Research there. Sullenger wrote many books and articles covering various aspects of sociological study.

interested in Psychology I applied for psychological work in the Navy. Was accepted and sent to this place for duty. I give psychological tests to determine the age of mentality of the soldiers and sailors before they are discharged from the hospital. I also have charge of a group of shell-shocked and gassed soldiers who are under observation. I feel that I am gaining some helpful information. I also am afforded a great opportunity of spending my leisure time visiting and studying our National Capital City.

It sure has been great to be in Washington these days of historic significance. Of course the museums, library and Congress take a good portion of my hours of liberty.

I have met some of my old O.U. friends since entering the service. I am always pleased to hear from the school. Am looking forward to the time when I shall be permitted to resume my work among the "Sooners."

Assuring you that I shall be pleased to hear from you again and with best wishes for O.U.

I am

Just a "Sooner",
T. Earl Sullenger

Ernest Wells Tallman

JEFFERSON HOTEL

JNO. CAIN, PRESIDENT

ABSOLUTELY FIRE-PROOF

180 ROOMS–EVERY ROOM WITH BATH

COLUMBIA, S.C.

Sunday Nov 4, 1918

Battery D. 13 Reg. F.A.R. D.

Camp Jackson, S.C[1]

Dr. Stratton D. Brooks.

Pres. Uni of Okla.

Dear Sir:

I've been hoping to have something of interest to write you but am still practically a Domestic Service man. We graduated in a class of 2600 Artillery Officers in Kentucky August 31st. They gave us 7 days to report to Camp Jackson, S.C. Some of us spent our spare days at Mammoth Cave Ky & around Lincoln's Birthplace. Those days were very restful after double-timing thru the hottest summer Kentucky had seen for many years.

If you have visited the Mammoth Cave you know that its size is its chief feature. The mineral formations are more beautiful in other caves.

Ernest Wells Tallman (1893–1986) was born in Illinois and graduated in 1918 from the University of Oklahoma School of Law. He emerged from the war a captain. Tallman worked for the federal government for the next 50 years, including an assignment as regional director of the Social Security Administration. Tallman was appointed to various public offices by 10 U.S. presidents.

1. Opened on June 2, 1917, Camp Jackson, located near Columbia, South Carolina, was an active training center during the war. It was closed in 1922, only to be reactivated in 1939 as World War II loomed.

Echo River[2] over 300 feet underground was very weird & felt like an uninhabited underworld. Our guide would <u>yoddle</u>? as he pushed our boat up the dark river channel & the tones would vibrate & echo & re-echo up & down the water in beautiful chords. There were about forty young Lieut[enant]s & tourists [who] explored those great caverns & passages & every hour was a happy one after our summer of training. We failed to find any of the little white eyeless fish in Echo River & as there is over one hundred miles to explore we did not cover it all. Broadway[3] which was four miles long was wide enough for a double track railroad.

There were old wooden pipes & remains of the salt-peter works used in the War of 1812. The Cave's surroundings were practically unimproved which added to its interesting features. As you strolled along a forest path you would meet bare-footed natives hunting with squirrel rifles & dogs. These natives are courteous & offered us everything they had to help us have a good time. Sometimes you wonder if they're not ninety-percent happier than the people who shift every where & really fail to get any where.

We ate corn bread three times a day at the hotel & fried chicken just as often but even out in those forest hills of Kentucky[,] Hoover had us pouring sugar out of a pen-point envelope.[4]

We were sorry to leave the quiet restful camp & hospitable simple people & take the little 2 × 4 train back to town. As we were rolling & rocking over the rails thru the woods a farmer came out of his cabin & waved at our train whereupon the train stopped. I was sitting in the front

---

2. Echo River runs underground through Mammoth Cave National Park. It is famous for its blind fish.

3. "Broadway" is the name given to the main, paved passageway through Mammoth Cave.

4. See the letter of Charles Robert Stephens, note 5, above. As head of the U.S. Food Administration, Herbert Hoover worked to conserve food resources in order both to assure food for the military and to avoid domestic shortages.

of the coach & couldn't see what he wanted but it looked as if he had stopped us to get the Conductor to change a bill for him. Four of us stopped over in Hodgeville near the Lincoln Farm & drove out thru the old farm to the big granite Lincoln Memorial. We perhaps had our own tho[ugh]ts as the big quaint guide unlocked the doors & permitted us to pass in where the old log cabin in which Lincoln was born, stood.[5]

The care taker had bro[ugh]t in the big silk flag & had spread it out to dry over one side of the cabin. (It had been raining all day). It was natural that he should remove the American flag behind which stood the birthplace of the first typical American product. Every day now the world is learning what is behind that old flag. It won[']t be many years till the world will appreciate & welcome the backing those colors can give.

We didn't find much to talk about as we walked around those old logs. Perhaps Abe had climbed up & down those corners & whittled on their edges. It is no more remarkable that the ruler of a nation came from those old rough logs than that a wonderful flower blooms from a homely stock since both are products of nature.

The more you wander around those logs & stand & look around the spring where the Lincoln family got their water the more you can appreciate certain elements in Lincoln. Ma[y]be his melancholy moods were filled with visions of that old cabin & spring & his early days. It was interesting to imagine. It was a privilege to visit that place & feed my imagination on such an American.

Well we traveled down thru Tennessee & North Carolina to our new camp & the awful lack of improvement in those hill states perhaps accounts for the illiterates they've furnished this camp.

5. Actually, the cabin Tallman and his companions toured was a replica of the original. Of course the Lincoln Memorial here is not to be confused with the Lincoln Memorial in Washington, D.C., which would become open to the public in May 1922.

Columbia is a southern town[,] the former hot bed of secession where the Articles of Confederation were started,[6] the capitol [*sic*] of the first state to secede, where Sherman made his headquarters on his march to the sea, where Woodrow Wilson's father preached for years & where his father & mother & sister are buried.[7]

I was talking to an elderly Presbyterian lady[,] a Mrs. McMasters who is closely related to President Wilson & she told me of the President when he was a homely young fellow going to see his girl in Columbia & bashfully offering bo[u]quets to her.

I was surprised at this lady when I mentioned visiting Lincoln's birthplace & she promptly instructed me not to tell her anything about Lincoln for that did not interest her. The old timers here certainly hate the name of Sherman & perhaps it is natural for them to hate one who took what they had & burned the rest even tho he was doing it in the interests of his country of which they are a part. The old southern spirit is still burning in many of these people & even one of my best friends, a Lieutenant Murphy in my Battery & a Ga. Tech boy is sensitive on Civil War subjects.

There are Virginia, Georgia, Tennessee & other southern officers in our Regiment & you have to admire their manners & soft southern accent. This Lieut Murphy is a black-haired blue eyed Irishman & a thorough southerner so you can imagine him. He keeps preaching South America & I [preach] Russia for an after the War tho[ugh]t so we've compromised on Alaska for Capital then Argentina for business. He is so

6. Tallman does not mean the Articles of Confederation that formed the government of the rebelling colonies in 1777. He means the declaration of the South Carolina Secession Convention on December 17, 1860, proclaiming the state's independence. South Carolina was the first state to secede from the Union.

7. Union general William Tecumseh Sherman (1820–1891) made the legendary march from Atlanta to Savannah in November and December 1864. His campaign is remembered for its brutal "scorched earth" policy. Woodrow Wilson's father, Joseph Ruggles Wilson (1822–1903), a Presbyterian minister, preached all over the South.

wrapped with the idea that he bo[ugh]t a map & planned the trip as we waited for dinner last night.

Dr. Brooks the finest thrill of all my army days came last week when I was drilling the 1st lain Platoon up & down the field. This platoon is mostly Chicago & northern boys & they are fine soldiers even this late in the draft[.] Well as they came down in platoon front & I was marching backwards to watch them, the Battery Commander called me so I halted the platoon & double timed over to him & was knocked cold when he informed me [that] four of us including Lt. Murphy were picked for immediate over seas duty. Can you feature that? After aching to go for sixteen months & peace rumors growing all the time the prospects were sure drab. We go this fall to a school of fire near Paris & as the old 40th Division is near there (according to today[']s papers) you can't imagine how we whistle & paint our baggage. I put red stripes on my stuff & stencil white arrows at intervals on the stripes to remind me of Oklahoma. Well a fellow is hardly responsible after such news & our only fear is that something might happen before we are out of sight of the Statue of Liberty. As I'm not telling when I'm going to leave I think this would pass the censor O.K.[8]

Went up & held my breath as the Overseas Board examined my heart & lungs [and] walked out with "Fit for overseas duty" slip in my hand & now all that's lacking is the spray from the salty Atlantic.

It does no good for me to wish for things any more as I always get double what I expect. The fellows used to joke about my horse shoes, when we came in after taps or beat our way to San Diego on the pilot of a Sante Fe engine.

Even during this awful disease our battery was more fortunate in number of cases than any other in the F.A.R.D.[9]

8. This letter was written only one week before the armistice, and it is unlikely that Tallman got to realize his hopes for going overseas.
9. "F.A.R.D." likely stands for "Field Artillery Rapid Deployment."

Well I hope my luck will always land me where I can do some good in the Service.

I wrote to Prof. Kulp[10] for the names of those who had paid you part of my obligation but he failed to send them. You don[']t know how I appreciate everything you've done for me. I wish there was something I could [do] for you that you would need me [to]. You're [*sic*] letter helped me land a place in the 20th Training Battery which was complimented by Gen. Snow[11] & dubbed the Ideal Battery by the Commandant of the 8000 picked candidates in the Central Officers Training School in Kentucky[.] We started from old Kearny with 176 men & turned out 176 officers. It was a privilege to be with such men for they were products of the West.

Well I get letters occasionally from around Oklahoma telling of O.U. & her part in the War. That Military training course in the University is all I could have wished for O.U. I hope the Govt. can train the Okla. nurses in the new Uni Hospital for it must be finished by this time.[12] I always know there's nothing available for O.U. that she doesn't get & usually her President is adding to the <u>available</u>.[13]

10. Victor Henry Kulp (1881–1967) was born in Illinois and practiced law there until joining the University of Oklahoma's law school faculty in 1911. For decades, he was a valued teacher and a world-renowned authority on oil and gas law. His precise service to Ernest Tallman is unknown but obviously involved the professor's supervising in some way the financial assistance provided to the student.

11. Major General William Josiah Snow (1868–1947), a West Point graduate (1890) and an experienced career officer, was the first Chief of Field Artillery.

12. In 1912, the University's School of Medicine, in Oklahoma City, lost its "A" ranking because of deficiencies in its clinical operation, principally the absence of a hospital for the training of young medical students. Finally, in 1917, the legislature appropriated both land and money for a hospital. After wartime delays in construction, the University Hospital building was completed in August 1919 and dedicated on November 13. On March 11, 1920, the "A" ranking was restored to the School of Medicine. See Everett, *Medical Education in Oklahoma*, ch. 8.

13. By this time, President Brooks, who had been in office since 1912, had gained a reputation for his unique ability to wring scarce funds out of the state legislature.

I hope to have something of interest for you by Xmas but just now there's little to tell you.

I hope the Influenza failed to visit any of your family and I wish for you every success[,] rather the continuance of success. Surely you're gratified to have your work felt all over a great state & know you've just well started.

I think of you & the Uni & its faculty often.

Sincerely,

Ernest W. Tallman

John Philip Toberman

Trier, Germany.[1]
February 21, 1919

Dr. S. D. Brooks,

Norman, Oklahoma.

My dear Dr. Brooks:

It has been a long time since I have been in Norman and from the prospects now it will be some time before I return, but I certainly will be a happy boy when I am again in the dear old U. S. A. and I will know how to appreciate it.

I received your letter some time ago and certainly was glad to hear from you but have been too busy to answer.

I landed in Liverpool, England Aug. 28, 1918, reached Southampton Sept. 1st., and landed in Cherbourg, France Sept. 3rd. I traveled through central and northern France in a French cattle car marked "8 Chevous or 48 Hom[m]es", in other words our side door pullman was supposed to hold eight horses or fourty [*sic*] eight men.[2] On the 28th of Sept. we reported for duty with the 1st Day Bombardment Group at Petite Maulan, Meuse, France[3] where we remained till the 20th of Dec. While there we were very busy with photographic work, wading mud, and

---

John Philip Toberman (1890–1950) was born in Texas, but came to Oklahoma with his family when his father entered the florist business in Norman in 1907. John was a junior in 1917, studying engineering. After returning from the war, Toberman joined his father as a florist ("Toberman and Toberman") and lived in Norman (on Toberman Drive) until moving to Texas, late in life.

1. Trier, an ancient city and once a Roman capital of Gaul, is located on the Moselle River, about 20 miles from the Luxembourg border. In 1919 its population was around 53,000.

2. Toberman mistook the marking, which specified "40 hommes," not 48.

3. Petite Maulan, in the Meuse region of northeastern France, was the site of an American and French air base, instrumental in the battles of St. Mihiel and the Meuse-Argonne offensive.

dodging through the woods at night when the HUNS came over with bombs. It was always lights out when Fritz was around with his old "egg" bus, but we had our fun nevertheless. On Dec. 21st we reported at Colombey-les-Belles,[4] our base, and were ordered home. That certainly was great news, BUT that was revoked and we were assigned to the 7th Corps, 3rd Army, and are now at Treves (Trier), Germany.

On New Years eve I had my first pass and spent New Years day in Paris and was at the University Union while there but as luck would have it I was the only O.U. boy present.

For military reasons I am not allowed to send any of the pictures that our section made while on the front, BUT I have a set of pictures which I got from a German and am sending them to you to be put in the University collection. I am enclosing a list of the names of the pictures. They are on post cards and will give you an idea of what I have seen on the front. I am sending the 51 pictures in ten envelopes numbered from 1 to 10. The only request I have to make is that no one be allowed to make copies of them but put them where they can be seen by the students as they are actual pictures of happenings in this little old scrap we have been having over here.

Please let me know if you get all the pictures.

Please have the University publications sent to me as reading matter is very scarce over here despite what the Y. M. C. A. has to say, infact [sic] they may have been a fizzle[5] over here holding us up like they have.

Hoping to hear from you soon, 1 beg to remain,

Yours truly,

J. P. Toberman

Cpl. J. P. Toberman

12th Photo Section,

P.O. 731-A., Am.E.F.

4. Colombey-les-Belles is a small town about 40 miles east of Maulan.
5. A failure after a promising beginning (as in to "fizzle out").

William Miller Vernor

My Experience in the Service

W. M. Vernor

B.S. in E.E. '16

On June 21st 1918 I was sworn into the Naval Reserve Force as Ensign for engineering duties on submarines.[1] I was told that applicants for this service would be trained eight months on shore at school and then sent out in submarines. One of the Reserve Officers classes had just started at Annapolis[;] however my entrance in the service was too late for me to enter that class so I was to be sent to sea in a submarine till the next class started.

William Miller Vernor (1893–1950) was born in Illinois, but came to Ardmore, Oklahoma, in 1900, when his father was appointed U.S. marshal to Indian Territory and placed in charge of the federal prison there. The son, who sometimes went by the name of Miller, entered the University as an unclassified student in September 1912. He graduated with a degree in Electrical Engineering on June 8, 1916. While on the campus he was active in various professional organizations. A description of him in the *Sooner Yearbook* states: "Might have been a farmer, but he left the A and M: Variety's his spice of life—has twenty girls per semester." After the war, Vernor traveled widely (Europe, New York City, Hong Kong) during some of his tenure as an employee of the Westinghouse Corporation. He lived in Houston for a time. Vernor died in Norman and was buried in Ardmore.

1. When the war began, the U.S. Navy had 42 submarines, the most modern of them in the smaller K and L classes. These were 165 feet long and could carry barely enough fuel to cross the Atlantic—hence the need for a "tender" ship to accompany them. But submarines in the N and O classes, which still required tenders, were soon being built. The O class boats on which Vernor served cost $550,000 each and had diesel engines. They were 172.3 feet long and had a crew of 29 men, each with his own berth. These vessels were, in turn, eventually surpassed by P and R class submarines. At the end of the war, the United States was operating 74 submarines and had another 59 under construction. Gary E. Weir, *Building American Submarines, 1914–1940* (Washington, D.C.: Naval Historical Center, 1991); and Edwin P. Hoyt, *Submarines at War: The History of American Silent Service* (New York: Stein and Day, 1983).

After a two weeks visit home in Ardmore I was ordered to report to the Commanding Officer of the U.S.S. 0-4 in "Boston or wherever she may be". I had no idea of the 0-4's exact location, however on July 9th I departed from home for Boston according to orders.

Upon arriving I found that the 0-4 was not there but the mother-ship or tender was being repaired in the Navy Yard. This flotilla was Division Eight, submarine force, of the Atlantic fleet, and was composed of the "Savannah"[2] as tender and seven submarines, the 0-3 to 0-9 inclusive. The Savannah was an eight or ten thousand ton ship, formerly the German liner and passenger ship "Saxonia". The submarines were at that time the best, and with the exception of one inferior boat, the largest afloat in our navy. However at that time larger submarines were being built.

The 0-8 was alongside of a pier and there I had my first long look at a submarine. My first impression was that it was small and fas[c]inating and I was very anxious to make a trip.

I was ordered, temporarily, to the Savannah till we again fell in with the 0-4. All officers and men of submarines have quarters aboard the tender.

Following a two weeks stay in Boston we put to sea bound for Delaware Waters.[3] At night we travelled with all lights out and in the daytime kept twelve special lookouts over which I stood one watch in three. Standing over these men was not as important as the duty the men themselves were doing. Each man was provided with a field glass and ordered to report everything he saw in the water, giving the bearing of the object. A sixty degree sector was covered by each man and he was relieved every fifteen minutes by a man standing behind him. During this uneventful

2. First launched in 1899 as the German freighter *Saxonia*, the ship was taken by the United States when the war began and was refitted and renamed the *Savannah*. The vessel served as a submarine tender during the war.

3. Up the Delaware River, the boundary between Pennsylvania and New Jersey.

trip we stopped at Newport and Provincetown and finally anchored or "dropped the hook" behind the break water at Lewes, Delaware.[4]

From this place the submarines were to patrol certain parts of the coast. Each submarine was assigned a certain area about one hundred miles out limited, of course, by latitude and longitude, in which they would stay for a week submerged during the day and running on the surface at night charging batteries. This was the most trying experience I had. In a submerged submarine it is excessively hot in summer and cold in the winter, therefore one is forced to live in temperature extremes, in this case a hot humid atmosphere. On these trips we were submerged fourteen hours a day without coming up for air, that is from sunrise to sunset, the idea being not to be seen on the surface. About 4 P.M. daily we would start an air purification system which had little noticeable effect. The system was circulating the air thru cans of soda compound which was intended to remove the carbon content.

After darkness we would come up and run on the surface with one engine and charge batteries with the other. There were three reasons for running submerged all day, namely, to find an enemy, to get in practice for the North Sea, and to avoid being sunk by our own surface ships. When the sea was smooth we ran at a depth of eighteen feet and stand [stood?] a periscope watch, revolving the periscope around the horizon about once in two minutes. When the sea was rough we would go down to about sixty feet and listen with our listening devices. We were supposed to be able to hear any ship within ten miles with this device although it was not considered thoroughly reliable by our captain. When we heard a ship we would always come up and take a peep with our periscope and usually be disappointed to find a tramp steamer or a merchant vessel. At one time when a ship was going over us everyone heard the swish of the propellers without the use of listening devices.

4. Lewes, Delaware, is located at the southernmost part of Delaware Bay, directly across the water from Cape May, New Jersey.

When submerged all day one becomes very weary, the days seem longer and there is nothing to do but stand watch, eat, sleep and read. Usually about noon I would develop a slight head-ache which would last until we came up into the fresh air at night. Although the food served in the wardroom on the tender was of good quality[,] that on the submarine was poor, the same for officers and men, being mostly canned goods in the summertime. Our ice wouldn[']t last over a day or two.

The officers quarters were cramped and we had to accustom ourselves to sleeping in a small space with lots of noise all-around. When submerged everything was usually quite [quiet?], the roughness of the sea being apparent but very little at a depth of sixty feet, however on the surface the ship rolls and pitches and the engines vibrate making noisy [*sic*].

On the surface the ventilation is almost perfect, the engines taking 1300 cu[bic] f[ee]t. of air per minute from the conning tower hatch, drawing it half way thru the boat. When submerged, however, the air circulated thru the boat continually there being no fresh air released. If fresh air were released the pressure would increase too much and the only way of reducing it would be the slow undesirable method of running the compressor. In the summertime after about six or eight hours down the air becomes foul and everything gets damp. Although the hull is corked inside[,] the ribs and other metal parts begin to drip with sweat. Under such circumstances one's garments are quite often damp from perspiration.

One morning about eight oclock, when we had been down about two hours and a half[,] the captain and I were eating breakfast on our small general-service table in the central operating compartment in which all the gauges and control mechanisms are located. The other two officers were asleep in their bunks which were athwartships.[5] We were moving along slowly at a depth of about sixty feet when the gauges began to show

5. "Athwartship" means from side to side of the vessel (i.e., at right angles from the line from front to rear of the ship).

that we were going down deeper. This was no cause for alarm but we usually liked to maintain a certain depth when we wanted to. "Ten degrees rise on the diving rudder" said the captain, but the boat continued to go down slowly. "Twenty degrees rise" and no effect. A little more speed on the motors was ordered by the captain, (this to make the rudders take effect) but no results. We were then about one hundred feet down and the skipper being a man who didn't like to take <u>unnecessary</u> chances ordered "Blow forward main ballast", and immediately following the execution of this order the boat started to the surface at an angle of fifteen degrees. This had blown forty some odd tons of water from the forward tanks. The captain[,] who had arisen[,] placed his arm along the after edge of the table, to keep the remaining dishes from sliding off[,] watched the gauges. A can of tomatoes turned over and ran down his sleeve but he didn't notice this during the boat[']s ascension. Upon arriving on the surface, he swore as he laughed and threw the tomatoes out of his sleeve. The second officer came in and said he thought we had been looping the loop as he had been rolled out on the deck.

The 0-4 was 173 feet long and the engines developed a total of 880 H[orse]P[ower]. She is capable of making 14 knots (or 16.1 land miles) on the surface and 10 knots submerged. We were rarely in need of more speed submerged than 2 or 3 knots unless in the vicinity of enemy craft in which case underwater maneuvering would be necessary. It should not be thought that the United States could not have built submarines as big and as good as Germany's. This could be more than accomplished if we had the incentive and one half the time Germany had.

One night when it was especially dark we saw a black object, about our size, on our right hand. We were pretty far out to sea to meet one of our own sub-chasers but we were not sure[,] and not desiring to attack without being sure[,] we dived. There was a good chance that it was a German and I think we should have taken some action. This is the only supposed sight of the enemy that we had in the two months and a half that I was attached to the flotilla.

The 0-6 came back to the tender one night with four five[-]inch shells thru her superstructure, one being only about six inches about [above?] her hull. This was done by a British Merchantman at about 3000 yards or a mile and a half. The 0-6 was in the setting sun and in spite of all her efforts to make signals the Englishman fired about twenty shots, and the sub finally dived in a leaking condition. The Merchantman pursued and in doing so picked up one of the 0-6 lifebelts, which came of[f] the bridge as she dived, and seeing then that it was an allied sub, went on about her business. That was a narrow escape. We were more afraid of our own surface craft than we were of the Hun. Nearly all of our subs had been fired at.

Later, in the Brooklyn Navy Yard, the 0-5 exploded and killed the captain and the third officer. It was an internal battery gas explosion, not injurious to the hull, but it wrecked one of the compartments.[6]

The 0-3 and 0-5 before this had gone out on a three week's trip with an old sailing vessel as a decoy for German raiders. They were unfortunate in not finding a Dutchman.[7] There were only a few sent over here and the Atlantic coast is quite long.

The questions that have been asked me most frequently, "How deep can a submarine dive?" and "How long can they stay down?" These questions are difficult to answer. They are supposed to be tested for three hundred feet, however they have gone deeper, seldom intentionally. Our submarines can stay down twenty four or thirty six hours or longer, and I can give hearsay from Navy officers that on a test stayed down one hundred hours.

Of course the depth reached and time under depend on how long it is necessary to stay under and how deep it is necessary to dive, also upon how much depends on results. The time of remaining submerged would be limited by the physical condition of the weakest man and the

6. The explosion on the O-5 occurred on October 6, 1918.
7. "Dutchman" in this context means a German.

depth reached is limited by the strength of the boat to resist high pressures of the sea. The ordinary submerged operating depth is less than a hundred feet.

The duties and activities of Allied Submarines were not fully appreciated by the public, very little having been published on the subject. The training of our submarines in doing patrol duty on this side was all in preparation for the North Sea or other more hostile waters.

A month or so after I was detached from the submarine force of division eight, they started across and were called back at the Azores, over half way across, due to the signing of the armistice. Nearly all subs operating on this side were fired on by their own or allied craft, and over there this condition was much worse. On this side we were told not to be seen, over there they were ordered not to be seen. It is true that we had several kinds of recognition signals but the surface craft often didn[']t wait to see or hear signals. They had the "submarine fever". The Irish third officer of the 0-5, who was later killed in the explosion, shouted to the skipper of a fishing vessel, one day as the 0-5 was returning to the Savannah. The next day the newspapers reported a fishing vessel's contact with an enemy submarine and one of the enemy officers "spoke English with a strong German accent". This caused much merriment in the ward room of the Savannah.

One of the higher officers from the Navy dept. at Washington, who was doing submarine duty ashore under naval operations, in an address to our class at the Naval Academy, stated that the total allied submarines sank forty four German submarines. This may be taken as an authentic statement.

The latter three months of my time in the service were spent in an intensive training class at the U.S. Navy Academy in Annapolis, Md. Here I studied Navigation, Ordnance and Seamanship with plenty [of] drill not only infantry but all kinds, boat & gun drills, etc.

I lead a quite different life from that on shipboard. The grounds are very beautiful and it is here that the customs, traditions and some of the slang of the Navy originates. When I was there, there were twenty two hundred midshipmen and four hundred in our Reserve Officers class. It is very interesting to observe the regular navy officers and the midshipmen on their home ground.

Following the signing of the armistice our morale dropped about one hundred and one percent and we were soon given a chance to return to civil life. After a two weeks stay in Philadelphia, to put the papers thru etc, I was disenrolled from the Naval Reserve Force on Jan. 7th 1919.

Clyde Herbert Whitwell

THE WESTINGHOUSE CLUB
Wilkinsburg, Pa.

December 24, 1918

Dr. Stratton D Brooks
University of Oklahoma.
Norman, Okla.

Dear Sir:

In reply to your request for a letter telling of my war time experiences, I submit the following.

I went to Camp Pike, Arkansas on August 28th., 1918 with the draft contingent from Norman.

For lack of better accom[m]odations the drafted men who came to Camp Pike in August were quartered in the mule sheds vacated by the Field Artillery when the 87th Division left the camp. We were fed, about seven thousand of us, at one big open air kitchen. When the K.P.'s were working good, they fed the bunch in twenty five or thirty minutes. The food was sometimes good and sometimes other-wise. Like the salt in the potatoes, it ran in streaks.

It took about two weeks to get into the army after coming to camp. Several times each day we were herded over the hill to the receiving station for an examination of some sort, or for a "shot."

After three weeks in the detention camp, I was transferred to a Receiving Battalion of the Depot Brigade, in which men with trades were held

---

Clyde Herbert Whitwell (1897–1999), from Norman, was a junior in 1917, studying engineering. He enlisted in August 1918 (infantry). He transferred to the Signal Corps and was discharged on December 11, 1918. Whitwell returned immediately to the University and, in June 1918, received a Bachelor of Science degree in Electrical Engineering. Whitwell, who lived to be 102, held various engineering jobs (Westinghouse; Equitable Gas Co.) in several places; he died in Fort Myers, Florida.

for assignment. Here the daily program was nine hours of drilling and hill climbing excursions.

Then the influenza epidemic hit the camp and drilling stopped, for those who were not sick were busy taking care of the sick ones, or doing guard duty. I kept well and consequently got lots of experience in "walking my post in a military manner."

On November 8th I was transferred to the Signal Corps Training School at Yale University. Unfortunately for my aspirations for a commission I arrived in New Haven just in time to participate in the celebration of the signing of the armistice. During the ensuing month I pursued the training course with as much interest as the circumstances would permit, and on December eleventh received my discharge from the army and returned to civil life.

I am now working with the Westinghouse Electric and Manufacturing Company at East Pittsburgh, Pa.

Respectfully
Clyde H. Whitwell

Virgle Glenn Wilhite

Dec. 11, 1918

Stratton D. Brooks

Pres. Okla. Uni.:

Your letter of the 6th of November reached me a few days ago. I appreciate very much the invitation to write of my experiences. I have inclination and will find time to write. As to my impressions during the war, I will not have much to say now because I feel that I can discuss them more freely when the censorship is completely removed. If circumstances permit I will try to send letters occasionally on various subjects.

Perhaps an account of a visit to the "front" would be of interest. Early Sunday morning the 17th of November, six days after the cessation of hostilities, Sgt. Leslie E. Salter[1] and I started out to see the last front

Virgle Glenn Wilhite (1895–1962), whose name occasionally appears as Glenn V. Wilhite. was born in Denton, Texas. He came to the University from Altus, Oklahoma. He enlisted on February 25, 1918, and was initially in the Corps of Engineers, but later transferred to the Transportation Corps. After the armistice, Wilhite studied for a short while at the University of Toulouse in France. He returned to Norman and finished his BA in the College of Arts and Sciences, graduating in June 1921. After a few years as a schoolteacher and principal, he joined the faculty of the University as a professor of Economics. He is best known for his book *The Founders of American Economic Thought and Policy* (New York: Bookman Associates, 1958). For the unusual spelling of his first name, see "Wilhite Tells Spelling Tale of First Name," *OD*, October 2, 1945, 5.

1. Leslie Earnest Salter (1896–1964) was one of the trio of Salter brothers who served during the war (see letter from Lewis, above). Leslie served in both the navy and the army during the Great War. He was part of the Army of Occupation (a member of the regimental band) before being discharged on March 30, 1919.

line. Salter is our First Sergeant, and is an exceptionally good one too. All the men have lots of confidence in his ability. Sgt. Salter and myself are the only members of the company from O.U. We derive a great deal of pleasure from talking over "old times" spent in the best institution in the best State of the best Nation on earth.

Our organization was doing railroad work back of the lines at the time the fighting was discontinued, so we took advantage of the first opportunity to go "see what we could see.["]. This entire country is infested with trenches[,] dug-outs and barbed wire entanglements[,] but they become more complex as one approaches the old line–part of the famous system of Hindenburg fortifications.

From our barracks we walked about a mile and a half to a little town called ROYAUMEIX. Here we were fortunate en[o]ugh to catch a truck going our direction. BERNECOURT was the next town, about fourteen kilometers fa[r]ther on. This place was near the front for a long time and is in a state of ruins. A few kilometers beyond BERNECOURT is the village of FLIERY. There is nothing left of it but the name.[2]

The ruins of the buildings are only a heap of powdered limestone. Like many other hamlets FLIERY was subject to cross-fire and from the looks of things both armies were doing a good job. Perhaps the villages in this section will be rebuilt in a more modern style. If so the destruction will prove a blessing. The archi[te]cture is very crude and the buildings were absolut[e]ly rotten with age. Many of the churches were constructed in

---

Salter graduated from the School of Law at the University on June 6, 1922. While still a student, he was elected to the state legislature and, in 1923, he played an active part in the impeachment and conviction of Governor John Walton. After moving to the Chicago area in the late 1930s, he tried a number of important and well-publicized cases. During his notable career, Salter held positions as a lawyer, government prosecutor, and judge. For a brief summary of his career, see *Who Was Who in America, Volume 4 (1961–68)* (Chicago: Marquis Who's Who, 1968).

2. The towns Wilhite mentions are all located along the same road. The distance between northernmost Firey and southernmost Royaumeix is less than eight miles. These villages are about 40 miles south of Metz and about 70 miles west of the closest German border.

the fifteenth and sixteenth centuries. I remember passing the wreck of one church building that was dated 1627. The enemy seem to have made targets of the churches. The reason they said was that the French and Americans used the steeples for observation purposes.

Beyond FLIERY all the towns have been in the possession of the Germans. All the directions and signs are written in the German language. The names of the streets and even of the towns themselves were changed to German. They are mostly called for the military and political leaders of Germany and her allies. About twelve oclock we reached BENNY[3] which is only a little way from the front of November 11, 1918. From here we proceeded on foot. We were getting hungry by this time and you can imagine how gl[a]d we were to come upon a company of American Engineers eating dinner. They gave us a good feed and told their experiences. That morning they had been digging up German mines.

About fifteen minute[']s walk brought us to the last battle field. On reaching the last American line a guard halted us so we did not get to see the scene of the Germans last stand. The guard said no one was allowed to pass until they were through "policing up", this phraze [sic] in the army is a very broad term and means any thing from gathering up match steem [sticks?] and cigarett[e]s to buryin[g] the dead. I don[']t know what kind of policing they were doing, but hardly think they were picking up German cigarett[e] snipes.

We were permitted to stroll about the American lines at will. It did not require a close observer to see that things had been rather exciting around there recently. The shell craters were fresh and the trees were newly torn by artillery fire. Fragments of high explosive shells could be gathered by the bushel. The ground was littered with abandoned equipment; rifles, bayonets, gas masks, tin derbies, raincoats, gloves etc.

On the side of a hill a little distance back of the lines a detachment of men had been encamped over night. Judging from appearances the

3. Benny is about 40 miles south of Fliery.

enemy had got the range and began firing on them while they were asleep. Everything indicated a hasty departure. Most of their equipment was left on the spot. I noticed a helmet that had been completely crushed by a piece of shell. If the fellow it belonged to had it on when that happened his troubles are all over now.

Things are shot up much worse on the old line than on the new. The country cover[e]d the last few weeks is not very badly devastated. The Germans were running to[o] fast to do much damage. I will describe one hill on the old front that is typical of the entire line. The trees along the road leading to it are stripped of limbs and even of bark for miles back. They are merely shattered stubs. Of course the roads were special objects of the artillery fire. The hill itself is a perfect chaos of shattered concrete trenches, shell torn earth and barbed wire. It somewhat resembles an orange peel looked at through a high powered magnifying glass. Scarcely a yard of the reinforced concrete trenches is left intact. On the top of the hill is a group of American graves. At the head of each is a plain wooden cross to which one of the man[']s identification disks is tacked. Not fifty feet distant is a similar group of German graves marked in like manner.

The roads all along the way were lined with the troops of the army of occupation moving to the German frontier. Another interesting and pathetic sight was the returning prisoners of war. They were poorly clad and thin but seemed to be in good spirits. The ones I saw were not in as bad condition as the news papers indicate.

On our return trip we were not so fortunate catching trucks as we were going, had to walk almost half of the way. About four oclock we got a free lunch at a Red Cross canteen. This was all the food we got until next day as it was to[o] late for supper when we reached camp. The day will always be regarded as one of the great events of my life.

With best wishes to the Faculty and students of O.U. I am,

Very truly,
Virgle Glenn Wilhite
Pvt. Co., A, 47 Rgt. T.C.

Burton Harris Witherspoon

HEADQUARTERS, SECOND ARMY
AMERICAN EXPEDITIONARY FORCES
OFFICE OF A.C. OF S., G-5

Jan 18, 1919

Editor,

"Sooners & War Service"

Norman, Okla.

Your excellent publication has reached me—that is two copies have—and I am very much pleased with the news of "Sooners" contained therein.

Personally I have only run across three of my old Oklahoma University fellows. I saw Major Artie Alden, M.C. in Paris last August, as sound and hearty as usual.[1] Sgt. "Bloke" Allen[2] I talked with for a couple of

---

Burton Harris Witherspoon (1889–1952) was born in Shawnee, Oklahoma. He graduated from the University in 1912. He was commissioned a first lieutenant, Field Artillery, on August 15, 1917, and sent overseas. He eventually rose to the rank of lieutenant colonel, and took part in several battles before becoming aide de camp to General Bullard (see note 5, below). After the war Witherspoon held various high-level management positions. He retired in Santa Barbara, California. On January 25, 1952, Witherspoon died in an airplane crash during a fishing trip in Mexico. This letter was addressed to the editor of the University's wartime publication.

1. Arthur Maxwell Alden (1885–1965) earned a bachelor's degree in 1907 and a Master of Arts degree two years later. He received his MD in 1915 from St. Louis University. He entered the military as a first lieutenant in the Medical Corps and was a major by the time he left the service in June 1919. From 1920 to 1922, Alden was the chief of Ear, Nose, and Throat services at Walter Reed Hospital in Washington, D.C. He entered private practice in St. Louis in 1922.

2. Sergeant Fred ("Bloke") Allen was a chemical engineer. He graduated in 1908. After enlisting in the war, he fought at Chateau-Thierry and St. Mihiel. He was awarded the Croix de Guerre in June 1918, for managing the first American gas attack at Pont-a-Mousson. On October 2, a gas shell exploded in the dugout where he was on duty. He died from the effects of that incident on October 15, 1918.

hours. At that time we were along the Vesle near Fismes.[3] "Bloke" has, as you since know, died of pneumonia. A fine man and a <u>soldier</u>. His commanding officers and the men under him, with whom I have spoken or written have all had the highest praise for "Bloke"—his soldierly bearing, his comradeship, his bravery in action. O.U. has lost a worthy son—this lad who gave all for a <u>cause</u> and for <u>right</u>.

Lieut Ray Evans, F.A.[4] I encountered during the first part of the fighting north of Verdun near the Argonne. That was about Oct. 1. Only had a chance to talk with him a moment. There was much going on.

As for myself, I was with the First Division from Jan to August, with Third Corps from Sept to Nov., and then with second army H.Q. Since August I have been aide de camp to Lt. Gen. R L Bullard.[5]

Many thanks for the "Sooners [and] W[ar]. S[ervice]." Pardon this long delay in telling you about some of the Sooners and giving my change of address.

B. H. Witherspoon
Lt. Col. A[ide] de C[amp].
Hq. Second Army
Amer. E. F

3. This was the site of an important battle fought through the whole month of August 1918, part of the Second Battle of the Marne. The town changed hands several times and American casualties were very heavy, but the German advance was finally stopped. The war would end three months later.

4. Ray Evans (1895–1935), from Shawnee, earned a bachelor's degree in 1917. He saw action in many key battles during his ten months in France. He was then part of the Army of Occupation. After the war he returned to the law school and graduated, as vice president of his class, on June 8, 1920. He went on to become a prominent attorney. Evans was murdered as part of a killing spree in which nine people were killed. See *The Orange Leader* (Orange, Texas), November 28, 1935, 1.

5. Lieutenant General Robert Lee Bullard (1861–1947) commanded the 1st Infantry Division ("the Big Red One") during the war. See Allan R. Millett, *The General: Robert L. Bullard and Officership in the United States Army* (Westport, Conn.: Greenwood Press, 1975).

Albert Lloyd Young

January 28, 1919
Germany

Comrades and Friends:

I have been asked to write about my experience in the war, so here it is up to date: I sailed from New York with the 90th Division on the 28th of June 1918, reached Bristol, England the 10th of July, and Havre, France, two days later; trained in the interior of France till August 23, when we took our position on the St. Mihiel sector; there we made the drive on Sept. 12, in company with other American Divisions, that wrested some 150 sq. miles of territory from the Hun; moved north of Verdun and were in line on the Argonne-Meuse sector from Nov. 1-11 where some of the severest artillery and machine-gun fire was encountered, which our Infantry passed thru and won great glory; marched thru Luxembourg into Germany here at Bernkastel-Cues, on the vine-clad banks of the Mosel.[1] Incidentally, the Division won three citations, and captured over 1800 prisoners.

Albert L. Young, A.B. '11
Pvt. Co. C, 315th Field Sig. Bn.
A.P.O. 770—A.E.F.

Albert Lloyd Young (1887–1976) was born in Iowa. He graduated from the University in 1911 and was in the Army of Occupation. After the war he was a teacher and principal for a while in Guymon, Oklahoma, before becoming proprietor of a grocery store in Oklahoma City.

1. Bernkastel-Kues is a German town about 65 miles east of the Luxembourg-French border and around 120 miles northwest of Heidelberg.

ACKNOWLEDGMENTS

I have accumulated numerous debts in the process of bringing this project to completion, and mentioning here the names of those who have helped me is one of the pleasures of creating this book. Part of that pleasure, I suspect, comes from the perverse delusion that printing their names and expressing gratitude somehow squares us, somehow evens things up, somehow compensates these individuals in full for all their good will, all the labor that they have generously expended on my behalf. Deep down, of course, I know better. I trust that those whose names appear below do not believe for a minute that I think these acknowledgments adequately measure what I owe them.

In 2017, I published seven of these letters together with notes and a brief introduction in the *Chronicles of Oklahoma*,[1] and I benefitted from the wise advice of the journal's editor, Elizabeth Bass.

The University of Oklahoma Press received a generous subvention to help defray some of the costs of producing this book. This subvention has enabled the Press to reduce the price of the book to potential readers. I am grateful for this support to multiple departments at the University of Oklahoma, namely the Office of the Provost, the Office of the Vice President for Research and Partnerships, the Dodge Family College of Arts and Sciences, and the Department of History. The subvention

---

1. "Sooner Doughboys: University of Oklahoma Students Describe Their Experiences in the Great War," *ChO* 17 (Spring 2017): 4–45.

was efficiently and helpfully administered by Melissa Seeyle, Director of Open Initiatives and Scholarly Communication, at the Bizzell Library. Others involved in providing these funds included Jenica Bachman, Dianna Crissman, Elyssa Faison, Lee Green, Michael Keeter, Danni McCutchen, Toni Pace, Heather Todd, David Wrobel, and Lizi Young.

As usual, the staff at the Bizzell Memorial Library has been unfailingly courteous, knowledgeable, and accommodating. I would especially like to acknowledge the help I received from Karen Rupp-Serano, Magen Bednar, Jeffrey Wilhite, and those competent and obliging student employees who help fix my computer. A special thanks must go to Laurie Scrivener, the indispensable expert and patient guide to the library's resources for historians.

For more than thirty years I have been the recipient of the expertise, the friendship, and the hospitality of the staff of the Western History Collections. The happy relations I have experienced under the administrations of Don DeWitt, John Lovett, and David Wrobel have continued down to the present generation at Monnet Hall. I owe much to the kindness and management skills of Todd Fuller, Curator of the Collections, and to Lina Ortega, Associate Curator. I will never be able to repay what I (and many others) owe to Jacquelyn Reese, the collection's Librarian. Her deep knowledge of the resources she manages is matched only by her remarkable readiness to help researchers in any way she can.

This is the seventh book I have published with the University of Oklahoma Press, and I continue to be astounded by the professionalism and kindness of the people who work there. In the case of this book, I am grateful to Promotions Manager Amy Hernandez, and Acquisitions Coordinator Upuli DeSilva, who, among other things, organized the volume's illustrations. It has been a privilege to know and work with Editorial Director Andrew Berzanskis and Managing Editor Steven Baker. It goes without saying that they know their business. But they also have the uncanny talent of making authors feel like friends and genuine partners in a common enterprise.

Once again, copyeditor Alice Stanton has saved me from numerous and embarrassing errors, countless infelicities of expression, and multiple incidents of unclear writing. There is no page (and few paragraphs) in this book that her intelligence and expertise and sensitivity has not substantially improved. If there is anybody out there more skilled at this work, I would like to meet that person someday.

Finally, as always, my chief debt is to my wife Lynne. I will not attempt to enumerate what I owe her. Partly because I don't have the words; partly because, even if I had the words, there is not enough space.

BIBLIOGRAPHICAL ESSAY

THE quantity of writing about World War I is, of course, enormous— far greater than anyone could expect to read in a lifetime. Readers of the letters in this volume will find in my notes more than two dozen citations to books and articles touching upon distinct and often narrow matters mentioned by one or another of the letter writers. What follows in this essay are some suggested general readings for those who wish to learn more about a war that ended decades of relative peace in Europe and changed in fundamental ways that continent and the world.

Readers who want to understand the Great War would be well advised to begin their exploration with a brief, one-volume overview, and there are several fine works along these lines from which to choose. The account of the distinguished military historian Sir Michael Howard, *The First World War: A Very Short Introduction* (New York: Oxford University Press, 2002), is the most concise, and while it is excellent, some readers may wish for a more detailed work. Other superb summaries of the war include Martin Gilbert, *The First World War: A Complete History* (New York: Henry Holt, 1994); John Keegan, *The First World War* (New York: Knopf, 1999); Adam Hochschild, *To End All Wars: A Story of Loyalty and Rebellion, 1914–1918* (Boston, New York: Harper Collins, 2011); and G. J. Meyer, *A World Undone: The Story of the Great War, 1914 to 1918* (New York: Delacorte Press, 2006). The last four of these offer extensive annotation and bibliographies for those who might want to delve deeper into particular aspects of the conflict.

No one interested in this war should fail to read two older books now considered classics: Barbara Tuchman, *The Guns of August* (New York: Macmillan, 1962), a beautifully written analysis of the coming of the war and its first battles; and Paul Fussell, *The Great War and Modern Memory* (New York: Oxford University Press, 1975), a brilliant exploration of the literary and cultural impact of the war.

Valuable reference works on the war include Spencer C. Tucker and Priscilla Mary Roberts, eds., *The Encyclopedia of World War I: A Political, Social, and Military History,* 5 vols. (Santa Barbara, Calif.: ABC-CLIO, 2005); Tucker, ed., *World War I: The Essential Reference Guide* (Santa Barbara, Calif.: ABC-CLIO, 2016); John Ellis and Michael Cox, *World War I Databook: The Essential Facts and Figures for All the Combatants* (London: Aurum Press, 2001); Martin Gilbert, ed., *Atlas of World War I* (New York: Oxford University Press, 1995); and Arthur Banks, *A Military Atlas of the First World War* (Yorkshire, England: Pen and Sword Publishers, rev. ed., 2000).

On America's role in the war, two useful reference works are Anne Cipriano Venzon, ed., *The United States in the First World War: An Encyclopedia* (New York: Garland, 1995), a collection of articles by around two hundred authors, with each offering a short bibliography; and David Woodward, ed., *America and World War I: A Selected Bibliography of English Language Sources* (Abingdon, Eng.: Routledge, 2007). Also helpful are Edward Coffman, *The War to End All Wars: The American Military Experience in World War I* (Cambridge, Mass: Belknap Press, 2004); Robert H. Zieger, *America's Great War: World War I and the American Experience* (Lanham, Md.: Rowan and Littlefield, 2001); and Justus D. Doenecke, *Nothing Less than War: A New History of America's Entry into World War I* (Lexington: University Press of Kentucky, 2011).

There have been excellent studies of the American home front during the war, starting with David M. Kennedy, *Over Here: The First World War and American Society* (New York: Oxford University Press, 1980). See also William J. Breen, *Uncle Sam at Home: Civilian Mobilization,*

Wartime Federalism, and the Council of National Defense, 1917–1919 (Westport, Conn.: Greenwood Press, 1984); Alan Axelrod, *Selling the Great War: The Making of American Propaganda* (New York: Palgrave Macmillan, 2009); Ronald Schaffer, *America in the Great War: The Rise of the War Welfare State* (New York: Oxford University Press, 1991); and Robert D. Cuff, *The War Industries Board: Business-Government Relations During World War I* (Baltimore: Johns Hopkins University Press, 1973). For engrossing studies of American opposition to the war, one should start with Horace C. Peterson and Gilbert C. Fite, *Opponents of War, 1917–1918* (Madison: University of Wisconsin Press, 1957); and Michael Kazin, *The War against War: The American Fight for Peace, 1914–1918* (New York: Simon and Schuster, 2017).

For the impact of the war on the University of Oklahoma, see Edwin K. Wood, "The University of Oklahoma in World War" (master's thesis: University of Oklahoma, 1923); David W. Levy, "'Practically a Military School': The University of Oklahoma and World War One," *ChO* 84 (Summer 2006): 132–61; Roy Gittinger, *The University of Oklahoma: A History of Fifty Years* (Norman: University of Oklahoma Press, 1942), 106–9, 214–15; or the University's yearbooks for 1918 and 1919, named *The Victory Sooner.*

The Great War left a legacy of remarkable international literature. In a class by itself is the novel *All Quiet on the Western Front,* by German author Erich Maria Remarque, first published in America by Little Brown in 1929. The moving work of British poets who were participants in the war, including Wilfred Owen, Siegfried Sassoon, Vera Brittain, Isaac Rosenberg, and Rupert Brooke, is well worth studying. A convenient sampling of these poets is George Walter, ed., *The Penguin Book of First World War Poetry* (London: Penguin Books, 2006). The highly acclaimed memoir of Robert Graves, *Goodbye to All That,* was published in 1929 and is available in several editions. Benjamin Britten's *War Requiem* (1962) was composed after World War II, but features the poetry of Wilfrid Owen, who died in combat a week before the 1918 armistice. The most widely known American novels of World War I, also available in many editions, are John Dos Passos, *Three Soldiers* (1921); Willa Cather, *One of Ours* (1923); and Ernest Hemingway, *A Farewell to Arms* (1929).

Readers intrigued by the letters in this book and wishing to know more about the American doughboys of World War 1 are directed to Jennifer D. Keene, *Doughboys: The Great War and the Remaking of America* (Baltimore: Johns Hopkins University Press, 2003); Keene, *World War I: The American Soldier Experience* (Lincoln, Neb.: Bison Books, 2011); Laurence Stallings, *The Doughboys: The Story of the AEF, 1917–18* (New York: Harper and Row, 1963); James H. Hallas, *Doughboy War: The American Expeditionary Force in World War I* (Mechanicsburg, Pa.: Stackpole Books, 2009); and Edward A. Gutiérrez, *Doughboys on the Great War: How American Soldiers Viewed Their Military Service* (Lawrence: University Press of Kansas, 2014).

The great influenza epidemic of 1918–19, which killed many more people than were killed by the war (around 50 million worldwide and more than 650,000 in the United States), is explored in Alfred W. Crosby, *America's Forgotten Pandemic: The Influenza of 1918*, 2nd ed. (New York: Cambridge University Press, 2003); A. A. Hoehling, *The Great Epidemic* (Boston: Little Brown, 1961); and J. M. Barry, *The Great Influenza: The Epic Story of the Greatest Plague in History* (New York: Viking Penguin, 2004).

On June 28, 1919, the controversial treaty ending the war was signed in France. Starting with John Maynard Keynes's influential analysis *The Economic Consequences of the Peace* (New York: Harcourt, Brace, and Howe, 1920), interpretations of the results of the Treaty of Versailles have abounded, with some writers blaming everything from the Great Depression to the rise of Naziism, the Holocaust, and the start of World War II on the measures agreed upon at Versailles, while others have defended various aspects of the treaty. For recent summaries and analyses surrounding the century-old settlement and its legacies, see David A. Andelman, *A Shattered Peace: Versailles 1919 and the Price We Pay Today*

(Nashville: Turner Publishing, 2014); Margaret MacMillan, *Paris 1919: Six Months That Changed the World* (New York: Random House, 2003); and Robert Gerwarth, "The Sky beyond Versailles: The Paris Peace Treaties in Recent Historiography," *Journal of Modern History* 93 (December 2021): 896–930.

INDEX

Brandeville, France, 59
Breheville, France, 72
Brest, France, 26n4, 37–38, 40, 51–52, 61, 70–71, 96, 98, 105, 154, 173, 196, 199
Brienne-le-Chateau, France, 62
Brieulles, France, 58
Brill, James A., 45, 188
Bristol, England, 230
Brooklyn, N.Y., 30
Brooks, Marian, 7
Brooks, Stratton D., 1, 6, 8, 14–15, 191, 210
Brussels, Belgium, 172
Buchanan, James, 6, 9
Bucklin, George A., 38–39
Bullard, Robert L., 229n5
Burke, John, 113n6

Caesar, Julius, 68
Camp A. A. Humphreys, 166–67
Campbell, Walter S., 48
Camp Bowie, 104–5, 153–54, 199
Camp Cody, 188
Camp Colt, 68
Camp Dick, 169
Camp Dix, 93–94, 136, 189
Camp Forrest, 179
Camp Freemont, 159
Camp Grant, 51–52
Camp Jackson, 205
Camp Lee, 166–67
Camp Lewis, 83–84
Camp Logan, 153, 199
Camp MacArthur, 138
Camp Merritt, 54, 56
Camp Mills, 154, 163–64
Camp Nicholls, 153
Camp Pantanezen, 154
Camp Pike, 173, 222
Camp Sheridan, 88
Camp St. Aignan, 74
Camp Stuart, 159, 163–64
Camp Taliaferro, Fort Worth, Tex., 169
Camp Travis, 79
Canadian River, 103
Cantigny, Battle of, 129n1
Cape Henry, Va., 39
Carmel, France, 58

Caskey, Glenn A., 51
casuals, 74–75, 93, 105, 160–61, 169
censorship, 49, 66, 99, 157, 224
Chalons-sur-Marne, France, 62, 199
Champagne, France, 45–46, 63, 199
Champlette, France, 71, 139
Chateau d'If, 117
Chateauoux, France, 48
Chateau Thierry, France, 54–58, 66, 69, 71, 77, 140–41
Chaumont, 140
Cherbourg, France, 84, 212
Chickamauga Park, Ga., 178, 180
Chickasha, Okla., 159
Chinon, France, 93
Cierges, France, 58
Cincinnati, Ohio, 88
Cirey-les-Mareilles, 101
Clare, Ross A., 54
Cleveland County, 3
Cleveland County Council of Defense, 9
Clichy, France, 176
Coblenz, Germany, 46, 56, 59, 146, 148, 187
Coetquidan, France, 56
Cohan, George M., 76
Colombey-les-Belles, 213
Colorado River, 81
Columbia, S.C., 208
Condi-in Barrios, France, 200
Construction Division, U.S. Army, 151–52
Contigny, France, 134
convoys, 35–37, 40–41, 96–98, 148, 154, 199
cooties, 48, 75, 146
Copeland, Fayette, 4–5
Corfu, Greece, 196
Corkill, William E., 56
Count of Monte Christo (Dumas), 117
Cowper, William, 28n14
Creager, Joe C., 60
currency, 148

Dale, Edward E., 9
Dammartin, France, 136
Dana, Richard Henry, 127
Dannemoine, France, 153, 155
Davis, Hughes B., 66
Davis, James C., 114n8

Newport News, Va., 34
Newport, R.I., 216
Nice, France, 186
Nogales, Ariz., 81
Noidant-Chatenoy, France, 66
Norfolk, Va., 30
North Carolina (ship), 96–97

Ober Wesel, Germany, 59
Oderman, Harry S., 151
Oklahoma City, 17
Oklahoma Council of Defense, 8–9
Oklahoma Daily, 4, 6–7, 10–11, 118, 185
Oklahomans opposed to the war, 2–4
Olympic (ship), 84
Orleans, France, 24
Osne-le-Val, France, 71
Oster, Clifford C., 153, 202
Owen, Benjamin, 7, 10, 91
Oxford, England, 138
Oyghem, Belgium, 85

Palais Des Glaces, France, 177
Paris, France, 17, 75, 176, 182
Pensacola, Fla., 193
Périgueux, France, 21–22, 189
Pershing, John J., 46n4, 54n3, 55n5, 64, 134n11, 141
Petit Maulan, France, 212
Phelan, Warren, 9
Philippines, 82
Pickering, Miss, 109
Pickett's charge, 67n5
Pierrefonds, France, 142
Pittsburgh, Pa., 152
Place de la Concorde, France, 146
Plymouth, England, 182
Pogoloff, Samuel H., 157
poison gas, 23n5, 63–64, 133
Pond Creek, Okla., 169
Post Field, Fort Sill, Okla., 113
Powers, Jesse L., 159
Press, Abraham, 111–12
Prince Edward (ship), 84
Prinz Eitel Friedrich (ship), 130
Proven, Belgium, 83
Provincetown, Mass., 216

Prussian Guards, 28, 85
Puderbach, Germany, 147

Qurcq River, 71

Reaves, Samuel W., 115
Red Cross, 4, 7, 52, 94, 161, 163, 182, 227
Reddy Farm, France, 141
Reeves, Edward H., 166
Rentfrow, Frank M., 169
Revelle, J. K., 175
Revelle, Wakefield, 175
Rheims, France, 26, 46, 63
Rhine River, 59, 72, 103
Riely, Leander A., 178
Rodetsky (ship), 195
Romorantin, France, 109, 170
Roosevelt, Theodore, 147
Rouen, France, 176
Royaumeix, France, 225
Rugny, France, 25
Rumley, Grover G., 181
Russell, Luther, 184

Sabinus, 68n8
Salter, Leslie E., 224–25
Salter, Lewis S., 23, 187
Salwaechter, Christian, 62
Sam Browne belt, 132
San Benito, Texas, 130
Sanger, Fenton M., 190
San Pedro, Calif., 127
Savannah (ship), 215, 220
Saxonia (ship), 215
Sayre, Robert M., 193
Schelt River, 85
Selective Service Act (May 1917), 13, 84n3
Selfridge Field, Mich., 111–13
Services of Supply (S.O.S.), 45n3, 64, 93, 146
Shelters, Germany, 148
Sherman, William T., 208
Sigma Nu fraternity, 65
slackers, 73n6
slackers' pen, 4
"slumgullion," 160
Snow, William J., 210
Soissons, France, 46, 71, 134, 142

The manufacturer's authorized representative in the EU for
product safety is Mare Nostrum Group B.V., Mauritskade 21D,
1091 GC Amsterdam, The Netherlands
email: gpsr@mare-nostrum.co.uk